WHOSE MIDDLE AGES?

Whose Middle Ages?

TEACHABLE MOMENTS FOR AN ILL-USED PAST

Andrew Albin
Mary C. Erler
Thomas O'Donnell
Nicholas L. Paul
Nina Rowe
EDITORS

INTRODUCTION BY DAVID PERRY
AFTERWORD BY GERALDINE HENG

FORDHAM UNIVERSITY PRESS NEW YORK 2019

Fordham Series in Medieval Studies

Copyright © 2019 Fordham University Press

Library of Congress Cataloging-in-Publication Data
available online at https://catalog.loc.gov.

Printed in the United States of America

21 20 19   5 4 3 2 1

First edition

Contents

Part III – #Hashtags

Appendixes

WHOSE MIDDLE AGES?

Introduction

David Perry

There's no such thing as the Middle Ages and there never was. The notion of a *medium aevum* that is neither one thing nor the other, permanently stagnating in the in-between, has always been a fiction. This isn't unusual. All eras are fictions. We humans love to apply our retrospective gaze on the sweeping vistas of the past, then chop them up into neat little periods to help us make sense of time. We allow periods to take shape in our cultural imagination when they serve a purpose, when we use them to define a present against its various pasts, whether through assertions of affinity or otherness. There's nothing necessarily wrong with these handy fictions about time, at least not until we allow the convenient shorthand to morph into something we mistake as objectively real. Here's the truth, at least for the way that most of us talk about truth: There never was any such thing as the Middle Ages.

And yet the Middle Ages undeniably exist. They've been roaring through cultural imaginations more or less constantly over the last five or six centuries. They started as a collection of years and peoples from whom thinkers in the Italian Renaissance wanted to distance themselves. In eighteenth- and nineteenth-century Western Europe, the imagined medieval occupied a more cherished space, a period of purity in comparison to perceptions of racial and cultural mixing that threatened Europeans' ideas about their superiority. Today, well, today things are as complicated as ever. But *studying* both the Middle Ages and how people have thought about and tried sometimes to appropriate them can pay enormous dividends for the understanding of both history and the present day. Scholars of this period not only get the pleasure of engaging with complex source material, sometimes even handling the raw stuff of the past themselves, but acquire technical and theoretical skills and habits of mind with broad applications.

For evidence, flip through the essays in this volume. In each case, consider the tools that these scholars of the Middle Ages and medievalism (the deliberate adoption, re-invention, and implementation of tropes the creator imagines to be "medieval") leverage in order to make their case and explore these questions of ownership and identity linked to modern exploitation of the medieval past.

Here's just one gem from this collection that we might pull out into the light and examine, the essay of Stephennie Mulder, "No, People in the Middle East Haven't Been Fighting Since the Beginning of Time." Mulder examines the narratives that identify the seventh-century Shi'a–Sunni schism as the source of modern conflict in the region. Historians have chosen to support the modern story of ancient origins and constant conflict through analysis of the extant primary written record. But Mulder is an art historian and leverages the history of the buildings she studies to complicate a simple narrative of conflict. She tells us that during this era of supposedly unending violence, Shi'a "shrines were endowed, patronized, and visited by both Sunnis and Shi'is: in many cases, by some of Islam's most illustrious Sunni rulers." A technical expertise in the history of buildings attained through careful study of the remaining structures and more quotidian sources — about the funding and attendance of those structures — would enable us to reimagine our whole history of the politics of the "Middle East."

The other essays in this volume offer similar gifts through a wide variety of tools. Helen Young explains why even people who aren't avowed white supremacists get uneasy when people of color appear in medieval fantasy settings (even though there were people of color, in fact, living in medieval Europe). Her tool isn't a technical expertise, but rather an engagement with critical race theory — a body of knowledge and methodological approach that instructs us to examine the power structures of societies as vehicles for maintaining racial hierarchies. Cord Whitaker's essay also relies on careful deployment of literary and cultural theory, but here he does something different. He applies his skill as a reader of medieval texts to works of medievalism that lie within — perhaps, he says, at the very heart of — the Harlem Renaissance. We cannot understand this flowering of black culture, Whitaker argues, without critical engagement with both medievalism and the Middle Ages. Medievalism in the nineteenth century is always linked with amateurism and fraud — the inventors of Scottish clan tartans, the founder of the semi-Masonic orders of the Knights Templar (unrelated to the crusading order), and so forth. Amateurish "revival" work could also provide a valuable bedrock for nationalism as the various European nations sought specific narratives of the past to unite diverse factions under the banner of the nation-state. Whitaker, however, places a romantic love of medieval texts and images within a transformative cultural moment in a marginalized population.

Over the last few hundred years, there were two dominant ways of putting notions about a "middle age" to use. Italian Renaissance thinkers who sought to craft a connection between themselves and the thinkers of classical Greece and Rome deployed a medievalism that distanced themselves from the more recent past. The Renaissance, itself a useful fiction, took place during a period of exceptional turbulence in politics, culture, and economics, yet also featured innovative intellectual and artistic practices that sought inspiration in the classical world. Hence, Renaissance artists and thinkers proposed that they had left behind a "middle age" between the cultural greatness of Rome and the greatness to which they aspired in their own time. In fact, historians can trace just as much continuity with the preceding "medieval" centuries as they can identify innovation during the Renaissance. Moreover, many of the features we most identify as belonging to the Renaissance found their origins not in ancient Rome but in the medieval Islamic world or even further afield.

While the thinkers of the Renaissance represented the Middle Ages in ways that put the Middle Ages at a distance, during the succeeding eras of European colonialism and imperialism thinkers placed the Middle Ages at the center of their new national histories. European nation-states sought hegemony over so much of the broader world, subjugating diverse peoples, engaging in mass enslavement and other forms of labor exploitation, and too often seeking to eradicate indigenous cultures, that intellectuals in Western Europe were less ready to erase the centuries during which the cultures that supposedly defined their nations coalesced. European thinkers instead sought a heritage — often a specifically white and Christian one — that used the Middle Ages to link the glories of the Pax Romana of the classical past to Rule Britannia and the continental empires (through

the distinct narratives that medieval Europeans themselves
told). New narratives of hereditary greatness and racial superiority required a history differentiating a white Christian
past from the narratives of other places and peoples. Thus,
the eighteenth- and nineteenth-century British invented an
isolated race they called the "Anglo-Saxons" as a white early
medieval heritage on their isolated, splendid island. The
French claimed Charles Martel's defeat of an Islamic raiding party in Tours in 732 CE as evidence that Carolingians
had staved off the Islamification of Europe. Nineteenth-
century German intellectuals, obsessed with a notion of a
German people and German state that transcended time,
found in the Holy Roman Empire after 1000 CE a *reich* to
remember.

Speaking of those German intellectuals, they were also
busy inventing the modern research university and codifying
the disciplines that still structure professional scholarly activity today. This, as much as any of the big cultural forces, is
why scholars keep this construct of time and place around.
It's useful. It explains why a good history department might
need a specialist in the millennium between 500 and 1500
CE, between the "Fall of Rome" (which didn't happen) and
the invention of the printing press (which did, though the
ensuing information revolution built on ideas about knowledge long resident in western Europe). I am a *medieval* historian because the jobs that I applied for were defined as
medieval history. These constructs shape how we make our
livings, what kinds of journals and publishing houses want
our work, the grants for which we can apply, the conferences
we attend, the classes we teach, and more. That's not all
bad, but the mundane details of how your professor gets a
paycheck can drive us to believe that the Middle Ages exist
as some kind of fundamental historical truth. If you are a
student, it may seem odd to think that entire eras of history

exist in your imagination largely because it makes for convenient field delineation among professional scholars, but that's what happened. There are worse reasons to believe in the Middle Ages.

This volume took shape in the weeks and months after a group of neo-Nazis marched through the college town of Charlottesville, Virginia, wielding clubs and shields bearing medieval insignia. During that march, one of the neo-Nazi demonstrators drove his car into a crowd of counter protesters and killed Heather Heyer, a peaceful counter-protestor. It would be a mistake to end without reckoning, briefly, with that beginning. Many people in the United States and the British Commonwealth still yearn for a homogeneously white, universally Christian, splendidly isolated Middle Ages that never existed. In Europe, men gather under crusader flags, arm themselves with assault rifles, and form militias to patrol their borders in hopes of turning away Islamic refugees from war in Syria in the name of that imaginary Middle Ages. In New Zealand, a white supremacist cited First Crusade rhetoric before murdering Muslims at prayer. In San Diego, another white supremacist wrote about medieval blood libel before murdering Jews. Narratives of European medieval whiteness continue to be used to support some of the most dangerous ideologies in the world.

Meanwhile, medieval studies as a field is slowly, haltingly, organizing itself against oppressive ideologies. New collectives of scholars have organized into communities working to transform and destabilize our notion of the Middle Ages and to whom they belong. In recent years, that movement has been led by the group Medievalists of Color, a community of deeply engaged scholars from diverse backgrounds working at all levels of the academy and writing both inside and outside academic contexts. The scholars in this group challenge the periodization and geographical separateness of a "medieval past" with an urgency fueled by discrimination both inside and outside the academy in an era of rising white supremacy. Sierra Lomuto, for instance, writes in "White Nationalism and the Ethics of Medieval Studies," that "when we refuse to see race in the Middle Ages, the stakes are much greater than etymology or linguistics; we are refusing to see how hierarchical structures of difference operate in all of their nuanced complexities, including within multicultural and transnational contexts. We are allowing the Middle Ages to be seen as a preracial space where whiteness can locate its ethnic heritage." Lomuto's call, echoed by other medievalists from a variety of marginalized backgrounds, connects the urgency in the streets of Charlottesville, the mosque in New Zealand, and the synagogue in San Diego to what happens in academic spaces. They are all connected. They always have been.

We are in an era of weaponized nostalgia, in which constructed pasts that may or may not bear much relationship to what scholars actually know about those pasts can shape the fate of nations. Medievalism can manifest as one of those nostalgias. Nostalgia can accelerate and intensify oppressive ideologies as forces react to stave off change through violence and bigotry. Nostalgia can provide models for resistance and resiliency in the face of oppression. But nostalgia always relies on the fabricated notions of the past with which I began this essay. It's fine to believe in the Middle Ages, as long as you remember they didn't exist.

Further Reading

An excellent book on the medieval in contemporary political discourse in the United States is Bruce W. Holsinger, *Neomedievalism, Neoconservatism, and the War on Terror*

(Chicago: Prickly Paradigm Press, 2007). For a number of European perspectives, see Robert John Weston Evans and Guy P. Machal, eds., *The Uses of the Middle Ages in Modern European States: History, Nationhood and the Search for Origins* (Basingstoke: Palgrave Macmillan, 2015).

Sierra Lomuto's essay can be found at the blog *In the Medieval Middle* at www.inthemedievalmiddle.com/2016/12/white-nationalism-and-ethics-of.html. Cord Whitaker's introduction to a special issue of the journal *Postmedieval* contains a powerful description of the experience of studying the Middle Ages as a scholar of color: "Race-ing the Dragon: the Middle Ages, race and trippin' into the future," *Postmedieval* 6, no. 1 (Spring 2015).

PART I
Stories

People never tire of telling stories about the Middle Ages. After all, the first stories that many of us hear as children are set in the Middle Ages — or in a fictional version of it, at least, studded with castles and crawling with dragons. There are grimmer accounts of the Middle Ages, too, that include superstition, racial apartheid, and unrestrained religious violence. The essays in this section therefore focus on the Middle Ages as an object of story-telling and fantasy. Frequently our stories dealing with the Middle Ages contradict the stories created by medieval people themselves and preserved or reflected in their own writing, documents, philosophy, and art. In the contributions here, experts in the field tell their own stories about the Middle Ages, sometimes to offer corrections and sometimes to explore just how fundamental storytelling is to the way we understand the Middle Ages today.

Sandy Bardsley's "The Invisible Peasantry" picks up where Renaissance fairs, with their focus on noble feasts and knightly jousts, leave off: with a gaze on medieval peasantry and "the labor of the 90%" that made medieval civilization possible. Given that most of the textual evidence for life in the Middle Ages was made by and for elites, Bardsley's essay is particularly interested in how we learn about rural society. By reading sources such as manorial accounts, poetry, and church art against the grain, Bardsley suggests, we get a glimpse of how medieval people — including the peasants themselves — viewed the economic and social bedrock of their world. In "The Hidden Narratives of Medieval Art," Katherine Anne Wilson looks at the paintings and tapestries of late medieval elites from late medieval France and Flanders (in modern Belgium) to explore the roles played by urban workers in creating the art that now defines our ideas of medieval elite culture. While modern museum-goers might focus exclusively on the aristocrats and rich burghers immortalized in the paintings or of a single artist who signed the piece, Wilson explains how a richer, more complex story of "collaboration and exploitation" between different socioeconomic groupings with different interests and different ideas about what the work meant can be discovered on the very surface of this art.

In some cases, stories about the Middle Ages offer false precedents for modern injustices. In his essay "Modern Intolerance and the Medieval Crusades," Nicholas L. Paul first discusses the impact that the memory of the crusades exerts on the modern day. The appeal of the crusades, as a "holy war" pitting "west" against "east," has inspired not just white supremacists in Europe and North America but also ISIS in the Middle East. Paul contrasts these views to those developed by historians based on the evidence left behind by medieval people themselves. The diversity and complexity of crusading movements discovered by scholars cannot bear the burden of precedent placed upon them by modern extremists. As Paul concludes, when we look to the crusades as a mirror for our own modern colonial or racial ideologies, they "reflect back to us only our own troubled image." In her essay, "Blood Libel, a Lie and Its Legacies," Magda Teter explores how medieval people themselves generated and sustained the false stories that have led to modern violence. Her focus is on the blood libel, the false accusation that Jewish people would ritually murder innocent Christian children, which first circulated in the Middle Ages and continues to attract attention from anti-Semites today. Teter traces the diffusion of these stories through the words and images in medieval and early modern chronicles that purport to tell world history. These chronicles did not just transmit older stories passively but originated another dangerous and false idea of "a European past as Christian, with Jews, or 'Jewish diaspora,' as sojourners in 'host nations.'"

In other cases, medieval stories can resolve modern anxieties and fears. In "Who's Afraid of Shari'a Law?," Fred M. Donner offers a corrective to worries expressed in Western news outlets about the influence of Islamic religious law in North American and European societies. Aside from reminding readers that modern constitutional governments guarantee freedom of conscience, Donner explains how Islamic law, whose origins lay in the eighth, ninth, and tenth centuries, has always been founded on public interest and open debates over precedents and rationale. And insofar as some Islamic legal ideas are based on memories of the life of Muhammad, stories prove central to its development in the Middle Ages to the modern day. W. Mark Ormrod's essay, "How Do We Find Out About Immigrants in Later Medieval England?," looks at the phenomena of migration and immigration in late medieval England. Ormrod describes how immigrants found an assured place in English society in the fifteenth century as a more-or-less accepted, and valued, part of the English kingdom. Modern debates about the place of immigration in English society distort the picture when they ignore this evidence, especially when they falsely imagine a time when England was not home to immigrants of many different colors and creeds.

Cord J. Whitaker's "The Middle Ages in the Harlem Renaissance" turns provocatively to the question of how people become attached to the stories that they tell about the Middle Ages. Whitaker's example is the prolific Harlem Renaissance writer and editor, Jessie Redmon Fauset. In her novels and journalistic pieces, Fauset seizes on ideas about the Middle Ages as a means to represent her own double consciousness as an African American, torn between who she knows she is and who others take her to be. In one of her journalistic pieces, "My House and a Glimpse of My Life Therein," Fauset contrasts the details of her inner rooms and private garden — described in terms redolent of medieval romance — to the grim life of the industrial city, which was beginning to take on new importance for African Americans after the Great Migration. Whitaker's essay is less interested in the means by which we establish what is objectively true about the Middle Ages (or any historical period or any person) than the value of telling new stories about the past to combat contemporary injustice. Fauset's subjective, creative approach to the Middle Ages permits her to contemplate alternatives to the disordered present and can raise questions about the why and the how of our own claims about the past.

In reading the essays in this section, we might first of all reflect on the basis of our understanding of the Middle Ages. How do we come to know what we think that we do about the Middle Ages, and how do the sources of our knowledge shape, implicitly or explicitly, our historical judgments? Do the sources and approaches presented by the essays of this volume themselves require multiplication or nuancing? What would that look like? Finally, with Fauset we might ask how stories about the Middle Ages are not just the products of historical scholarship (or the fantasies of bad-faith actors) but also opportunities to experience the present in new ways. What do the fictional, the playful, and the visionary Middle Ages share with the fact-checked and the rigorously argued? What are some ways in which they work together?

The Invisible Peasantry

Sandy Bardsley

Go to any medieval festival or Renaissance faire and you will see an interesting cast of characters. Inevitably, you will find representation of royalty. Kings and queens help structure the day with special events requiring elaborate clothing and ceremonies. These royal personages frequently preside over tournaments in which well-trained horses and knights wow the audience with bravery in the face of apparent danger. Lesser nobles, dressed in silks and fine jewelry, attend their majesties. Meanwhile, scruffier townspeople staff the booths designed to empty your pockets and send you home with souvenirs and full bellies. If peasants appear on the scene at all, they are likely swelling the ranks of the crowd, shouting protest from the stocks, or entertaining imbibers at taverns. The peasantry, according to modern popular representations, are often absent; when they do appear, they are depicted mostly as stupid bumpkins or lascivious lasses.

To be fair, the medieval nobility didn't think much differently about their underlings. Although she is better known for her love stories of aristocrats (*lais*) Marie de France wrote several Aesop-like fables in which sly, lustful wives outsmarted dopey peasant husbands who thought they had caught their wives out in adultery. In "About a Woman and Her Paramour," the wife makes her husband look into a barrel of water and explains patiently that just as the reflection he sees there is not real, nor was the sight he glimpsed of her with her lover. Another gullible husband is led to believe that the sight of his wife and a lover was, in fact, an omen of her imminent death and vows never to mention it again. Marie does not talk directly about buxom tavern wenches, but chances are that she would happily have accepted this stereotype for her unfaithful peasant wives. Nor would she likely have been surprised to see bumpkin husbands protesting from the stocks, stashed away from the main action of the tournament.

What neither Marie nor the planners of medieval festivals appreciate, however, is just how many peasants dominated the landscapes of medieval Europe nor how varied their lives were. Throughout the Middle Ages, peasants accounted for at least 90 percent—often as much as 95 percent—of the population. Their labor made possible the silks and jewelry of the elites, as well as the fine food of their feasts and the elaborate tapestries of their manor houses and castles. The system of manorialism meant that the nobility's livelihood depended largely on the labor of the peasantry. That is, peasants lived in small communities called manors. Typically—and there were indeed exceptions to this rule—these consisted of villages surrounded by unfenced fields. Some peasants were regarded as attached to the land in much the same way as buildings. Thus, if a piece of land was transferred from one lord to another, the peasants went along with it and paid their rents to the new lord. Manorialism meant payment of rents, in either cash or crops, but it also meant peasants must work for a certain number of days each week on land that the lord did not rent out. In addition, lords claimed special fees and services, such as extra work days during harvest time or fines paid in manorial courts. Lords thus received income, either in cash or in kind, from rents, from the courts, from extra payments, and from the produce of lands not rented to peasants. They took whatever food-stuffs they needed for themselves and sold the remainder to places such as towns and monasteries. The money they received in return paid for luxury goods — fine clothing, food (beyond the necessities), wine, tapestries, buildings, employ-ment of servants, upkeep of knights and horses, and more. When we admire the finery of the royal procession at a Re-naissance faire (or in a medieval manuscript), we are really looking, then, at the labor of the 90 percent.

Up until now, we've been approaching the peasantry from the perspective of the nobility — noble stereotypes of peas-ants and the economic function of the peasantry from the perspective of lords. Much of the telling of medieval history has, indeed, taken this perspective, and has justified it on the grounds that we lack sufficient documents to do otherwise. Medieval documents, certainly, were written by or on behalf of the nobility. Literacy rates were very low, and documents were usually written either for royal or noble bureaucra-cies, the church, or entertainment of the elites. Beyond the manor house, many villages lacked anyone capable of read-ing and writing except the parish priest, and thus he was of-ten drafted into service to record documents concerning the peasantry but for the explicit benefit of the manorial lord. These very documents nonetheless give us many insights into the lives of the 90 percent and allow us better to see the middle ages from their perspective. For one thing, we must realize that the 90 percent are no uniform group. The size and frequency of what they owed varied from one peasant to another, even within the same village. Some peasants (also known as serfs or villeins) were unfree and, along with their descendants, were required always to work the same land; they could not carry weapons, send their sons to school, or permit their daughters to marry someone outside the manor without the explicit and expensive permission of their lords. But this did not necessarily preclude their influence within the manor. Other peasants were free and had greater rights, albeit less economic security; when times were tough, some even chose to give away their freedom in return for a piece of land to rent. Although free and unfree peasants mixed in daily social interactions, each person in the village would have been well aware of the status of the others.

For many places, records involving the peasantry have been lost or destroyed. Late medieval England, for which tens of thousands of manorial documents survive, is an exception. The immediate purpose of these parchment rolls was to record noble income and expenditure, such as peasant rents, fines for misbehavior, or regular fees paid for various rights. Yet reading these documents against the grain—that is, in a way other than intended—tells us a great deal about the everyday lives of the peasantry and helps challenge the stereotypes of buxom wench and dumb bumpkin. We can supplement these with unwritten sources, especially artistic representations and archaeological finds.

Since the 1970s, historians have used court records and other manorial documents to collect large amounts of data about relatively ordinary individual peasants. This technique, known as prosopography, or collective biography, involves focusing on a specific place (often just one manor) and recording each time a peasant name is mentioned. Over many, many court rolls, account rolls, lists of rent, and other documents, a historian can accumulate substantial information about individuals and about the dynamics of a community. Thus, we might learn that a hypothetical William Smith, a serf, works three days a week on his lord's land and pays 2 shillings a year to rent his own plot. We might

discover that he is a butcher, because he pays a fee for practicing this trade, that his wife, Matilda, sells ale and also
pays a fee, that the land they rent has a drain that sometimes
blocks and must, by order of the court, be cleaned out, that
William often serves as member of a jury (implying he is respected), and that their eldest daughter marries a man from
a different manor. On its own, this information is interesting
enough, but the work of accumulating data pays off when
the biographies of Matilda and William are combined with
those of other peasants. For example, by noting the number
of young women, like their daughter, who marry outside of
the manor, we get some sense of patterns such as endogamy
and exogamy (marrying within and beyond the local community). If the Smiths are charged only once with a failure
to clear a blocked drain and no one faces similar charges,
then we may think little of it. However, if drain blockages
are a frequent concern then we may look again. Is this issue
purely practical (it creates flooding above, perhaps?) or do
charges of blocked drains fit a pattern of increasing attention
to the physical surroundings and order of the community?
Patterns identified from scarce scraps of data have enabled
historians to identify cultural shifts in peasant communities (although in many cases historians continue to argue
over the extent of these shifts). For example, was there a loss
in community identity after the fourteenth-century Black
Death as survivors scrambled to put their lives back together
and workers moved around the country in search of higher
wages? Was there a general shift from community policing
in the form of the hue and cry (shouting out to others to
pursue wrongdoers when someone saw a crime being committed) to policing by village elites?

Accumulation of scarce data has enabled historians to appreciate that peasants were anything but dumb yokels when
it came to manipulating the various legal systems they encountered. Many, in fact, were quite shrewd. The English

judicial system was complex, consisting not only of manorial courts but also church courts, borough courts, and various levels of royal jurisdiction. In some cases, the jurisdiction was clear. Church courts, for instance, dealt with matters of adultery or heresy as part of their jurisdiction over marriage and morality. But the crime of "scolding" (abusing someone publicly) might be seen by some as moral—as slandering the character of another—and thus belonging in a church court but by others as proper business for a local manorial or borough court and by others still as fair game for a lower-level king's court, such as that run by a sheriff. If prosecuting a potential scold, a local official could pull strings to get the case into the court most likely to convict. Peasants made similar choices when it came to inheritance of land. When a peasant householder died, that person's heirs had to pay the lord a fee, called a heriot, for the right to rent the same piece of land. Heriots traditionally took the form of the highest-valued animal owned by the family, although as time went on they were increasingly commuted to a monetary fee. But peasants nearing the ends of their lives did their heirs the favor of getting around the heriot fee by gifting them the lands and paying a lower fee for this transaction. Sometimes, in return, members of the younger generation agreed to supply relatives with stipulated amounts of food, clothing, and a seat near the hearth in their homes. In other words, peasants used the court systems imposed on them to meet their own needs and even manipulated them to their own benefit. They were well informed and made choices based on their assessment of the best outcomes.

The method of collective biography tells us much, and where there are gaps, we can often fill them with other written and unwritten sources. For instance, we can learn from court rolls about alliances among peasant men, who needed to list "pledges," other men who would guarantee their attendance at the next court. This pledging system, however, usually omitted women. But networks of female support and friendship typically existed beyond the scope of the court. Traces of female friendship can thus be found in poems and plays, such as those depicting the rowdy Wife of Noah, who prefers to stay and drown with her friends than join Noah on the ark. Peasant women and men, especially those near towns that performed the annual mystery plays, may well have watched the actor playing Noah ask the audience to empathize with him as his Wife defected to her gossipy friends. Recent work on the frequency of interactions between town and village make it hard to imagine that these representations existed only in an urban bubble, and thus we might infer that they had currency, too, for rural peasant women and men. Poems such as "A Tale of Ten Wives on Their Husbands' Ware" similarly evoke strong communities of women as they giggled over the size and shape of their husbands' "tools." (The double entendre was very much intended here; medieval people were seldom prudish.) Artistic representations—especially crude wall paintings from the fourteenth and fifteenth centuries found in parish churches and seen on a regular basis by peasant women and men—further suggest a familiarity with the discourse on strong female friendship communities. Indeed, one frequently painted scene makes a clear link with literary stereotypes. Poems and sermons tell of the demon Tutivillus who lingers behind women who gossip during church services and writes the words they speak onto a scroll. Tutivillus and the gossiping women appear in a number of surviving wall paintings. The depiction of this theme across a variety of media—wall paintings, wood and stone carvings in cathedrals, poems, and sermons—points again to discursive connections between town and countryside. One final example casts women's friendships in a more positive light: A frequent theme in parish church wall paintings is that of

Mary and St. Elizabeth confiding the news of their respective pregnancies. Here there is no lingering demon, only a focus on two women exchanging meaningful news in a sisterly embrace. The frequency with which female friendship is depicted in these sources makes it likely that peasant women experienced friendships and networks similar to those of their husbands' pledges but invisible in the court rolls. Collective biography may come up short in showing us the particulars in this instance, but examination of other types of sources can help fill in the gaps.

One type of primary source that historians have only recently begun to explore is that of archaeological remains. Skeletons from parish cemeteries, in particular, can provide a great deal of data about the health and lifespan of medieval women and men. Stable isotope studies on collagen can reveal aspects of medieval peasant diets, such as access to marine and freshwater fish, and they can give evidence of migration. Marks on bones can show prevalence of illnesses such as arthritis, tuberculosis, and chronic sinusitis. Indeed, examination of the maxillary sinuses for evidence of chronic sinusitis has revealed just how much the lives of peasant men and women were hampered by inhabiting smoky houses without chimneys. Inhalation of carbon monoxide and particulate matter almost certainly played a role in shortening the lives of peasants and may have affected women more than men. More collaboration between historians and archaeologists will certainly result in a great deal more data concerning the lives of the peasantry.

In short, the full range of peasant experiences may not be depicted at medieval festivals and Renaissance faires, but this is not because we don't know anything about them. Rather, we make choices about whose lives are worthy of depiction and commemoration, and the drama and romance we attribute to the sword-wielding knight or the eyelash-fluttering damsel tells us more about the twenty-first century than it does about the twelfth. Narratives of individuals and their impact on history perhaps help us feel included in moments of real import and bolster the sense that anyone can play a role in producing change. Yet all the elite adventures depicted in festivals take place on the backs, as it were, of the invisible peasantry. Techniques such as collective biography and use of non-documentary sources show us that this peasantry by no means consisted entirely of bumpkins and wenches. Medieval peasants, in all their variety, made smart choices and used their resources in smart ways. Their lives were often physically tough, but they softened the rough contours with friendships and humor.

Further Reading

Paul Freedman's *Images of the Medieval Peasant* (Stanford: Stanford University Press, 1999) summarizes well the varying ways in which medieval elites regarded the peasantry. For a discussion of family life of both peasants and townspeople, as extrapolated largely from coroners' rolls, see Barbara A. Hanawalt, *The Ties That Bound: Peasant Families in Medieval England* (Oxford: Oxford University Press, 1986). Judith M. Bennett's *A Medieval Life: Cecilia Penifader of Brigstock c. 1295–1344* (Boston: McGraw-Hill College, 1998) uses the life of an individual English peasant and her family as an entry point into explaining structures of life surrounding peasant communities. These three books emphasize the continuities in peasant life over the centuries. By contrast, Marjorie K. McIntosh, *Controlling Misbehavior in England, 1370–1600* (Cambridge: Cambridge University Press, 1997) considers changes in local control and courts following the Black Death.

The Hidden Narratives of Medieval Art

Katherine Anne Wilson

Two figures dressed in the height of mid-fifteenth-century fashion dominate the Arnolfini portrait in the National Art Gallery of London. Thought to represent Giovanni di Nicolao Arnolfini (ca. 1400–ca. 1460s), supplier to the court of Burgundy, and his wife, in their residence in Bruges, it is recognized as one of the finest products of fifteenth-century art, an early example of oil painting. A master of realism and perspective, Jan van Eyck of Bruges signed the portrait and is glimpsed in the mirror behind the couple. In the nineteenth century, scholars classified these paintings as "fine art": They were coveted on the burgeoning art market, gazed at and wondered upon, and academic scholars claimed a monopoly on understanding their various mysteries and possible symbolisms. The Château of Angers, France, exhibits tapestries depicting the Apocalypse. Encountering these textiles as a visitor, their sheer scale is overwhelming. Even incomplete, the set measures 144 square meters. Commissioned by Louis I, Duke of Anjou (1339–84), between 1377 and 1382, from Nicholas Bataille, a Parisian tapestry supplier, the tapestries depict the Apocalypse as taken from the Book of Revelation by St. John the Divine. Another set of tapestries, only known from documentary evidence, was commissioned to depict a contemporary battle. Paid for by the Burgundian duke, John the Fearless (1371–1419), in 1411, the five textiles commemorated his victory over the city of Liège in 1408. Gold and silver threads made the figure of John the Fearless a focal point in each tapestry, which measured 11 meters by 5 meters. In contrast to paintings, which were "fine art," nineteenth-century scholars classified medieval tapestry as "decorative art." Thus, we are less likely to revere textiles than oil paintings, even though tapestries were produced in greater numbers in the later Middle Ages and were used as cushion, bench, and table covers in homes of the middle and elite classes.

To modern viewers and readers, the Arnolfini portrait, the Angers Apocalypse tapestry series, and the documents recording the purchase of the Liège tapestries appear to be the product and preserve of an elite class of consumers in the late Middle Ages. Members of the Arnolfini family supplied luxury textiles to Philip the Good, Duke of Burgundy (1419–67), the most powerful ruler in Western Europe. Jan van Eyck was painter to the court of Burgundy at the same time and produced portraits of ruling members of the Burgundian dynasty. Louis I, Duke of Anjou, ruled alongside his nephews (Philip the Bold of Burgundy and the Duke of Berry) as regent to the French King, Charles IV (1380–1422). Louis's nephew, Philip the Bold, was father to John the Fearless. We often interpret paintings and tapestries in light of the social position of their owners. We describe the Arnolfini painting as a projection of the couple's status and wealth. We present Louis, John the Fearless, and their noble family as being in "artistic" competition with each other through their purchase of various luxury objects, and we describe tapestry commissions of this size and scale as functioning as "propaganda" statements about rule and status.

But our analyses of these objects should not focus exclusively, or perhaps even predominantly, on such elites. Our tendency to venerate these objects has obscured the layered networks of individuals whose labor was crucial to their creation and who ultimately created demand for these products that crossed borders. This essay begins by giving a "voice" and a "place" to the workers behind these products, examining the economic uncertainty and instability of employment that underpinned their production. It proceeds by considering the entrepreneurs who saw medieval courts and elite customers as commercial opportunities to be exploited. It ends by examining the elite users of these products to complicate the narratives of their consumption. Far from simply reflecting the power and status of their owners, objects such as the Arnolfini portrait or the Apocalypse tapestry also conveyed the uncertainty of everyday life and the fragility of princely rule during the Middle Ages.

One of the dangerous misconceptions of medieval products such as painting and tapestry is that one male "master artist" produced them. However, in the fourteenth and fifteenth centuries, the conception of the "artist" differed from ours today. Recent research underlines that the notion of "the master" at work on a commission in a workshop is an incorrect way to view the production of textiles or painting in the late Middle Ages. In fact, the collaboration and competition of multiple individuals over geographic and linguistic boundaries produced items such as the Arnolfini portrait and the Apocalypse tapestries. Individuals cooperated across social divisions to produce portraits and tapestries. Many designers, painters, carpenters, and gilders created an altarpiece for the Florentine church of San Pier Maggiore in 1370–71, not the single male painter, Jacopo di Cione, as scholars once suggested. Merchants traded raw materials to create paintings, such as lapis and indigo (deep blues), from Alexandria (Egypt) and Asia to Northern Italy. Many people and processes underpinned the production of textiles, including large tapestry sets. An entrepreneur or guild master oversaw the commission; a painter or draughtsman made initial drawings; weavers hung large cartoons to weave the finished textile. Teams of weavers and finishers operating multiple looms and finishing textiles produced larger commissions. Gold and silver threads from Cyprus, and silk threads from Italy, China, and Central Asia, provided expensive textiles with visual luminosity and sheen. Carders and dyers in England, Scotland, and Spain disentangled, cleaned, and dyed wool, which merchants imported and weavers used to add structural integrity to the textiles and to pick out visual programs. Finally, finishers, fullers, liners, and hangers completed, cleaned, lined, edged, and prepared the textiles and added ropes and hooks. Although these processes were essential to the finish of the final objects, they frequently involved workers excluded from formal organizations who were hired and fired when consumer demand dictated. These individuals were medieval "gig economy" workers, and without their contributions our "works of art" would not exist.

The women among these producers often disappear from view in modern accounts. In the period spanning from 1250 to 1500, men generally controlled the methods of production and the materials for the manufacture of textiles. Yet women's participation in the production of textiles does emerge in historical records. Often cited are the rare examples of women's silk guilds operating in thirteenth-century Cologne, Paris, and Rouen. Individual women operated in certain trades after the death of a husband or father. Between 1407 and 1419, Burgundian and Orléans noble households commissioned "Marguerite, widow of Colin Bataille, tapestry supplier" in her own right for textiles to be used on walls and as bed covers. Women also provided cheap labor for spinning threads and finishing textiles. However, the ability of women to operate in the workplace often depended on their relationships to successful male guild members, as daughters or wives. Even when women supplied textiles to noble households, contracts often designated them simply as "the wife of X." Some women undoubtedly exploited opportunities in the textile industry to their advantage. Their contribution deserves recognition, even if those opportunities were limited within a male-dominated industry and the records deny us their individual identities.

Urban guilds — associations of craftsmen who oversaw the various stages of industrial production — closely monitored the making of textiles. Guilds subcontracted and outsourced work when additional labor was needed and paid laborers per day or by piece produced. Though this subcontracting allowed employers to be flexible in the face of fluctuating market demand, it did not necessarily benefit those dependent on piecework. Weavers' statutes from the city of Mechelen in 1270 tell us that weavers, masters, and journeymen requiring work should stand each week at the graveyard of the local parish church to wait for the offer of a job and that they should not take any initiative in sourcing employment by talking to potential employers. These rules give a glimpse into a world of male and female textile workers who were hired and fired as needed, and who were not allowed access to formal guild structures. They remained outside of any of the guild's fiscal support networks that were especially useful in times of economic hardship. The revolt of the Ypres drapers in 1281, the revolt of the Tournai fullers in 1307, the revolt of Bruges weavers and fullers in 1360, and of the Sienese wool workers and carders in 1371 should be viewed, in part, as a symptom of the precarious circumstances faced by many of these "gig" workers. Laborers seeking to achieve representation from guilds and town authorities or to demand higher wages frequently drove urban revolts across late medieval Europe. At times, these revolts achieved their goals. Yet several revolts ended with loss of life. On Wednesday, December 4, 1280, three weavers, Haneton Lauwier, Jehan Boucery, and Collart Caullet, were decapitated for their role in preventing and disrupting work as well as causing injuries to ruling elites of the city. Their end is a salutary reminder of the hardships workers endured and the risks laborers took to make their voices heard to the elites for whom they worked.

The individuals at the top of guild structures who acted as a point of contact for customers who commissioned paintings or tapestries enjoyed far more protection. They could possess multiple guild memberships, were often the owners and renters of urban properties, and served on local government committees. However, they also navigated uncertainty. The medieval world, like so many economies today, provided no social safety net, and even individuals who had climbed to the top of the urban ladder in trade and commerce had to consider the prospect of a fall. We have records of a master draper of Verona who, in the thirteenth century, left the city due to poverty, and Parisian trade statutes from 1272 reveal masters who had to drop down to the status of journeymen as a result of financial hardship. Indeed, complex commissions such as large-scale tapestries or paintings created inherent financial and personal risk. Clients — especially noble clients — were frequently late in settling debts. Thus, collaboration made sense for large-scale products, such as the Apocalypse or Liège tapestries, to spread risk. Surviving payments for weavings occasionally record contracts for two individuals to produce large-scale textiles. Guild statutes from Bruges in the fourteenth century expressly forbid guild masters to pool resources and share weaving looms, a rule likely made because such sharing was occurring with great frequency.

If production of these items was risky, then why undertake it? In a sense, producers were exploiting customers to create their own economic security net. We might consider noble households as nodes in commercial networks rather than centers of art production or patronage, providing a mass of wealthy customers with money to burn and reputation to bestow. Medieval courts presented commercial opportunities for aspiring suppliers of luxury objects. Supplying nobility within a courtly network, even once, with good quality products, was a means by which an individual supplier (male or female) might enhance their mercantile reputation. They could then carry this reputation back to their centers of production to obtain more monetary credit, which in turn might lead to more commissions, more networks, and further economic security. Individuals who could maintain the quality of products might establish a monopoly of supply at certain medieval courts. Jan van Eyck, our painter of the Arnolfini portrait was one, his subject Giovanni Arnolfini another. Van Eyck was given an official position at the court of Burgundy and was sent on diplomatic visits. The Arnolfini family established a monopoly on the supply of silks to the Burgundian court.

But what, then, of the users of textiles and painting? Surely given all the individuals, labor, and materials involved in their production, patrons commissioned and used these objects to project their power and authority. However, consumption, use, and display are far more complicated than this. Two considerations are important here. First, objects do not remain static once created. Second, objects can escape the intentions of their creators. If we stand in front of medieval products today, it is important to recognize the claims that paintings and tapestries made might have been at odds with the social and political realities surrounding those who owned and displayed them, as well as the perceptions of those people and their objects by those visiting their households. Two case studies can serve to illuminate these points.

First, the Arnolfini portrait depicts the uncertainty of everyday life as much as it projects the power and success of the Arnolfini family, which included Giovanni di Nicolao Arnolfini and his younger cousin, Giovanni de Arrigo Arnolfini. After several initial commissions to the Burgundian household, supplying luxury textiles in the 1420s and founding a silk shop in Bruges in the 1430s, the Arnolfinis had established a monopoly of supply to the Burgundian household of silks and velvets. Between 1439 and 1455, Giovanni de Arrigo Arnolfini sold 19,352 ells (about 21,000 meters in total) of textiles for £131,568. In the portrait, the objects of the room visually embody the commercial success of the family. Textiles are a dominant object in the chamber: They are present on the bed as blood red backings, curtains, ceiling, and cover, on the chair as components of a seat and cushion cover, and on the floor. The couple is draped in heavy woolen broadcloths, one of the finest textiles produced in the Low Countries. Fresh oranges under the window signal the Arnolfini ability to access wider markets. The Arnolfini portrait, painted around the time the family were tightening their monopoly at the Burgundian household, might well be described as a "snapshot" of Arnolfini power and status.

However, we can also read from the painting the motto of late medieval merchants, that the only thing to rely on in life was the "certainty of uncertainty." Scholars have debated the identity of the female figure in the portrait: It might be a memorial portrait of Constanza Trenta, Giovanni di Nicolao Arnolfini's first wife who died (possibly in childbirth) in 1433. Whether is it Constanza or a later partner, here is the first hint of the uncertainty of life, the tragic death of a female and child in spite of the narrative of commercial success embedded in the portrait. Another "uncertainty" comes in the narrative of the Arnolfini family career. In 1461, at the height of Arnolfini success, Giovanni de Arrigo Arnolfini defected to the "archenemy" of the Burgundian duke, the French King Louis XI. What prompted this significant change remains unclear.

The second example concerns an artistic production whose pictorial claims were at odds with its political reality — the set of textiles paid for by the Burgundian duke, John the Fearless, in 1411 to commemorate his victory over the city of Liège in 1408. Unlike the Apocalypse textiles, John the Fearless's tapestries no longer exist. However, documentary evidence of their purchase and visual programs remains. Even when medieval objects do not survive, documentary evidence needs to be used to study them further and shed light on their multiple uses. The first hanging in the series represented John the Fearless mustering his army, the second showed the siege of the town of Maastricht, the third depicted the battle and the "manner by which they [the Liégeois] were chased away," the fourth had scenes of submission of the towns involved, and the fifth offered a vision of the repentance of the key figures in the rebellion and the revocation of city privileges. Each hanging was 55 square meters, woven with gold and silver threads. It is tempting to see these objects as depicting "propagandist subject matter" or functioning as a "portable propaganda" imposing upon viewers a central message of Burgundian authority and the consequences of challenging that rule.

However, the commissioner faced significant political insecurities at the point of production, when there was strong political opposition to the Burgundian duke. In 1411, John the Fearless was in a significant struggle for control of the crown of France. King Charles VI was mentally incapacitated and unable to rule. Other members of the French royal family were seeking to usurp John's dominance over the French King and heir, and the political situation in Paris was deteriorating into open civil war. John the Fearless was himself murdered in 1419 as a direct result of these political conflicts. When commissioned, these textiles may have been intended to represent an ideal past, but they also reflected political uncertainty and the instability of princely rule. Medieval audiences were by no means passive consumers of visual narratives.

When we examine surviving objects like the Arnolfini portrait or the Apocalypse tapestries, we need to see multiple hands involved in their production, use, and reception. They refract to us a far more diverse past than just the triumph and passive acceptance of power, wealth, and elitism. Instead, they present to us a more interesting Middle Ages of collaboration and exploitation, inclusion and exclusion, stability and instability. As students of these objects, we must represent all the individuals and narratives involved in their creation, reception, and use to ask far more carefully: Whose Middle Ages do these objects reflect?

Further Reading

The student will find useful evidence on later medieval European revolts in Samuel K. Cohn, *Popular Protest in Late Medieval Europe, Italy, France and Flanders* (Manchester, UK: Manchester University Press, 2004). For women as producers and workers, see both Martha Howell, *Women, Production and Patriarchy in Late Medieval Cities* (Chicago: University of Chicago Press, 1986) and Sharon Farmer, *The*

Silk Industries of Medieval Paris: Artisanal Migration, Technological Innovation, and Gendered Experience (Philadelphia: University of Pennsylvania Press, 2016). For analysis of the Arnolfini family as merchants and of the Arnolfini portrait itself, students will find useful discussions in Bart Lambert, *The City, the Duke and Their Banker: The Rapondi Family and the Formation of the Burgundian State (1384–1430)* (Turnhout, Belgium: Brepols, 2006); Margaret D. Carroll, "In the name of God and Profit: Jan Van Eyck's Arnolfini Portrait," *Representations* 44 (1993), 96–132; and Craig Harbison, *Jan Van Eyck: The Play of Realism*, 2nd Expanded Edition (London, UK: Reaktion Books, 2011). Useful information on the collaborative processes behind products in the Middle Ages, on the guild producers, apprentices, and other labor can be found in Gervase Rosser, "Crafts, Guilds and the Negotiation of Work in the Medieval Town," *Past and Present* 154 (1997), 3–31; and Peter Stabel, "The Move to Quality Cloth: Luxury Textiles, Labour Markets and Middle Class Identity in a Medieval Textile City. Mechelen in the Late Thirteenth and Early Fourteenth Centuries," in Bart Lambert and Katherine Anne Wilson, *Europe's Rich Fabric: The Consumption, Commercialisation, and Production of Luxury Textiles in Italy, the Low Countries and Neighbouring Territories (Fourteenth-Sixteenth Centuries)* (Farnham, UK: Ashgate Books, 2016). On challenging the concept of tapestry as a "decorative art" and examining textiles from documentary evidence, see Laura Weigert, "Tapestry Exposed," *The Art Bulletin* 4 (1994): 784–96, and Katherine Anne Wilson, *The Power of Textiles: Tapestries of the Burgundian Dominions (1363–1477)* (Turnhout, Belgium: Brepols, 2018).

Modern Intolerance
and the Medieval Crusades

Nicholas L. Paul

Among the events and ideas we link with the Middle Ages perhaps none is invoked as frequently, as forcefully, and in as bewildering an array of circumstances as the Christian holy wars known as crusades. Epic battles pitting helmeted knights against turbaned adversaries in dusty settings are the backdrop for popular movies, TV shows, novels, and massively popular electronic games; figures from the crusades are held up as mascots for sports teams and as iconic figures in the histories of nations and religious and cultural groups. Memories of the crusades are not just popular — they are also powerful, and claims about the meaning and legacy of the crusades have never been as contentious, nor as potentially explosive, as they are today.

Although the crusades have always occupied an outsized place in popular perceptions of the Middle Ages, in the Western world the term "crusade" gained a new political currency after the September 11, 2001, terrorist attacks in the United States. Only five days later, U.S. President George W. Bush famously quipped that "this crusade, this war on terror, is going to take a while." The remark appeared to have been unscripted, and the administration did not take long to apologize, but none of this made the comment any less momentous. For one thing, the president's words came at a moment marked by extreme statements about Islam and its relationship to Christianity and the Western world. Two days earlier, columnist Ann Coulter — still a frequent invitee to speak on American college campuses — had written in the *National Review Online* that rather than worrying about offending Muslims through racial or religious profiling at airports, "we should invade their countries, kill their leaders, and convert them to Christianity." Bush's words were also an omen, for they heralded a new appropriation of the crusades among some white Europeans and Americans who saw themselves as locked in a global struggle against a resurgent and threatening Islam.

In Europe and the United States, anti-immigrant activists and white supremacists have explicitly associated themselves and their actions with the crusades. Anders Behring Breivik, a Norwegian ethno-nationalist terrorist who murdered 77 people in 2011, wrote a manifesto that made extensive reference to the crusades. Breivik claimed to be a member of an organization that was called the "Knights Templar" after a medieval crusading military order. In 2016, members of a Kansas militia calling themselves "The Crusaders" were arrested plotting to blow up mosques in the United States. At the time of this writing, online neo-Nazi discussion forums brim with discussions of the history of the crusades. Images of armored knights sporting the banner of the cross are frequently deployed as memes on social media, often with anti-immigrant or fascist connotations.

The widespread perception of the crusades as a "clash of civilizations" in which white Europeans supposedly resisted or even subjugated non-whites, non-Christians, and especially Muslims has become an inspiration to those inclined to racist ideologies. A similar intensification of references to the crusading past in terms of existential conflict can be observed in the media of Islamist extremist militants. While "crusade" and "crusader" have long been familiar epithets cast at perceived enemies of the Muslim world, in the age of international terrorism these terms have been directed at perceived "crusader" enemies, such as the United States, Europe, and Israel. The neo-medieval Islamist group known in the United States as ISIS made the West's "Failed Crusade" against them a cover story of the October 2014 issue of their magazine *Dabiq*.

The fiery language of Islamic extremists and European ethno-nationalists is only the most recent chapter in a longer story of the appropriation and reinterpretation of the crusades over time. The representation of the crusades in the most extreme rhetoric of the present moment is most often drawn not from a direct engagement with medieval materials, but from centuries of modern remembering, reassigning, and reinterpreting, much of it carried out in art and literature. In the eighteenth century, French Enlightenment philosophers used the crusades as an example of the ignorance and superstition of traditional religion. In the mid-nineteenth century, readers thrilled to the novels of the British author Walter Scott, who used the crusades as the backdrop for tales of chivalry and romantic adventure. Not long afterwards, European writers celebrated their newly won empires in North Africa, the Middle East, and (in the case of Germany) Central and Eastern Europe, by comparing their troops to conquering crusaders, finishing the job of colonization that their crusading ancestors had started. But by the same token, children educated under colonial occupation grew up to understand the crusades as evidence of the timeless drive by European powers to conquer and subject others to their will. This sense of having been "crusaded" is no less important in the Orthodox Christian world, where the memory of invasion of Orthodox Slavic territory by the German crusading order of the Teutonic Knights in 1240 was a key element in Soviet propaganda during the Second World War. The sack of Constantinople by the Fourth Crusade in 1204 and the failure of crusaders to prevent the Ottoman conquest of the Byzantine empire have also played an important role in modern Greek national history and identity.

All of these interpretations of medieval Christian Holy War, rationalist and romantic, colonial and nationalist, now co-exist in a kind of muddy soup from which modern impressions of the crusades are formed. So muddled had even the scholarly situation become in the later twentieth century that one medieval historian thought it necessary to return to the basic question: *What were the crusades?* It is a more challenging question than might be apparent at first glance. Although we can find the origins of the word "crusade" in terms that appear in the later Middle Ages (*cruzada/ crozada* or *crucesignati*, for its warriors who were "signed with the cross"), the medieval terminology was applied inconsistently. The large military expeditions we might call the "First Crusade" or the "Third Crusade" were as likely to be known to contemporaries simply as a "journey" or a "[sea] crossing" made by "pilgrims" or "soldiers of Christ."

Like any important historical question, we still debate how best to define the crusades, but most specialists have settled on four main characteristics:

Crusades originated with the authority of the church; the call to arms was issued by the papacy and announced by the church through preaching.

Like initiation into a monastic order, becoming a crusader involved a major change in status that was signaled through rituals. Crusaders often took

a solemn vow, symbolized by the sign of the cross
worn on their clothing.

The assumption of crusading status was recognized in turn
by the extension of valuable privileges:

With regard to worldly goods, crusaders could expect
protections for their family and property while
they were preparing to depart and, most important, while they were away.
Arguably the most valuable of all privileges was the
plenary indulgence. Offered to crusaders upon
successful completion of their vow or in death, the
indulgence meant that crusaders would not have
to fear God's punishment for any sins they had
confessed.

Nothing as complicated and new as this could emerge out of
thin air — it took time for the fundamental ideas to develop
and the practices to spread. Some aspects, such as the vow,
the change of clothing and status, and the indulgence were
clearly related to the practice of pilgrimage. The first key
architect of the crusading idea was Pope Urban II (reigned
1088–1099). It was Urban who first called upon Latin Christians to march to the East at the Council of Clermont —
in modern-day France — on November 27, 1095. We actually have very little idea about what precisely Urban said
that day, but he likely combined a proposal to defend the
Christian Church in the East with the notion of penitence
(suffering to alleviate the consequences of sinful behavior). Penitence was already a very popular idea — it enjoyed
widespread popularity in pilgrimage — and this was a potent
combination of penitence and violence, of pilgrimage and
war. The idea was an instant success, generating an enormous popular response in the chain of events that we call
the "First Crusade."

The four-point definition of *crusade* offered here (known as the "pluralist" definition) is perhaps most notable for what it does *not* include. There is, for instance, nothing about crusading being directed at a particular target, be that a region (the Holy Land), holy site (Jerusalem), or avowed enemy (followers of Islam). Crusading could and did happen anywhere in the medieval world within Christian reach, including the Iberian Peninsula, the Baltic region, North Africa, and the Canary Islands in the North Atlantic. It could also take place within Christendom against those viewed as schismatics like the Orthodox population of the Byzantine Empire, against those seen as supporters of heretics such as the Catholic population of southern France, and political enemies of the Roman Church such as the Holy Roman Emperor Frederick II. The latter case is a reminder that crusades were directed not only against Christians, but even against other crusaders.

The medieval experience of crusading, then, differs in very significant ways from many modern representations, and most starkly from the ideas of today's racist ideologues. Racial and religious hatred did exist in the Middle Ages, and it was certainly marshaled as a tool of recruitment for particular crusade expeditions. But in this harnessing of ideas of difference, of "us vs. them," the promoters of one or another crusade expedition did not differ very much from the promoters of war in other periods and throughout the world. Campaigns to recruit crusaders and the crusade armies themselves could occasion considerable violence toward vulnerable communities caught in the path of crusading armies or para-military groups hoping to join or support crusades. The preaching of several major crusade expedition destined for the East and also the "popular crusades" — grassroots movements undertaken without papal sanction — inspired massacres of Jewish communities within Europe, for instance. But this violence toward minority groups, such as the steadily rising rhetoric of fear, anger, and hatred directed at non-Christians, existed both before the coming of the First Crusade and long after the papacy ceased to make calls for new crusades. Crusades were only one avenue of opportunity for the types of violence and intolerance that were (and still are) carried out locally by individuals acting to their own advantage and by states and elites seeking to extend and consolidate power over their subjects. Violence and oppression are major features of the history of the crusades, but they are far from the most distinctive features of the broader crusade phenomenon, which owed its longevity and popularity to its engagement with the devotional lives of individual Christians, their concern over the implications of their sinful lives, and their desire to leave those lives behind and participate in the drama of salvation on an epic stage.

From the modern perspective, that epic stage of crusading conflict is made up of the famous, large-scale military expeditions under the command of kings such as Richard the Lionheart, Frederick Barbarossa, or Saint Louis. These are the crusades to which we attach a canonical number ("First" "Second" "Third," and so on) and which were fought predominantly by Latin (Roman Catholic) Christians against Muslim Arab and Turkish armies. Apart from common adherence to the Roman Christian religious tradition, however, the crusader armies that were drawn from many different regions and kingdoms had little in common and often could not agree on either the objective or basic strategy of the expedition. Both Muslim and Christian armies hired mercenaries and recruited allies of different faiths; crusader armies in the Near East were diverse, composed of Armenian engineers, Arab scribes, and mixed-race "Turcopole" auxiliary troops. Writing decades after he was held captive in Egypt in 1250, the crusader John of Joinville recalled the man he called "my Saracen" who had provided him security and comfort in his darkest hours. In a work he dedicated to Saladin, arch-enemy of the crusaders who reconquered Jerusalem in 1187, the Syrian Muslim writer Usama ibn Munqidh remembered the many friendships he had with Latin Europeans living in the crusader kingdoms, including those he had with the Knights Templar. Crusading was a Pan-European phenomenon, but it was not a project for the defense of Europe or Europeans, and crusaders collaborated with and even befriended those who did not look or worship as they did.

Taking the long view, it is easy to see how the crusades became associated with the later familiar story of European colonization and conquest. A unified project of overseas European conquest and domination was, in fact, how some contemporary Muslim observers perceived the coming of the crusaders. Living as they did in what was undeniably an era of expansion and territorial consolidation along the frontiers of Christendom (of the *Making of Europe*, to cite the title of a now famous book), the Muslims of the Near East such as the jurist 'Ali ibn Tahir al-Sulami (d. 1106) understandably assumed that the First Crusade was just another element of a global drive for mastery. But al-Sulami was far better informed about what was happening across the Mediterranean than the crusaders, most of whom would have been only dimly aware of what their co-religionists were up to in northeastern Spain or Sicily. Theirs was not a coordinated effort. Where coordination did come, it was to rationalize crusading as part of a larger effort of ecclesiastical reform and to ensure papal sovereignty over the earth: a kingdom of heaven rather than a terrestrial empire. In the minds of some, crusading was both an agent and a sign of the end of time, which further supports the idea that what the crusaders sought was the installation of a heavenly kingdom in place of the corrupt empires of mankind.

I have suggested above that crusade commanders (at least those fighting in the Near East) rarely agreed upon a clear strategy, but it is nevertheless true that crusades in the eastern Mediterranean resulted in the conquest of territory in areas of modern-day Syria, Palestine, Turkey, Lebanon, Israel, Egypt, Greece, and Cyprus. The later modern history of colonialism probably has much to teach us about the experiences of those living under crusader dominion. Nevertheless, specialists in the study of these territories strongly object to the idea of continuity or even similarity between the crusader conquests, which yielded no clear economic benefit to the patchwork of communities that sustained them, and later European colonization, which went hand-in-glove with economic exploitation and the construction of great national overseas empires by organized, centralized states.

The romance and the horror of the crusades, and so their fascination, are undeniable and enduring. For the student of history, this fascination only grows as we learn more about the shaping of ideologies of religious violence; the challenge of travel over great distances; the experience of colliding cultures, languages, and beliefs; and the countless human stories caught up in the first truly global drama of the Middle Ages. But just as the memory of the crusades belongs to myriad communities across the world, the identities of "crusader" and "crusaded" are worlds away. The complex devotional frameworks that made crusading possible are as alien today as the social and political structures that elevated lords in stone towers or the technologies that made a mounted warrior a preeminent force in war. Past stories provide no salve nor excuse for those who would seek to legitimize or explain the violence and intolerance of the present. Viewed in the medieval mirror, the demands of our own ideologies reflect back to us only our own troubled image.

Further Reading

A thoughtful, recent introduction to the history of the crusades is provided by Susanna Throop, *The Crusades: An Epitome* (Leeds, UK: Kismet Press, 2018). Jonathan Riley-Smith's *The Crusades: A History* 3rd ed. (New York: Bloomsbury, 2014) is the best comprehensive account of the crusades from the "pluralist" perspective. It is also possible to write a history of the crusades from other points of view, including from the perspective of the Islamic world, and this has been masterfully done by Paul Cobb, *The Race for Paradise: An Islamic History of the Crusades* (Oxford: Oxford University Press, 2014). An account of the changing attitudes of historians toward the crusades from the Middle Ages to the modern era is provided in Christopher Tyerman, *The Debate on the Crusades* (Manchester: Manchester University Press, 2011). For a focused study of the reception of crusading in the nineteenth and early twentieth centuries, see Mike Horswell, *The Rise and Fall of British Crusader Medievalism: c. 1825–1945* (Andover: Routledge, 2018). An important recent contribution to understanding contemporary challenges of talking about the crusades can be found in Matthew Gabriele, "Debating the 'Crusade' in Contemporary America," in *The Mediaeval Journal* (2016). For the crusades in contemporary media and politics, see Bruce Holsinger, *Neomedievalism, Neoconservatism, and the War on Terror* (Chicago: Prickly Paradigm Press, 2007) and Andrew B. R. Elliott, *Medievalism, Politics, and Mass Media: Appropriating the Middle Ages in the Twenty-First Century* (Cambridge: D. S. Brewer, 2017).

The author thanks William Purkis and Matthew Gabriele for their helpful comments on this piece.

Blood Libel, a Lie and Its Legacies

Magda Teter

In 2014, the Anti-Defamation League appealed to Facebook to take down a page titled "Jewish Ritual Murder." A year later, in May 2015, members of the British Movement (BM), a white supremacist group in the United Kingdom, gathered in the town of Lincoln to "revive a tradition of the English Middle Ages." The group proceeded to the Lincoln Cathedral, where they wanted to honor "Little Hugh of Lincoln," a nine-year old boy who died in 1255. Little Hugh's death was blamed on Jews and became the first case in England that resulted in their execution, though not the first case of such an accusation against them. A shrine devoted to "Little Hugh" emerged, and the story was soon included in contemporary chronicles, among them by Benedictine chronicler Matthew Paris, and local ballads. In the fourteenth century, the story entered more popular works of literature, the most famous being Chaucer's "Prioress' Tale." While "Little Hugh of Lincoln" became a site of popular devotion, he was never officially recognized as a saint by church authorities, Catholic, or, later, Anglican.

At their arrival in the Cathedral, the BM group was confronted by a priest who informed them that "Little Hugh of Lincoln" was not a saint. In fact, since 1959, a time when Europe was reckoning with the enormity of the Nazi destruction of Jews and beginning to reexamine Christian anti-Jewish sentiments in culture and prayers, a plaque has been placed at the site of Little Hugh's tomb. It calls the accusations "trumped-up stories" and "fictions" that "cost many innocent Jews their lives," and includes a prayer: "Such stories do not redound to the credit of Christendom, and so we pray: Lord, forgive what we have been, amend what we are, and direct what we shall be."

The neo-Nazi men in Lincoln rejected this rebuttal, gave their own counter-prayer, and left offerings of flowers (symbolic red and white roses) at the remnants of the burial site of "Little St. Hugh of Lincoln": "We are here today in memory of Little Saint Hugh, who was murdered in the year 1255 by Jews, he was just 9 years old. The medieval historian Mathew Paris recorded the event. A Jew named Jopin confessed to the murder and implicated the wider Jewish community of the time in this crime, Jopin suggested that the killing of Hugh was a ritual religious sacrifice. The modern statement here is an abomination and an insult to the memory of Little Saint Hugh." Though Lincoln Cathedral contains sites of burial of two other venerated figures — Bishop Hugh of Lincoln who died in 1200 and was officially canonized in 1220, and Bishop Edward King who died in 1910 — that the group would target the remnants of the shrine of Little Hugh of Lincoln reveals the enduring power and attraction of anti-Jewish elements of medieval history.

While other medieval anti-Jewish tales waned, as did those of the desecration of the consecrated communion wafer, or of poisoning of wells, the tale that Jews killed Christian children, known as the "ritual murder" or "blood libel" survived, adapting to changing cultural and political climates, surviving into the twenty-first century. In the Middle East, the iconography of ritual murder has become a visual tool for anti-Israeli cartoons. In Europe, these stories and sites associated with them have become, as the May 2015 encounter in Lincoln demonstrates, magnets for fascist and white supremacists groups. The British Movement is not the only group embracing this narrow part of the medieval past in seeking to revive cults grounded in the anti-Jewish tales accusing Jews of murdering Christian children. In 2007 a group emerged seeking to revive the cult of Simon of Trent, abolished in 1965. Simon's death in 1475 resulted in one of the most notorious persecutions of Jews. The story left a lasting literary, visual, and even legal legacy.

The attraction of the blood libel legend for fascist and white supremacist groups has a longer history than their twenty-first-century revival. On May 1, 1934, the Nazi paper *Der Stürmer* published a special issue devoted to "Ritual Murder." The headline in big red letters was screaming "A Jewish Plan to Murder Non-Jews Uncovered!" Below was an image of Jews filling basins with the purported blood of Christian children, with three crosses in the background. The caption read: "Throughout the millennia, the Jews, following the secret rite, shed human blood. The devil is still sitting on our necks today, it's up to you to pack the devil's brood." Stories and images of Jews killing Christians filled the rest of the issue — nearly twenty pages (see Figure 1). Three more such issues would follow in 1937, 1939, and 1942. Soon, the Italian fascist publication *La difesa della razza* also devoted part of its issue to ritual murder and blood libels.

The 1934 publication elicited a swift response. From May 11 through the next few days, the *Times* of London carried an article and a number letters of protest from prom-

Figure 1. Der Stürmer, May 1, 1934, page 7.

inent figures, including the Chief Rabbi, the Archbishop of Canterbury, and the President of the Folklore Society, alarmed by this "revival" of "the worst excesses of medieval fanaticism." The Mayor of Lincoln and the Chancellor of the Lincoln Cathedral also joined in "to disavow the legend of 'Little St. Hugh.'"

But if *Der Stürmer* exploited the deeply rooted tropes of ritual murder, they did not invent them. In fact, the May 1, 1934 issue went out of its way to provide what they deemed historical evidence of "the Jewish plan to murder mankind." The issue included "A Compilation of Jewish Ritual Mur-

ders from the Time of Christ until 1932," with 131 examples,
along with sources aimed at their validation. For the medieval and early modern period, *Der Stürmer*'s sources were
early modern printed books — chronicles, annals, polemical anti-Jewish works, and lives of saints, among them the
notorious Alfonso Espina's *Fortalitium Fidei*, the widely
respected Cesare Baronio's *Annales Ecclesiastici*, and the
Bollandist *Acta Sanctorum*, as well as the more local Mat-
thäus Rader's *Bavaria Sacra*. Modern examples were in turn
supported by references to press coverage and contemporary
works, among them the Jesuit *Civiltà Cattolica*. In this presentation, Julius Streicher sought to impress on his readers
the "millennia"-long Jewish "plot" against Christians. And
in a sophisticated propagandistic move, Streicher provided
"visual evidence" of diverse historical images depicting Jews
killing Christians. Among them were paintings and sculptures from churches, for example, of Werner of Oberwesel
and Andreas von Rinn; reproductions of woodcuts and cop-
perplates from premodern books (among them the iconic
image of Simon of Trent from Hartmann Schedel's 1493
chronicle, which had incidentally been republished in a
splendid facsimile in 1933 in Leipzig, and a vivid illustration of an accusation in Regensburg from *Bavaria Sacra*),
and nineteenth-century cartoons from the press covering the
murders in Tisza-Eszlar and Konitz. For propagandistic purposes, *Der Stürmer* did not turn just to premodern literature
for historical proofs but also to premodern methodologies.
Der Stürmer's sources did indeed contain the stories included in the May 1934 issue. But the paper took them — as
many premoderns did — as *prima facie* authoritative sources
of historical knowledge.

In complex ways, these premodern chronicles shaped the
way future generations would remember the past, as they,
according to historian Heinrich Schmidt, wrote events "into

a future," making "their presence last." European chronicles, rooted in biblical and Roman models, formed what Judith Pollmann called "an archive" of "useful knowledge that was considered to be 'true.'" They recorded "what was memorable and therefore important," mentioned, or even inscribed, crucial documents, and narrated power relations. They had a choice to omit events and stories or to include them, to leave them for posterity or to doom them into oblivion. Chronicle narratives also supplied morality tales through stories of disorder that always ended with a resolution and return to order.

Scattered among thousands of events and stories, sometimes from the creation of the world to the contemporary moment, are dozens of seemingly random tales about Jews, exposing a reader not interested in specifically Jewish topics to Jews in word and sometimes images. Just glancing at premodern indexes, which frequently did not include all stories, provides a taste of what European readers could see Jews historically "did" and what was done to them. The *Liber chronicarum*, a chronicle of the world, by Hartmann Schedel, published in Nuremberg in 1493—arguably most famous for thousands of woodcut illustrations, though not the most popular—included eleven stories about Jews for the post-biblical period. Ten were listed in the index under the heading "Jews." Those included: "Jews were expelled from France"; "Jews treat the venerable sacrament irreverently in the town of Deckendorff"; "Jews were burned throughout Germany because they poisoned Christian springs"; "Jews were killed and plundered by the inhabitants of Prague"; "Jews were burned by the order of Albert, the Duke of Austria"; "Jews killed a boy named Simon in the city of Trent"; "Jews in these times pierced sacred Eucharist with blood pouring"; "Jews in Nuremberg and other adjacent places were sent to fire"; "A Jew stabbed an image

of Christ and blood flowed"; "A baptized Jew returned to
Judaism and was sent to fire." In short, in Schedel's world
chronicle, post-biblical Jews kill; desecrate images and the
Eucharist; poison wells and springs; and convert, but then
revert, to Judaism. In return, they are expelled, burned,
plundered, and killed. The verbs used in relation to Jews are
ominous. Only occasionally did Jews convert and become
good Christians, like Petrus Alphonsi. The Jews of Christian chronicles are not the Jews Christians actually encountered every day as their neighbors, with whom they shared
towns, neighborhoods, even homes. These were dangerous,
demonic figures, enemies, who needed to be contained and
punished. Also missing in this imagined medieval past is the
fact that while the Middle Ages are marked by the beginning
of the ritual murder and blood libel accusations — Christian
narratives and persistent beliefs about Jews killing Christian
children — the period is also notable for the most explicit
defense of Jews by both secular and ecclesiastical authorities
against these accusations.

Amplifying the impact of these ghastly stories about Jews,
Hartmann Schedel and his printer, Anton Koberger, added
images — images that stand out on the page as larger and
more detailed than others. For example, the story of a Jew
desecrating a crucifix in the early seventh century is only
seven lines long, but the image is the largest on the page,
nineteen lines in height. Similarly, William of Norwich, the
first European story of ritual accusation, is mentioned in
just one sentence — "Boy William in England was crucified
by Jews on Good Friday in the town of Norwich, of whose
subsequent wonderful sight one can read," an allusion to
the story in Vincent of Beauvais's *Speculum historiale* — on
a page containing stories of prominent Christians: Hilde-
gard of Bingen (seven lines), Gratian (fifteen lines), Peter
Lombard (nine lines), and Peter Comestor (eleven lines).
But the image depicting William's crucifixion is the largest

Das sechſt alter

hildegardis

Jlbegardis ein iunckfraw gůts alters hat in teütſchen landen bey dem Rheyn wunderperlicher weyſe gereichſinet. vnnd het auß gőtlicher kraft die gnad. das ſie (wiewol ſie ein layin vnd vngelert was) offt wunderperlich an ſchlaff entzugt. ler net nicht allain latein reden ſunder auch ſchreyben vnnd tichten. alſo das ſie etliche bücher crıſtenlicher lere machet. Von der ſagt man das ſie künftige ding verkündmet hab. Je hab auch ſamnt Bernhart etliche brieff geſchriben. So hab ſie auch an die von Cőlne von künftiger betrübnus der pfaſheit geſchriben. wie die pfaſheit ere vnd rům on verdienſt. vnd verdienſtnus on das werck haben wőllen.

Gracianus

Gracianus ein cloſterman wardt in dem iar des herren M.c.xlv. zu Bononia von ſeiner groſſe ſynnreichig keit vnd ſchaftlicher lere vnnd weyßheit wegen zu groſſer achtung vñ wird en gehalten. Der hat vnder andern wer ken ſeiner kunſt das buch gaiſtlicher rechten Decretows ge nant gar maiſterlich geſamlet. das daß durch babſt Euge nium beſtettigt vnd in den hohen ſchůlen zeleſen verlihen iſt. das hat er in ſchőner art zu vnderſchaid vnd merckung der puncten. artickel vnd maynung darin begriffen ge ordnet. vnnd in drey tayl geſündert inmaſſen die rechtgelerten deß gůts wiſſen haben. Darüber haben auch nachfolgend etlich lere der recht außlegung vnd erklerung ge ſchriben.

Petrus lombardus

Petrus lombardus biſchoff zu Parys ein Lombardi er iſt diſer zeit (als Vincentius gallus ſeyt) zu Parys vnder den gelerten. mit allain ſeiner ſunder auch dauo ver ſchyner zeit an güther des lebens vnd ſcheypffe der ſynnreichigen hohberümbt vnd achtper geweſt. vnnd hat die bücher der hohen ſynne gar treffenlich geſchriben. das daſn ein mülſiams werck auß vil heiliger vater ſpruchen müglich zuſame gebracht iſt. Er hat auch die grőſſern gloß des pſalters vnd ſant paulſen epiſtel auß vil ſprüchen geordnet. vñ ſunſt vil gaiſtlichs treffenlichs gůts vnd tapffers dings gemacht vñ ge ſchriben vnd auch gar ſchőn lőblich vñ fruchtpar predig vñ lere vor dē vo lck getan.

Petrus comeſtor

Petrus comeſtor der vorgenantē zwayer brüder nicht des flaſchs ſunder der tugent halben hat diſer zeit gelebet. vnd (als Vincentius Gallus melder. hiſtoriā ſco laſticam gemacht. vnd darin die hiſtorien vnd geſchichten beder teſtament floſſigclich vnd zierlich außgedruckt. vnd dabey auch allſpald etlicher haydon hiſtorien vnd geſchichtē an bequemlichen enden eingeſüert vnd eingezogen vñ auch etlich ſchőn verlų zu lob vnd preiſe der iunck/ frawen marie gemacht. Alſo iſt diſer zeit die kirch mit lere faſt erleüchtet worden. Er lich ſagen diſe vorgenanten drey lere ſeyen drey leyplich brüder doch auß eebuch ge
poru ge
weſen.
vnd als
ir muter
darumb nicht rew haben mocht.
do wardt ir zu bůß geſetzt das ſie
doch deß rew habe ſolt dz ſie nicht
rew haben mőcht.

Gwilhelmus ein kind

Gwilhelm us ein kind in engel/ land wardt diſer zeit von dē iuden an karfreytag in der ſtatt nor wico gecreützgt. von dem liſet man darnach ein wunderliche geſchee.

Je renniſer warō diſer zeit an reichthümern vnnd rům alſo achtper das ſie von kőnig Cunaten ein freyheit gold vnd ſilber zemding en erlangten mit ſeinem pild die ſie noch heut beytag gebrauchen.

image on the page, twenty-three lines high (see Figure 2). Three stories are accompanied by a prominent image of Jews being burned, also the largest on the page (twenty-two lines high): the 1298 persecution of Jews by Albert I; the 1337 Deckendorff host desecration mentioned together with the 1348 persecutions during the black death; and the 1492 host desecration in Sternberg. And, of course, there is the iconic image of Simon of Trent, more than a half-page large at thirty-seven lines high (see Figure 3).

Figure 3. Depiction of Simon of Trent, Hartmann Schedel, *Weltchronik* [German edition of *Liber chronicarum*] (Nuremberg: Anton Koberger, 1493) fol. CCLIIIIv.

Schedel was not the first to use images to depict Jews — some of the earliest depictions of Jews in print come from works published in the aftermath of the Trent trial in 1475. But he was the first to use such prominent and detailed images of Jews in a book in which Jews appear only as side topics (the pirated, less splendid versions of Schedel's chronicle included crude copies of the original images). Still, Schedel's model of signaling a story through an image would become influential. The sixteenth-century publisher of Sebastian Münster's *Cosmographia* later also included several recurring images to alert readers to stories about Jews.

Although some of the tales about Jews appear only in Schedel's *Liber chronicarum*, he did not start the trend. Since the invention of movable type in the middle of the fifteenth century, thanks to the increased availability of books through print, authors interacted more with previously published works, creating a veritable chain of historical memory. Schedel's work was based on material found in earlier chronicles, most notably the exceedingly popular Werner Rolevinck's *Fasciculus temporum*, which went through nearly forty printed editions between its first printing in 1474 and Rolevinck's death in 1502, and Jacob Philip Foresti of Bergamo's *Supplementum chronicarum*, which first appeared in 1483 in Venice and was likewise quite popular with over twenty editions between 1483 and 1581. They in turn had benefited from the medieval work by Vincent of Beauvais, *Speculum historiale*, first printed in 1473 and then in 1474 (this edition was also owned and used by Bishop Hinderbach of Trent during the notorious trial of the Jews in 1475; stories about Jews therein were used to justify the trial). Some of the stories Schedel included had already appeared in Vincent of Beauvais's, and then in Rolevinck's and sometimes also Foresti's, works. For example, William of Norwich, Richard of Pontoise (or of Paris), and Werner of Bachrach, found in *Speculum historiale*, were included only in Rolevinck and then Schedel but not Foresti, while the desecration of the crucifix appeared only in Foresti and in Schedel, but not in Rolevinck.

Not surprisingly, in Schedel's predecessors, post-biblical Jews were also confined to roles of vicious killers, enemies of Christians, sometimes deceived by a devil; they were, in turn, killed and burned, or, if they were allowed to live, converted. In Rolevinck, for example, there is a quick succession of tales about Jews: desecration of the crucifix, a Jewish father burning his son after he took communion with Christian children, William of Norwich, Richard of Pontoise, a conversion of a Jew in Toledo, Werner of Bachrach, expulsion of Jews from France, and the burning of Jews for poisoning wells.

By the second half of the sixteenth century, printers and scholars began to explore archives, where they discovered medieval chronicles holding local memories of the medieval past. Now made available through print, these medieval monastic chronicles were, in turn, used in the nineteenth century as historical primary sources for national histories. For example, monastic chronicles published by Christian Wurtisen in the second half of the sixteenth century entered the majestic *Monumenta Germaniae Historica* (MGH), conceived as a printed repository of historical sources in 1819, after the fall of the Holy Roman Empire, and published since 1826. The availability of such sources in authoritative publications had an impact on shaping and reinforcing the image of Jews in the newly emerging national story. The stories of the horrifying and the unusual that had piqued the attention of medieval chroniclers now became part of the known record, with Jews said to be committing horrendous deeds, for which they were — as the chroniclers asserted — "justly" punished. The readers and scholars of the national pasts were now exposed to repeated stories of massacres and burnings of Jews; of Jews committing suicide rather than converting to Christianity; of Jews poisoning wells; of Jews killing Christians and defiling the sacred. As these historical sources created new national memories, Jews did not fit as full members of the newly emerging nations. Instead, they were a historical enemy within, hateful and being hated, a people who kill and who are being killed. In 1934, Julius Streicher thus stepped into an existing epistemological framework and used it for propagandistic purposes. But Streicher is only the most extreme example of this legacy.

Modern historians also became trapped in this epistemological framework. In scholarly studies, including textbooks, the Middle Ages have been represented as a Christian story. Jews, if they are present at all, appear as a hated and persecuted minority, engaged in usury and other unrespectable activities. For example, in the book *Economic and Social History of Later Medieval Europe*, published as recently as 2009, Stephen Epstein presented Jews as a separate group, maintaining their own language and culture. The book emphasized the Jews' "exclusion," described them as "scapegoats," and noted "massacres" of them. Monarchs, for example, "squeezed the Jews to skim off the profits, when the Jews could yield no more they were expelled." This was the case in England, and France where Louis IX's bureaucracy "went to work and increased regular tax income. Jews were particularly hard-pressed — money lenders were expropriated and expelled." Epstein, perhaps unwittingly, used nearly the same verbs as the medieval and early modern chroniclers, without integrating Jews into a larger story as key and integral actors in the European past. (But can some clauses in the pivotal document of European jurisprudence, the 1215 Magna Carta, for example, be understood without a nuanced discussion of Jews in English economy?)

This scholarly approach is not without consequences. Conservative and extremist right-wing groups frequently stress Europe's "Christian roots." Their selective and narrow vision of the European past is inadvertently reinforced by published, and therefore accessible, historical sources, usually Christian, and by scholarship so predominantly focused on Christian culture of the European Middle Ages. In these scholarly works, with few exceptions, Jews are almost entirely missing as historical actors embedded in the fabric of medieval European society. Instead, they remain a hated minority, victims of persecutions, and, in their economic activity, marginal usurers. Interpreted differently and more ex-

Figure 4. An example of the reuse of the same fifteenth-century woodcut in 2017 in an online forum.

tremely, among white supremacists, they are, as in premodern chronicles, enemies of Christian Europe (see Figure 4).

The medieval and early modern epistemologies thus continue their imprint on scholarship and teaching today, perpetuating the understanding and presentation of the European past as Christian, with Jews — sometimes referred to as the "Jewish diaspora" — as sojourners in "host nations," and with Muslims as unwelcome invaders on European land. It is only recently that some medieval historians have begun to look into the more complicated medieval past by mining archives and material objects to view the past more fully and include Jews and other non-Christians as integral to European history and culture.

Further Reading

This essay uses quotes from Steven A. Epstein, *An Economic and Social History of Later Medieval Europe: 1000–1500* (Cambridge: Cambridge University Press, 2009); Judith

Pollmann, "Archiving the Present and Chronicling for the Future in Early Modern Europe," *Past & Present* 230, Supplement 11 (2016): 231–52; Nicholas Sagovsky, "What Makes a Saint? A Lincoln Case Study in the Communion of the Local and the Universal Church," *International Journal for the Study of the Christian Church* 17 no. 30 (2017): 173–83; and "Christians and Jews: Towards Better Understanding," *The Wiener Library Bulletin* 13, no. 3–4 (1959). For a modern edition of Hartman Schedel's chronicle and images, see Hartmann Schedel and Stephan Füssel, *Chronicle of the World: The Complete and Annotated Nuremberg Chronicle of 1493* (Köln, London, New York: Taschen, 2001).

For literature on medieval and early modern anti-Jewish accusations, see R. Po-chia Hsia, *The Myth of Ritual Murder: Jews and Magic in Reformation Germany* (New Haven: Yale University Press, 1988); and *Trent 1475: Stories of a Ritual Murder Trial* (New Haven: Yeshiva University Library and Yale University Press, 1992); Gavin I. Langmuir, *History, Religion, and Antisemitism* (Berkeley: University of California Press, 1990); and Israel Yuval, *Two Nations in Your Womb: Perceptions of Jews and Christians in Late Antiquity and the Middle Ages* (Berkeley: University of California Press, 2006).

For recent works on Jews in Christian Europe, and works that integrate Jews into the broader discussion of European Christian culture, see William Chester Jordan, "Jewish Studies and the Medieval Historian," *Exemplaria* 12, no. 1 (2000): 7–20; Ivan G. Marcus, *Rituals of Childhood: Jewish Culture and Acculturation in the Middle Ages* (New Haven: Yale University Press, 1996); David Nirenberg, *Communities of Violence: Persecution of Minorities in the Middle Ages*, 2nd ed. (Princeton, N.J.: Princeton University Press, 1998); and Ephraim Shoham-Steiner, *Intricate Interfaith Networks in the Middle Ages: Quotidian Jewish-Christian Contacts* (Turnhout, Belgium: Brepols, 2016).

Who's Afraid of Shari'a Law?

Fred M. Donner

In recent years, the Western press has published expressions of deep concern over the threat of "shari'a law"—or what we might more simply call Islamic law. Some critics express fear that certain distinctive practices found in some Muslim societies, such as the veiling and seclusion of women, may somehow become a routine part of Western life through the efforts of Muslims living in the West; or, going even farther, they raise the specter of Muslims transforming Western countries into theocratic Islamic states governed by shari'a law—which is viewed as some kind of rigid medieval code. In the United States and the United Kingdom, websites such as Creeping Shari'a and Shari'a Watch attempt to spread alarm among the general population on this issue by highlighting extreme personal situations or gruesome cases of abuse, which, they imply, are normative in shari'a law, or caused by it.

Such alarms are sensationalist and overblown. First, they suppress the basic fact that in the United States, at least, the U.S. Constitution bars the establishment of any religion as an official religion of the state. In most Western countries, shariʻa is something that can affect only Muslims who choose voluntarily to follow it on personal matters such as diet, ritual observance (fasting, prayer), dress, sexual preferences, and so on — akin to rabbinic law in Jewish communities in the West. It cannot be imposed on non-Muslims, or even on Muslims who do not wish to observe it. Beyond this, however, such pronouncements are based on a profound misunderstanding of the nature and historical development of Islamic law, and of its relationship to Muslim societies, the social practices of which have, from their medieval origins to the present day, varied greatly from one another and continue to evolve. The aim of the present chapter is to provide, in brief compass, some sense of how Islamic law developed and the reasons for its diverse and often flexible character.

The term *shariʻa* comes from a word in Islam's sacred scripture, the Qur'an, that refers to what God ordains, so Islamic law was conceived by Muslims as "God's law." This may cause some to imagine that Islamic law is a list of rigid and inflexible rules, like the Ten Commandments engraved in stone. But Islamic law is not a closed corpus of regulations, and it is far from monolithic. It is, instead, a dynamic system that provides rules for making laws — as well as for reconsidering and modifying them — so that it includes many different, even contradictory, legal opinions on almost every given question.

Islamic law first developed in the eighth, ninth, and tenth centuries, but it has been continually debated and refined ever since and, like any legal system, will always be subject to further evolution. The first Muslims, living in western Arabia in the time of Muhammad (d. 632), presumably had a clear sense of how they should live, based on traditional Arabian social practices as modified directly by the teachings of the prophet and the injunctions of the Qur'an. As the early

community of Muslims expanded from Arabia and took political control of adjacent lands in Syria, Iraq, Iran, Egypt,
and other nearby areas, it found itself governing populations
with many social practices that differed greatly from those
of Arabia. For example, the question of whether a widowed
woman needed the permission of a male "guardian" from
her family to remarry, as Arabian tribal custom demanded,
was much debated because in areas outside Arabia widows
often did not need a male "guardian," so no such permission
was required. In time, such practices came into the *shari'a*
as new converts to Islam brought them into the heart of the
Muslim community.

Islamic law was thus born out of the need felt by early
Muslims to establish what was essential to the proper way of
life for a Muslim. If the Qur'an gave relevant guidance, there
was usually no problem. For example, the Qur'an enjoins
Muslims to make themselves ritually pure before engaging
in prayer and gives some instructions on what this entails:
performing ablutions by washing the hands and feet, and so
on. But for many day-to-day social practices, and even many
ritual practices (such as prayer or pilgrimage), only general
guidance is found in the Qur'an. On the vexed question
of veiling, for example, the Qur'an says only that women
should dress modestly and cover their breasts and private
parts; face-veils, head covering, and other restrictive clothing are not stipulated. Learned Muslims therefore faced the
challenge of determining how Muslims should behave in
various situations in order to live in an appropriately righ-
teous and properly "Islamic" manner

Over many years, Muslim scholars developed a systematic approach to grapple with this challenge. This system —
known as *fiqh*, roughly translatable as "jurisprudence" —
established a hierarchy of sources for deciding whether a
practice was acceptable in Islam or not. The most obvi-

ous source of guidance in this system was, of course, the Qur'an, but a second major source consisted of sayings of the prophet Muhammad, called *hadith*. These were transmitted to later generations by people who had known him and remembered his actions and sayings, and they sometimes gave clear guidance on some issue that may have been ambiguous (or not mentioned) in the Qur'an. A third important source was analogical reasoning — that is, logical extrapolation from one case to others that seem comparable. (This practice, of course, is also a cornerstone of legal analysis in European jurisprudence.) For example, the Qur'an states clearly that wine (*khamr*) is harmful and to be avoided by believers. It does not mention beer, or whisky, or narcotics, but many jurists argued that these substances, because they have effects resembling those of wine, should also be discouraged or forbidden. A fourth source came to be known as *ijma'* the consensus of those learned in the Qur'an, *hadith*, and existing Islamic law. If all well-meaning scholars agreed on the permissibility of a certain practice, then that was sufficient to establish the practice's standing in the law. A fifth principle was sometimes brought to bear: *maslaha*, or the "public interest": If something was deemed good for the Muslim community, then it was in the interest of the community that it be allowed. (This is a kind of subset of *ijma'* because it requires that many scholars agree that something is in the community's interest.)

These five basic sources, then — the Qur'an, prophetic *hadith*, analogy, consensus, and public interest — have, for centuries, been the bases on which Islamic law developed; in Islamic parlance, they are called the "roots" (*usul*) of Islamic jurisprudence. It is easy to see, however, that these roots do not provide clear directions or easy answers. Many — indeed, most — issues could be endlessly debated because in reality, each of these sources was subject to interpretation and re-

interpretation by individual scholars. Even something based
on a relatively straightforward injunction in the least controversial of the sources, the Qur'an, could be far from clear. As
we have seen, the Qur'an says clearly that wine has harmful
effects and should be avoided, but one might question exactly what the Qur'an means by "wine," or note that because the proscription invokes harmful effects, the stricture
might not apply when wine serves as a beneficial element
in medical treatment. Similarly, jurists sometimes disagreed
profoundly on the applicability of analogical reasoning in a
particular case. For example, even if they agreed that drinking wine should not be allowed, was the prohibition also
applicable to coffee? To tobacco products? to marijuana? to
opium? Over the centuries, different jurists have argued for
and against these substances depending on how they wished
to apply analogical reasoning (and more recently, in light of
evidence of adverse health effects). Moreover, some of the
Qur'an's injunctions are incomplete, or not entirely clear.
For example, the Qur'an repeatedly enjoins believers to pray,
but it never states exactly how often one should pray. It mentions as desirable prayers made toward the beginning of the
day and at night, and refers once to the "middle prayer,"
which implies an odd number of required prayers daily, but
this leaves many possibilities open. The long-standard practice of praying five times every day, for instance, is something that jurists worked out among themselves through
argument and counter-argument. Veiling — which was practiced in the Near East long before Islam — was mentioned
in the Hebrew Bible and in early Christian literature, and is
a subject on which the Qur'an provides little guidance. Different Muslim jurists have recommended a wide range of
practices, from full coverage of the face, head, body, hands,
and feet, all the way to no head covering at all.

Laws based on the *hadiths* are even more open to interpretation and legal argument. These statements or actions

attributed to the prophet Muhammad supposedly illustrate the prophet's *sunna*, or preferred practice. Because the Qur'an is a relatively short book, there are innumerable everyday issues on which it offers no guidance at all, so Muslim thinkers of the eighth and later centuries came to draw more and more on *hadiths* as the source of their legal guidance, arguing that whatever the prophet did, his *sunna*, was effectively legal precedent for later Muslims. The problem — as medieval Muslim scholars themselves clearly recognized — is that it is difficult to know which ones among the plethora of reports about the prophet that circulated are actually reliable. The first collections of such reports do not appear until over a century after the prophet's death, by which time many spurious reports had been created, often in order to provide support for particular legal arguments. Medieval Muslim scholars recognized that faked *hadiths* were a problem and developed an elaborate system of evaluating *hadiths* by checking the names of the people who are said to have transmitted them from the prophet's day down to their own time (a process called *jarh wa ta'dil*, "challenging and confirming as trustworthy"). Some reports were dismissed as weak or invalid because one of its transmitters could not have known another in the supposed chain of transmitters, or because a transmitter in the chain was known to be unreliable in memory, prone to inventing things, or of dubious morality. Scrutinizing *hadiths* to establish prophetic *sunna* thus required knowledge of which transmitters — earlier scholars — had taught whom and so could plausibly have conveyed a report to his student. This gave birth to a voluminous corpus of relevant biographical information about these scholars of *hadith*, eventually compiled into multivolume biographical dictionaries that provide us with rich information on the intellectual history of the Muslim community over the centuries.

The criticism of *hadiths* was thus the key method for determining what was, and what was not, reliable information about what the prophet had said and done — about what was *sunna*. Only *hadiths* that were deemed "sound" (*sahih*) were acceptable as the basis for legal reasoning, and it became commonly accepted that only a small fraction of the hundreds of thousands of *hadiths* in circulation were actually sound. By the middle of the ninth century CE, various leading scholars of *fiqh* came to compile select collections of *hadiths* that they deemed sound — above all the famous books entitled *Sahih* by al-Bukhari and Muslim, and four other compilations, which together comprise the "Six Books" of authoritative *hadith* recognized by Sunni Muslims. (Sunni Muslims are so-called because they emphasize that their approach to the law is based on the *sunna*, or practice of the prophet, as established by the study of *hadith*. Shi'i Muslims developed a rather different approach to *hadith*, considering sayings of their *imams* or early religious leaders also valid as legal precedent.) Although the Qur'an is generally regarded as the primary source of Islamic law, the wealth of material in *hadith* often means that when the Qur'an is ambiguous on a certain point, its meaning is deduced by consulting what the prophet had said or done, so that, in effect, the *hadith* is almost more influential in shaping the legal practices of Muslims. The admissibility of *ijma'* also opens the door to differences in opinion among scholars because while scholars of one city, one legal tradition, or one era might all agree on a certain practice, scholars from another background often hold a different opinion.

The elaboration of Islamic law has thus always been a very complicated matter, despite the popular misconception that it is based on a simple, coherent reading of the Qur'an. The natural tendency of different scholars to see things in different ways and the opportunities the material offers for divergent interpretations mean that many different approaches to the elaboration of the law emerged among Sunni Muslims between the middle of the eighth and the ninth centuries, from which four major "schools" of legal interpretation eventually coalesced: the Maliki, Hanafi, Hanbali, and Shafi'i schools, each named after its founder. They differ somewhat in their approach to jurisprudence — the conservative Hanbali school, for example, rejects reasoning by analogy completely, arguing that it is too dependent on the whim of the interpreter. Hanbali jurisprudence emphasizes more than any other school the role of sound *hadith* as a source of legal authority.

What this all means is that virtually any precept of the religion — except the axiomatic Muslim belief that God is one, and that Muhammad was God's messenger — can be challenged or reinterpreted; and historically, almost all have been at one time or another. For many centuries, for example, one quite consistent precept of Islamic law in all schools was the prohibition on making loans with interest, derived from a Qur'anic verse that forbids the taking of usury. But around 1900, the reform-minded Egyptian jurist Muhammad 'Abduh, at the time head of the famed al-Azhar University in Cairo and effectively the leading Sunni cleric of his day, argued from *maslaha* that modern circumstances required the creation of savings banks with interest-bearing accounts. He also argued, among other things, that Islamic law should adopt much more liberal attitudes toward women than had been the norm among devout Muslims.

It is not easy — or perhaps, even possible — to know exactly what is the relationship between Islamic law and the social practices of Islamic societies. It seems certain that because the prophet Muhammad and the first Muslims were from Arabia, the very conservative practices of seventh-century Arabian society (in particular, its restrictive views on women) came to occupy an important place in Islamic law as it first developed. And we can certainly say that Islamic law has sometimes exercised a conservative influence on social practices in different parts of the Muslim world. That is, after all, the function of all systems of law — to provide an accepted set of rules according to which everyone agrees to live, an essentially conservative agenda. But as noted previously, it is also true that the various Islamic societies found throughout the world have, for centuries, differed, sometimes profoundly, in many of their social practices. The reality is that, as noted, almost every principle or practice set out in Islamic law can be challenged within the workings of the system of interpretation itself. Which particular legal positions on a certain issue are favored, then, often depends on the social values of the society in which it is being discussed and to which it is being applied. Paradoxically, Islamic law is thus shaped by prevailing social norms, even as Islamic societies are shaped by the law.

As in many societies, the Islamic community contains a perpetual tension between conservative and progressive views, and social practices swing like a pendulum back and forth over the generations. We can take the seclusion of women as an indicator of such trends. In the late nineteenth and first half of the twentieth centuries, many Muslim societies gradually embraced more relaxed social practices, and by the mid-twentieth century in many large urban centers of the Islamic world, women were mostly unveiled even in public and were active in the workforce. This trend toward a more "progressive" Islam may have been generated in part by the intrusion of Western powers, and their values, into many parts of the Islamic world as colonial overlords. Since about 1970, veiling has become increasingly prevalent, and a more "traditional" variety of Islam seems to have made a resurgence. This may be due, in part, to a natural reaction among Muslims against what are seen as the values of the Western world, which, for so long, dominated them. But it is also the result of a half-century of aggressive proselytizing by the Kingdom of Saudi Arabia, which has advanced its very conservative Wahhabi interpretation of Islam (an offshoot of Hanbali law) throughout the world.

Working through such organizations as the International Islamic Relief Organization and the World Muslim League — both bankrolled by the Kingdom's burgeoning oil wealth — the Saudi government has built over a thousand mosques, hundreds of schools, Islamic centers, and Islamic colleges throughout the world, and staffed them with clerics trained in Saudi Arabia's conservative form of Sunni Islam. These efforts are part of a determined effort by the Saudis to undermine or denigrate more liberal interpretations of Islam that had taken root in various countries, and to thwart Shi'ism in particular. This development, however, is the product of a unique set of historical circumstances, and not evidence that Islamic societies must adhere to such a restrictive interpretation of Islam. Muslim scholars in many countries, such as Indonesia, are simultaneously advancing more open and progressive interpretations of Islam that have roots just as deeply embedded in medieval practices of legal interpretation as the very conservative practices favored by Wahhabi clerics, whose approach reflects more the traditional Arabian social environment than any supposed Islamic "essence." As in many societies, the perennial tension between conservative and progressive trends will doubtless continue to play out in the realm of Islamic law as well. The important thing to remember is that Muslim societies the world over are highly diverse, so in practice there is really no single thing as "Islamic law"; rather, there coexist innumerable different approaches developed by Muslims to the challenge of living in an "Islamic" manner, all of them reflecting in varying degrees the basic sources and the interpretive principles of Islamic jurisprudence.

Further Reading

A concise overview can be found in Wael Hallaq, *Introduction to Islamic Law* (Cambridge: Cambridge University Press, 2009). An excellent introduction to the *hadith*, an important source for legal reasoning, is Jonathan A. C. Brown, *Hadith: Muhammad's legacy in the medieval and modern world* (Oxford: Oneworld, 2008).

Exemplary on the social and political context of the early development of Shafi'i law is Ahmed El-Shamsy, *The Canonization of Islamic Law* (New York: Cambridge University Press, 2013). A perceptive synthesis of the topic is Bernard Weiss, *The Spirit of Islamic Law* (Athens: University of Georgia Press, 1998).

A collection of excellent articles on many aspects of Islamic law can be found in A. Kevin Reinhart and Robert Gleave (eds.), *Islamic Law in theory: Studies on jurisprudence in honor of Bernard Weiss* (Leiden: Brill, 2014). A well-informed and engagingly written introduction to how Islamic law evolved and continues to do so, with many contemporary examples, is Rumee Ahmed, *Sharia Compliant: A User's Guide to Hacking Islamic Law* (Stanford: Stanford University Press, 2018).

How Do We Find Out About Immigrants in Later Medieval England?

W. Mark Ormrod

Introduction

Researching immigration in premodern contexts is a huge methodological challenge. For the European Middle Ages, we lack anything akin to the kind of records that are compiled by modern immigration services, let alone the statistical and cultural information about settled immigrants that are gathered in modern censuses. Very often, then, the study of immigration in the Middle Ages has to be done indirectly, by inference. For example, analyzing the style of artifacts and architecture and identifying loan words in a language or dialect allow us to spot external influences on a given group of people and to hypothesize the presence of immigrants in their midst.

Fortunately, however, there is one case, from fifteenth-century England, where a political initiative left an archive of documents sufficient to provide a detailed snapshot of the immigrant presence across an entire kingdom. In 1440, the English government decided to impose a new tax levied only on foreign-born people living in the realm. Because so many of the detailed fiscal records of this period survive today in the National Archives of the United Kingdom, we can use this tax as a means of recovering the names, nationalities, places of residence, occupations, and family and household structures of the thousands of people who, in each generation, made their way into England in the later Middle Ages.

Before we proceed to discuss that evidence in detail, however, we need a clearer sense of the concepts that underpin the process of immigration, and of the wider medieval context in which the English material needs to be read.

Migration in Medieval Europe: An Overview

In the modern world, *immigration* is understood as the process by which *aliens* (people of other nationalities) move into one country from another. Today, the word "immigrant" often has connotations of difference: Immigrants are sometimes classified as formal *minorities* on the basis of the host society's prevailing views about race and ethnicity. *Immigration* (arrival and settlement) is the end-point of a process of *migration* (movement) that begins with the act of *emigration* (leaving the place of birth). Migration can be large- and small-scale and can result both in well-established routes between particular regions and in wider diasporas within and over entire continents.

It is necessary at the outset to confront and dismantle any notions of the supposed ethnic "purity" of European society in the Middle Ages. The period from around 300 to 1000 CE marked a veritable "Migration Age" that witnessed the invasion and settlement of Europe by a multitude of new people. These included the so-called Germanic tribes and the Slavs (originally from the central Eurasian landmass) who inhabited large parts of eastern, central, and western Europe; the Vikings (from Scandinavia) whose descendants settled in many areas of northwestern Europe; and the Arabs (from the Arabian peninsula), who migrated via North Africa into various European lands bordering the Mediterranean. Almost all the Germanic and Viking settlers converted, over the course of time, from paganism to Christianity. The Arabs and other settlers from Africa and the Near and Middle East continued to practice Islam, and some of their subject people in southern Europe became Muslim, too. The diaspora of the Jews from the Near East, which began in Roman times, also continued during the Middle Ages, with the result that Jewish people were found in almost all parts of Europe by the twelfth century CE. Modern multicultural Europe is therefore the direct heir of migration in the early Middle Ages.

During the later Middle Ages, too, there were major movements of population in Europe. Both the so-called "commercial revolution" of the thirteenth century and the arrival of the Black Death in the fourteenth century resulted in significant mobility. The opening up of new trade routes between Europe and North and West Africa in the late fifteenth and sixteenth centuries led to a substantial influx of Africans into northern Europe. Religious persecution also played a role in migration. Jews and Muslims were subject to persecution and, in some cases, expelled from particular kingdoms. The Ottoman state, whose rulers were Muslim, expanded into the Balkans, resulting in the displacement of large numbers of Christian Orthodox Serbians. Finally, the European Reformation in the early sixteenth century brought about persecution within Christian communities and resulted in the migration of minority groups such as the Huguenots, who fled from Catholic France to Protestant England.

Finding Immigrants: Sources and Their Interpretation

Throughout the Middle Ages, the movement of people across Europe and the wider world remained largely unregulated. The modern notion that everyone has a single or primary nationality defined by identification papers and passports simply did not apply. And in the general absence of border controls, the vast majority of people who moved between different jurisdictions did so without any formal questioning or written permission.

In the thirteenth and fourteenth centuries, however, in various parts of western Europe, public authorities began to find it necessary to define the rights of more prominent foreigners, especially merchants, churchmen, and nobles. Self-governing towns allowed alien immigrants to enter the "freedom" or "franchise" of the place, and kings began to allow people born under other jurisdictions to take an oath of loyalty and enjoy what we would call "full citizenship." In England the latter process was known as "denization" (and later as "naturalization"). The records of civic and royal governments, which survive in larger numbers from the thirteenth century onwards, can therefore yield many details of named individuals who used such new legal opportunities to change nationality in the later Middle Ages.

The only example of a census of all foreigners living under a sovereign jurisdiction in this period, however, is the English tax on foreigners — the so-called "alien subsidy" — instituted in 1440. The tax was a short-term response to public concerns over the economic advantages that foreigners were supposedly enjoying within the realm. Once the first collection proved the extent of immigration, much of the original impetus dissipated; and although the tax was repeated on numerous occasions over the following two generations, many national and occupational groups secured exemption. It is therefore the first assessment, in 1440, that provides us with the best analysis of an alien presence not just in medieval England, but in the whole of Europe before the nineteenth century.

Who Were England's Immigrants in 1440?

The records of the alien subsidy of 1440 suggest that first-generation immigrants numbered between 1.0 and 1.5 percent of the overall population of England, a proportion roughly equivalent to that found in the United Kingdom censuses as late as 1901. In some of the major towns in the south, the figures were significantly higher, at 10 percent or more. But it is important to acknowledge that immigrants were located throughout the realm, in inland as well as coastal districts, and in rural as well as in urban society. Almost everyone in fifteenth-century England must have encountered people of foreign birth at some point in their lives.

The various nationalities represented in this total had different distributions and profiles. People from other parts of the British Isles — Wales and Ireland (which were dependencies of the English crown) and Scotland (which was still a separate kingdom) — accounted for the largest numbers of immigrants. There were also significant numbers of French and "Dutch" (a term that denoted a large area covering the Low Countries and western Germany). Smaller numbers of people migrated to England from the Iberian kingdoms, from Italy, and from "Greece" (a label used to denote much of the European eastern Mediterranean), as well as from Scandinavia and Iceland.

The status and occupations of these people were diverse. Many of the Welsh, Irish, Scots, and French were agricultural laborers eking out an existence through casual work and often moving on or returning to their places of birth when the harvest season ended. It has been suggested that some of the Icelanders may have been trafficked against their will and were thus effectively slaves. The Iberians, the Italians, and the Greeks, by contrast, were mostly prosperous people with high levels of skill: clergy, doctors, merchants, craftspeople, and so on. People from the Low Countries were particularly prominent in the manufacture of luxury goods. Women feature significantly in the 1440 tax returns, not just as the wives of foreigners but also as independent singletons in search of skilled and unskilled employment.

Minorities in England

The people who made the records of the English alien subsidy used labels that denoted people's origins in terms both of political units and of linguistic and cultural zones. In general, they did *not* define people by race, creed, or color. There are a handful of cases in later collections of the tax where people were described as coming from "Inde," a generalized term used to describe the whole of the Eurasian landmass beyond the Near East. The use of the description "black" and its various linguistic equivalents as a surname for foreigners may also, in a few cases, indicate African or Middle Eastern descent. In one case, these phenomena intersect: "James Black of Inde," who lived at Dartmouth in Devon in 1484, seems highly likely to have been of non-European descent. However, the records yield virtually no other instances where such designations can be made with any level of certainty.

The absence of systematic labeling for non-European and/or non-Christian religion minorities should not be taken as denoting a liberal and inclusive attitude. In many respects, indeed, the very opposite was the case. All Jews were expelled from England in 1290, and a formal ban on the practice of Judaism continued through the seventeenth century. The imaginative literature and drama of the later medieval period show that England remained deeply anti-Semitic. Muslims, usually referred to as "Saracens," were never excluded; but, like the handful of Jews who remained after 1290, they were only tolerated if they converted to Christianity. The forenames of Benedict and Antonia Cala-man, a husband and wife described as coming from "Inde" in the London alien subsidy of 1483, indicate that they were certainly Christians. They could have been born into the Coptic, Nestorian, or Syrian Churches, but it is also possible that they had been born to Jewish or Muslim parents and had converted to Christianity before or after entering England. Romany people (pejoratively called "gypsies"), who originated from Northern India, also found their way into the British Isles at the very beginning of the sixteenth century. In 1531, however, they were officially ordered to leave England because the ruling elite saw them as vagrants and criminals. The myth that Elizabeth I forcibly expelled all "blackamoors" from England in 1596 has been decisively dispelled, though it often continues to be cited as an example of what some see as a broader issue around racism in Tudor England.

Xenophobia in England

English people could be almost equally suspicious of ethnic or national groups from within Europe, exhibiting traits associated today with the term "xenophobia"—the fear, or hatred, of foreigners. Recorded physical violence was remarkably rare, but verbal abuse was probably relatively common: Medieval English literature is full of derogatory ethnic stereotypes, such as the uncouth Scots, the drunken "Dutch," the effeminate French, and so on. Occasionally, these prejudices were written into law. In 1377, for example, at a very tense moment in the so-called Hundred Years' War with France (1337–1453), the English Parliament agreed that all French-born people living in the kingdom should be forcibly repatriated. Individual towns also passed legislation preventing foreigners from having a vote in civic government: In 1419, for example, the city of York barred Scottish men from being admitted to the franchise. By the end of the fifteenth century, when the government became increasingly protectionist in its economic policy, there was an increasing body of national legislation restricting the kinds of skilled work open to aliens within the kingdom.

In their encounters with immigrants, English people's attitudes were often conditioned by language. The ability and willingness to communicate in English was taken as a marker of trustworthiness. In 1347, for example, the authorities in Salisbury recommended to the royal government that a French man dwelling in their city be exempt from a recent expulsion order on the grounds that he was only there "to improve his English." The flip side to this was that, if immigrants could not speak the English vernacular, or did so imperfectly, they were assumed to be suspect. During the popular uprising known as the Peasants' Revolt in 1381, it was said that the rebels in London had required people to speak the words "cheese and bread" so that they could identify foreigners in the city.

Under exceptional circumstances, medieval English people might make organized attacks on immigrants. Those from the Low Countries were particularly marked out in this respect. The "cheese and bread" episode of 1381 arose because the cloth merchants of London were jealous of the special privileges given to weavers from Flanders (modern Belgium and northern France), and stirred up the mob to attack this high-profile immigrant group. The defection of the Duke of Burgundy, the ruler of Flanders, from the English cause in the Hundred Years' War after 1435 intensified anti-Flemish sentiment and resulted in a number of further affrays in London. In 1517 came the largest anti-alien demonstration of the period, when Londoners, frustrated at the perceived advantages enjoyed by foreign craftspeople in the city again prompted attacks on immigrants in a riot known as the Evil May Day.

Integrating Immigrants in England

It is striking, however, that — with the exception of 1381 — virtually no Flemish or other aliens lost their lives in these moments of organized violence. It is also to be noted that such disturbances were almost entirely confined to the capital city. Overall, the evidence suggests that host communities across England regarded foreign immigrants as an inevitable and generally positive presence. In 1369, Parliament resisted a government initiative to expel Scottish people living in the north of England on the grounds that their presence there was "to the common profit." Much of the national and civic legislation against foreigners was either only half-heartedly enforced or was subject to many formal exemptions. For example, early sixteenth-century parliaments had to admit that it was not in the national interest to forbid foreigners from working as beer brewers and bakers in England.

This generally accommodating attitude had much to do with the settlement patterns of immigrants. English towns did not develop ghettos for particular racial or ethnic groups, as were found in other parts of Europe during the later Middle Ages. In major cities such as London, Bristol, and York, aliens were widely dispersed across both the richer and poorer parts of the townscape. The general absence of segregation also calls into question the degree to which immigrants of the same ethnicity actively perpetuated their distinctive customs into the second and subsequent generations. In the countryside in particular, aliens enumerated in 1440 were often the only people of their declared nationality for many miles around. Such incomers had very little choice but to accept the dominant culture of the English host community.

There were two fundamental reasons why the model of integration ultimately prevailed in England during the later Middle Ages. The first was that the English openly acknowledged that their own ethnic origins were very diverse and that they were a hybrid people formed from successive migrations of Celts, Romans, Anglo-Saxons, Vikings, and Normans. The fourteenth-century chronicler Peter Langtoft (who wrote in the Anglo-Norman French language, which had been adopted by the upper levels of society since the Norman Conquest) stated that England was "filled with people of divers birth." Immigrants were therefore no threat to a fantasy of ethnic "purity"; they could intermarry freely with the host community and produce children who enjoyed full status as English nationals.

The second crucial factor was religion. Late medieval England's immigrants were, or became, members of the single, Catholic, tradition of Christianity then authorized in the European West. The richest among them, such as the Italian merchants living in London, were able to employ priests from their homelands and create their own religious organizations. But the vast majority attended the local parish church and depended on the spiritual services provided by English clergy. This made immigration to England a very different cultural phenomenon than found, for example, in multi-faith medieval Iberia. In the sixteenth and seventeenth centuries, the position in England would also change, as Protestant Christian groups formed their own "stranger" churches in some of the larger English towns, and Judaism was once more sanctioned as a permitted religion. Perversely, the advent of religious freedom then meant that immigrant communities were increasingly seen as separated off from their English neighbors, and led to accusations that they served only their own interests and were disloyal to their adopted home.

Further Reading

For medieval migration in general and its historiographical impact, see Patrick J. Geary, *The Myth of Nations: The Medieval Origins of Europe* (Princeton: Princeton University Press, 2002). Full information on the English alien subsidies can be found in the online database "England's Immigrants, 1330–1550," www.englandsimmigrants.com. For a comprehensive analysis of this material, see W. Mark Ormrod, Bart Lambert, and Jonathan Mackman, *Immigrant England, 1300–1550* (Manchester: Manchester University Press, 2019). The African presence in the sixteenth century is discussed by Miranda Kauffmann, *Black Tudors: The Untold Story* (London: Oneworld, 2017). Essential to an understanding of English ethnicity in the later Middle Ages, and of English views of other ethnicities, is Andrea Ruddick, *English Identity in the Fourteenth Century* (Cambridge: Cambridge University Press, 2013).

The Middle Ages
in the Harlem Renaissance

Cord J. Whitaker

W. E. B. Du Bois writes that every African American lives a "double life . . . as a Negro and as an American, as swept on by the current of the nineteenth while yet struggling in the eddies of the fifteenth century." This, he contends, leads to a "painful self-consciousness . . . fatal to self confidence." This is one way that he describes "double consciousness," the dynamic of seeing oneself *as oneself* and simultaneously seeing oneself through the eyes of another who has a very different vision. Double consciousness has become a dominant theoretical paradigm in critical race and African American studies. Medieval studies today is in a similar double bind: The field today is swept on by the current of the twenty-first while yet struggling in the eddies of the *nineteenth* century — a time especially concerned with its own modernity. University disciplines still reflect the view, increasingly prominent in the nineteenth century, that the present moment only improves upon a benighted past consisting of discrete periods to be treated with objective scientific study, including ever more discrete historical specialization and rigid philological methods.

Medievalism has long troubled the waters of academic culture: A field that often demonstrates the surprising similarity between modernity and premodernity, it is also a discipline born of passionate interest. The early twentieth-century African American scholar and artist Jessie Redmon Fauset, the subject of this chapter, knew this all too well. When she used the European Middle Ages to stake African Americans' claim to the history and culture of the European Middle Ages and the entirety of the English literary canon, her amateurism — where *amateur* is true to its original meaning: *lover* — was fully in line with the history of medieval studies. The field owes its very existence to "amateur" medievalists such as Frederick James Furnivall "who wore their passions on their sleeves" and sought no detachment from their objects of study. Furnivall was anything but unproductive. He was editor and a principal contributor to what would eventually become the *Oxford English Dictionary*; he founded the Chaucer Society, the Wyclif Society, the Ballad Society, the New Shakspere Society, the Browning Society, and the Shelley Society. He also founded the Early English Text Society, for which he edited some 100 medieval texts himself. It now contains as many as 495 editions. It was a sense of pleasure "borne of connectedness to the people" that propelled Furnivall's work. His intimate attachments to objects of study also informed Furnivall's projects of social improvement: the London Working Men's College and the Girls' Sculling Club. Furnivall's work evidences that subjective love of the medieval past or, as Carolyn Dinshaw stirringly puts it, "[A]synchrony, in the form of restless ghosts haunting the present, can be the means of calling for justice for past exclusions and injustice." Racial injustice is included.

Fauset recognized that the Middle Ages — what Du Bois calls the "fifteenth century" representatively — is inextricably bound with double consciousness. When terrorism appears to threaten at every turn, when students of color report regularly feeling disenfranchised on college campuses, when respect for women's self-determination is so low that one in six first-year college women report having been raped while incapacitated, the doubleness of medieval studies — its aptitude for disrupting divisions between the premodern and the modern, the subjective and objective, the disempowered and the empowered, and between white and black — is instructive. Fauset recognized and used the Middle Ages' peculiar power, born of the "amateur" scholarship of the late Victorian popular "medieval revival," in building the foundations of the African American literary and cultural movement known as the Harlem Renaissance.

In 1914, Fauset was rising to some prominence on the literary scene when she published a piece that deploys the medieval past as a "restless ghost" to call for present justice. In *The Crisis*, the magazine of the National Association for the Advancement of Colored People, she placed a short vignette called "My House and a Glimpse of My Life Therein." In it, the narrative speaker situates her home and her life between a manicured private garden, a bustling industrialized city, and an enchanted forest. Her story manipulates the medieval past in order to ameliorate the psychological and spiritual pain of double consciousness by asserting the black reader's relationship to America's medieval English literary pre-history.

Fauset went on to become the most published female novelist of the Harlem Renaissance. Often called the Renaissance's "midwife," she was literary editor of *The Crisis*, under W. E. B. Du Bois, from 1919 until 1926. As the first editor to accept the work of Langston Hughes, she shepherded his career, along with those of other black literati such as Claude McKay and Jean Toomer. Yet, because critics of African American literature in the mid-twentieth century sought forms that challenged convention over and above those that sought to deploy conventional forms, Fauset's impact was minimized. Indeed, according to Robert Bone's 1958 study, Fauset's work amounted to naught but "vapidly genteel lace-curtain romances." The misread conventionality of her work has not a little to do with prejudices against the medievalizing nature of her gardens and forests.

In "My House," the narrator takes the reader on a tour of her whimsical, magical house. She describes it as "An irregular, rambling building . . . built on no particular plan, following no order save that of desire and fancy. Peculiarly jutting rooms appear, and unsuspected towers and bay-windows . . ." (143). The journey gives the reader access to the garden, the city, and the forest.

The narrator's is a symmetrical pleasure garden, and Fauset writes, "Surely, no parterre of the East, perfumed with all the odors of Arab[ia], and peopled with *houris* [the beautiful women who inhabit paradise] was ever so fair as my garden!" (143). Fauset's parterre owes its integral role in Western European medieval culture to the influence of Islamic Arab culture in Spain and southern Europe. As garden historian John Harvey puts it, in the case of the garden "medieval *Christian* sensibility was at one with Islam" (my emphasis).

"My House" continues to reference the Middle Ages once the narrator is inside. Chased inside by a surprise rainstorm, she peers through her windows in reverie. Out of one, she sees a busy town. She muses:

I perch myself on a window-seat and look toward
the town. Tall spires and godly church steeples rise

> before me; high above all climbs the town clock;
> farther over in the west, smoke is curling from the
> foundries. (144)

Out of another window she sees "the friendly nodding of tall trees and the tender intercourse of all this beautiful green life." The conceit registers the tension between modern industrial reality and the quaint medieval ideal. Indeed, still looking out the window, the narrator exclaims:

> Suddenly the place becomes transformed — this is an
> enchanted forest, the Forest Morgraunt — in and out
> among the trees pass valiant knights and distressed
> ladies. Prosper le Gai rides to the rescue of Isoult la
> Desirous. (144)

The Forest Morgraunt, Prosper le Gai, and Isoult la Desirous are from Maurice Hewlett's 1898 *Forest Lovers*, one of the most popular medievalist romances of the late nineteenth and early twentieth centuries. It was so well praised that, in 1899, a reviewer for the *New York Times* wrote that "Not since Spenser's *Faerie Queene* first delighted the world have we had such recountings of heroic deeds and manifest chivalry as are contained in these few hundred pages." In other words, it was a huge success surely headed for canonization. Scholar, editor, and writer Fauset could not help but know the novel. Nor would she, or other writers of her time, have been able to avoid the nineteenth-century popular medievalism now known as the Medieval Revival.

After her reverie, the narrator heads up to her library near the top of the house. *The Arabian Nights* and modern stories bookend the medievalizing texts that interest — and comfort — the narrator most. Fauset writes:

> But when a storm rises at night, say, and the rain
> beats and dashes, and all without is raging, I draw a

huge, red armchair before the fire and curl into its hospitable depths,

"And there I sit
Reading old things,
Of knights and lorn damsels,
While the wind sings—
Oh, drearily sings!" (144)

The poetic excerpt is taken from "The Meadows in Spring," first published in 1831 and republished, sometimes under other titles such as "Song of the Fire," in various anthologies throughout the nineteenth century. The poem, by the writer and orientalist Edward Fitzgerald, explicitly proclaims its medievalism a few lines after those that Fauset quotes. Fitzgerald writes: "sit I; / Reading of summer / And chivalry— / Gallant chivalry!" Medieval chivalry is what protects the narrator-reader. The storm—those things that make her uneasy, that put her out of sorts, including the industrialized city—is turned out of doors by the medieval past that helps her feel safe and at home. As Alice Chandler puts it, the Medieval Revival sought to substitute "the vision of a more stable and harmonious social order [and] the clear air and open fields of the medieval past in place of the blackening skies of England." Fauset's Forest Morgraunt represents idyllic pleasure in place of "blackening skies."

The Middle Ages are not the only ghost in Fauset's story. Industrialization not only undergirds the Medieval Revival but also drives the Great Migration of African Americans from the rural South to the urban North with the promise of economic improvement. This urbanizing trend provides the conditions for the Harlem Renaissance. The garden and forest point not only backward but also southward—toward the plantation South. The black philosopher Alain Locke, in his famed 1925 essay "The New Negro," identifies the Great

Migration as "in the Negro's case a deliberate flight not only from country side to city, but from *medieval* America to modern." The plantation South, which was often idealized as a medieval pastoral space by nineteenth-century defenders of slavery, is, because it was supposedly idyllic and because it was agricultural, linked with the medieval. Locke, however, turns the idyll on its head: The garden space invokes, for black readers, the history of enslavement and oppression.

Fauset takes a different approach to double consciousness when she depicts herself as a medieval lady in this photo that she publishes with "My House" (see Figure 1). Even though she is of light complexion, Fauset is still discernably African American, and the image makes visible the claim that the black woman has just as much right as the white woman to imagine herself a lady deserving of knights, jewels, fancy gowns, and all the other trappings of romance. What's more, by invoking her parterre's Eastern origins, Fauset has already disturbed the supposed whiteness of the Romantic Middle Ages. The modern late nineteenth and early twentieth-century African American woman claims her place, along with that of the "darker peoples of the world"—to use one of Du Bois's terms—in the idyllic Middle Ages so prized in the popular culture of her day. When Fauset lays claim to and changes the idyllic Middle Ages, she experiments with reunifying a double, or split, consciousness. No longer does the American black person have to see him or herself through the eyes of another who looks on in "amused contempt and pity." Instead, by combining the white American or European's popular view of herself as a medieval romance heroine with Fauset's own view of herself as a black woman, "My House" strives to depict a consciousness that sees itself clearly and as a fully unified being.

Fauset's subjective love of the Middle Ages, also borne out in other of her works, such as her most popular novel

Figure 1. Jessie Redmon Fauset, "My House and a Glimpse of My Life Therein," *The Crisis* 8 (July 1914): 144.

Plum Bun, evidences the strategic viability of medievalism as a tool for the advancement of racial justice. Fauset's "My House" is closer to *playing* in the Middle Ages rather than *struggling* "in the eddies of the fifteenth century." Her subjective love of the Middle Ages is not unlike Furnivall's, and her medievalism is a model for those who would ask "Whose Middle Ages is this?" in order to criticize and influence the politics and ethics of the present. It is a model for the student of medieval studies who would advance racial justice by ameliorating the dissonance of racial double consciousness while assuaging the discord of her own temporal double consciousness as a modern person who aims to analyze, criticize, and, at least occasionally, intellectually inhabit the Middle Ages.

Further Reading

For Du Bois's theory of double-consciousness and reflec-
tions on its role in the African American experience, see
W. E. B. Du Bois, *The Souls of Black Folk* (New York: Barnes
& Noble, 2003 [1903]). In addition to Fauset's writings, a notable example of Harlem Renaissance medievalism is found
in W. E. B. Du Bois, *Dark Princess: A Romance* (Jackson,
MS: Banner Books/ University Press of Mississippi, 2014
[1928]). The mid-twentieth-century reception of Fauset's
work is typified by its treatment in Robert Bone, *The Negro
Novel in America* (New Haven: Yale University Press, 1965).
For the nineteenth-century development of the medieval
idyll, see Alice Chandler, *A Dream of Order: The Medieval
Ideal in Nineteenth-Century English Literature* (London:
Routledge & Paul, 1970). Finally, for a contemporary view of
the Harlem Renaissance, and one that exhibits medievalism,
see Alain Locke, "The New Negro," *The New Negro: Readings on Race, Representation, and African-American Culture,
1892–1938* (Princeton: Princeton University Press, 2007).

PART II
Origins

Among our great narrative impulses is the desire to tell where we came from. Creation myth and national anthem and family tree all share an attraction to beginnings, to where it all began, to where I come from and to whom I belong, and so ultimately to who I am, as a person with a history. The search for origins is deep-rooted, but it is never a neutral project. What we seek out from the past and how we tell what we discover about our past always redounds on who we are, who we wish to be, and how we wish to imagine our future.

Claims to origins and the narratives built around those claims are thus much more powerful than we assume simple stories to be. They shape our sense of historical and present belonging; they delineate the boundaries of communal identity; they stand guard at the gates of group membership; they confer and bar access to the benefits, privileges, and rights that that membership entails. Every October, for example, American schoolchildren learn the story of the Nina, the Pinta, and the Santa Maria, knowledge that informs them of who they are, how they came to be American, and what it means to be an American. While origin narratives often pin their truth to the facticity of historical data, they also tend to treat historical fact with a light hand, adding in details that resonate and erasing details that interfere with the cultural work such narratives seek to perform in their day. It aids the project of American identity-building to award Columbus with the discovery that the globe is round, even though Greek geometers and their medieval readers knew this fact quite well. That project is marred once we recall that the Niña, Pinta, and Santa Maria are Spanish ships with Spanish names (and a telltale tilde), that the Italian who captained them never set foot on the soil of the continental United States, that his mission instituted the traumas of the transatlantic slave trade, or that Norse voyagers beat him to North America by nearly 500 years. Restoring these details opens alternative narratives of origin that are obscured by, or lost to, the predominant narrative. Our shared stories of belonging are not the only stories we can tell.

To put it more simply, origins help orient us, in history and in the present alike. And in the modern Western world, the Middle Ages serve as a gravitational point of history in relation to which subsequent cultural orientations seem to consistently emerge. The medieval is simultaneously familiar and strange, not so different from our world as to produce acute culture shock, but distant enough to function as a foreign epoch against which modernity may define itself. As a result, in popular usage the Middle Ages cease to refer to the span of over a thousand years during which diversities of people lived out their lives but instead become a collection of texts, images, objects, and ideas later historical periods can draw on to tell themselves about themselves. When certain of these narratives become ascendant, others fall away, often in service to powerful demographics and institutions, often to the detriment of those with lesser access to power, deep though their own legitimate medieval roots may be.

The essays in this section examine some of the ways Western nations, communities, and persons have seized upon the Middle Ages as a site of origin, as a potent place and time to which they lay self-narrating claim. Each essay draws attention to the light hand with which latter-day story-makers rummage through the Middle Ages, to the way those story-makers' choices obscure certain narratives of origin in favor of others, and to the political, cultural, and economic interests their preferred narratives shore up. The first four essays examine how influential narrative-spinners have culled from and selectively forgotten the medieval textual, historical, and artistic record to orient their audiences toward modern ends. Ryan Szpiech unearths the medieval bedrock of Thomas Jefferson's 1764 edition of the Qur'an with which Rep. Keith Ellison was sworn into office in 2007, both to counter the anti-Muslim smearing Ellison underwent and to trouble simplistic interpretations of Jefferson's Qur'an as an emblem of American religious pluralism. William J. Diebold traces the historical unmooring of an Alemanni symbol that appeared on white supremacists' shields during the 2017 Unite the Right rally in Charlottesville, locating the so-called Black Sun on the floor of Nazi Germany's shrine to the SS, Wewelsburg Castle. Diebold demonstrates how Heinrich Himmler's self-aggrandizing and grossly ideological fabrication of the Third Reich's medieval origins depended on the destruction of Germany's architectural heritage and the labor of countless human beings murdered in concentration camps. Turning to the religious sphere, Lauren Mancia grapples with Rod Dreher's proposal in *The Benedict Option* that Christians ought to withdraw into monastic isolation to eschew the depravity of a secularized United States. In turn, Mancia explains how this fantasy of retreat does not reflect the actual lives of medieval monks who were committedly in, if not of, their larger social world. Stephennie Mulder's essay similarly corrects common misapprehensions about medieval religious practices, here with respect to the seemingly unending sectarian strife between Sunni and Shi'a Islam. By studying one of medieval Syria's great architectural wonders, the Mashhad al-Husayn, she tells a different story of cooperation and coexistence, inviting us to query where our mistaken notions arise from.

The remaining four essays in this section all seek to recover medieval origins that dominant narratives about the Middle Ages have largely obscured. Sarah M. Guérin maps out the trade routes that intertwined Western Europe with the Mediterranean, Near East, Indian subcontinent, Eastern Asia, and especially Africa, source of over half of medieval Europe's gold, much of the alum needed for its textile production, and most of its ivory. Examining the materials from which medieval artwork was made reveals a global Middle Ages that brought diverse people into social and economic contact. The impact of this contact on medieval European perceptions comes to life in Pamela A. Patton's essay, which studies what and how black skin color meant during the Middle Ages, in dialogue with modern epidermal understandings of race. Patton warns us against finding an origin story for modern racism in medieval Europe, recognizing that, though we rightly see medieval attitudes toward skin color as racist, more often than not, dark skin did not itself function as the marker of race as it does for more modern systems of racial difference. The section's final two essays consider how contemporary European nationalist movements require a version of history that forgets the heterogeneity of their lands during the Middle Ages. In response to the nationalist politicking of Brexit, Elizabeth M. Tyler reanimates the diverse linguistic, ethnic, and cultural makeup of Anglo-Saxon England, revealing how that diversity was forcibly subordinated and subsumed to imperial West Saxon ambitions that foreclosed a more plural concept of the nation. David Wacks draws similar attention to the diversity of medieval Spain, whose vibrant Jewish and Muslim traditions saw expulsion by the same king who sent Columbus across the Atlantic and have since been written out of the nation's school curricula.

Taken together, these essays intersect and overlap in ways that raise a range of pressing questions we might consider today: How do the lived diversities of past historical moments, as witnessed by texts, objects, buildings, and other archives, lose their legibility over time? How do we best approach the project of recovering these obscured lives, and how do we account for the inevitable historical losses that make their recovery challenging? Why are narratives of origin important, why are they dangerous, and how do we negotiate their telling in ways that are responsible to their power to both inspire and destroy? Why are the Middle Ages such a potent site for our latter-day quest for origins, and can we disentangle the medieval on its own terms from our use of the medieval on ours? As the essays here reveal, the accurate telling of more complicated medieval histories and the revision of our received narratives about the period stand to reorient us toward the Middle Ages. As a result, we are invited to query our assumptions about the Middle Ages as a point of origin and to restore to the Middle Ages origins that have, for too long, been left out of the narrative.

Three Ways of Misreading Thomas Jefferson's Qur'an

Ryan Szpiech

On January 4, 2007, the first Muslim to be elected to the United States Congress — Democratic representative from Minnesota Keith Ellison — was sworn in, but not without some controversy. In the press photos of such events in Washington, it is customary for public servants to choose if they want to place their hand on a Bible (or another text, or no text at all) while vowing to do their duty. Because Ellison is a convert to Islam, he opted to use the Qur'an rather than the Bible, laying his hand on no less than the personal copy of the Qur'an in English translation that once belonged to Thomas Jefferson. Jefferson's Qur'an, having surviving multiple fires in the Capitol, is now housed in the Library of Congress.

This use of the Qur'an was criticized by some, spurring Republican pundit Dennis Prager to declare in an editorial that "America, not Keith Ellison, decides what book a congressman takes his oath on." To allow Ellison to use the Qur'an, he claimed, "will embolden Islamic extremists" to pursue "their greatest goal — the Islamicization of America."

Although his remarks were denounced by the Anti-Defamation League as "intolerant, misinformed, and downright un-American," Prager's views fell on some sympathetic ears, and, possibly as a result, a rumor started circulating online a few years later alleging that U.S. president Barack Obama had similarly been sworn in on a Qur'an. This claim overlapped with conspiracy theories about Obama's place of birth and citizenship, including later accusations by Donald Trump that Obama was not born in the United States, that he "founded ISIS," and even the speculation that "maybe . . . he is a Muslim." Such remarks might interest students of the Middle Ages because Trump has repeatedly asserted that the violent tactics used by ISIS are "medieval" in nature and "when we have a world where you have ISIS chopping off heads . . . this is like medieval times." A closer look at Jefferson's Qur'an — both at its medieval roots and its relevance to modern Muslims such as Ellison — can help us understand the logic of such facile contrasts between "the medieval" and "the modern," and also help us develop a nuanced view of Islam's complex role in American history, both in Jefferson's day and in our own.

Ellison served in Congress until 2018, when he was elected as Minnesota Attorney General. While the story of his swearing-in to congress is well known — it resurfaced in the news in 2015 when a New York trial court judge, Carolyn Walker-Diallo, similarly took her oath of office on a Qur'an — what is less known is that Jefferson's Qur'an, a 1764 printing of an English translation made by English orientalist George Sale in 1734, also contains an introduction and explanatory notes to help the reader understand the book in its historical context. Jefferson had a lasting curiosity about Islam, and he may have made use of his Qur'an during his law career as part of his comparative study of various law codes from different world civilizations. Jefferson's Qur'an has been interpreted by historians in the context of Enlightenment debates about religion in general and Islam in particular, and especially with respect to the place of Islam in Colonial America.

Yet less attention has been paid to Sale's medieval roots. As he explains, he made his translation as a response to medieval and early modern translations of the Qur'an. In particular, the introduction and notes in the 1734 Qur'an contain references to European Christian readers of the Islamic holy book as far back as the twelfth century. In his prologue, Sale refers to the first Latin Qur'an, translated by the Englishman Robert of Ketton in Toledo around 1143, as well as numerous later translations into Latin and various European vernaculars over subsequent centuries. Ketton's Qur'an was translated at the behest of Peter the Venerable, abbot of Cluny, for explicitly anti-Muslim purposes. In the twelfth century, Islamic civilization was at its zenith, spreading from southern Iberia to northern India and covering all of the southern shores of the Mediterranean and Middle East. Ketton and Peter were only two of numerous medieval Christians who began engaging more directly with Islamic writing in the wake of Christian–Muslim conflicts, including the Christian "re-conquest" of Iberia and the Christian conquest of Jerusalem and the Holy Land during the crusades. Demand for Latin translations of Arabic books grew in the twelfth century as students at Europe's earliest universities first encountered Arabic texts of science and philosophy, while Christian churchmen, working to define religious dogma (and infidelity) more explicitly, first translated Jewish and Muslim holy books in order to refute them.

In keeping with this medieval polemical spirit, Sale next names one "Johannes Andraes, a native of Xativa, in the kingdom of Valencia, who from a Mohammedan doctor became a Christian priest, translated not only the Koran but also its glosses." This "Johannes Andraes" is none other than Juan Andrés, the purported fifteenth-century author of the Spanish anti-Muslim treatise *Confusion or Confutation of the Muhammadan Sect and of the Qur'an*, published in Valencia in 1515. Sale returns to Juan Andrés again in a comment on verse 16:103, which describes how Muhammad was accused of being told what to say not by God but by some clever mortal. Sale explains that "some Christian writers" even suggest he was instructed by a Jew, among whom he names Juan Andrés as well as the thirteenth-century Dominican friar Riccoldo da Monte di Croce (d. 1320). Riccoldo's best-known work, *Against the Law of the Saracens* ("Saracen" was the common medieval Christian term for a Muslim) was one of numerous medieval treatises written to attack Islam and promote Christianity, using for that purpose quotations from Islamic sources about the Prophet Muhammad.

The fact that George Sale mentions these medieval names in the eighteenth century is not an anomaly, since such texts were widely available in Western Europe at that time. Ketton's Qur'an was copied repeatedly and was printed at least twice in the sixteenth century (including one edition that even reproduced the angry marginal comments of a medieval Christian reader attacking Islam). Similarly, Riccoldo's and Juan Andrés's diatribes were among the most widely distributed Christian books written against Islam. Riccoldo's Latin attack on the Qur'an was copied and printed many times, most famously in a German translation by Martin Luther from 1543. The text by Juan Andrés also circulated widely throughout Europe, being printed over a dozen times in at least six languages. These books were, by the standards of the day, veritable best sellers.

And so they remained for centuries. Juan Andrés and Riccoldo were not only printed and sold widely all the way to

the end of the eighteenth century, but they were even cited
on occasion in the twentieth and twenty-first centuries. For
example, in 1931, the *Islamic Review*, the official magazine
of the UK-based Woking Muslim Mission, copied Sale's description of Juan Andrés as part of a history of Qur'an translation in the West. In 1939, the American missionary (and
Princeton professor) Samuel Marinus Zwemer copied the
same description in his history of Christian missionaries in
Islamic lands over the ages. In 2002, in the wake of the attacks on the World Trade Center in New York, a Lutheran
minister in Missouri, Thomas Pfotenhauer, published an
English translation of Luther's German version of Riccoldo's book (under the title *Islam in the Crucible: Can It Pass
the Test?*). And in 2007, the same year as Keith Ellison's historic election to Congress, another translation of the Latin
original appeared in print, translated by one Londini Ensis,
a charged Latin pun meaning both "Londoner" and "The
Sword of London." The legacies of Riccoldo and Juan Andrés span centuries and reach all the way to the present.

Sale's use of these texts in his day was thus unsurpris-
ing not only because of their widespread popularity but also
because of their anti-Muslim views. In comparison to medieval and early modern Qur'an translations, Sale's version —
translated directly from Arabic, following the original text
closely, and including comments on grammar and interpretation — has been lauded as fair minded and even "scholarly." However, Dennis Prager and his readers might be
pleased to know that Sale himself also reveals some sympa-
thies with his medieval precursors. To be sure, Sale does seek
to correct numerous misunderstandings about Islam (such
as the widespread misconception that it was spread by coer-
cion), and he also affirms that Muhammad, as a leader and
lawgiver, deserves his readers' respect. Yet in expressing such
favorable views, Sale talks out of both sides of his mouth,
making it very clear that he considered Muhammad, as a

prophet and religious leader, to be fraudulent and worthy of condemnation. How are we to understand him when he remarks, "For how criminal soever Mohammad may have been in imposing a false religion on mankind, the praises due to his real virtues ought not to be denied him"? As for the Qur'an itself, although Sale recognizes its elegance, he also affirms that "it is absolutely necessary to undeceive those who, from the ignorant or unfair translations [of the Qur'an] which have appeared, have entertained too favourable an opinion of the original, and also to enable us effectually to expose the imposture."

In such statements, Sale shows himself — his occasional favorable observations notwithstanding — to share the view of his medieval sources that only one religion — Christianity — can claim to teach the whole truth. Despite this, modern commentators have stressed the ecumenical value of Jefferson's Qur'an in helping to forge common ground between Christians and Muslims, being apparently unaware of its polemical pedigree. President Obama himself, in a 2009 speech at Al-Azhar University in Cairo, Egypt, made reference to Ellison's use of Sale's translation, citing it as an example of how "Islam is a part of America." Ellison too, in responding to his critics (*Washington Post*, January 4, 2007), affirmed "a new politics of generosity and inclusion."

It is ironic that Jefferson's copy of Sale's translation has come to symbolize inclusivity for some when it carries within it the indelible marks of a medieval polemical tradition at odds with the modern notion of religious pluralism. The juxtaposition of Sale's remarks about Islam with the remarks of Ellison's defenders and critics presents us with three distinct sorts of misreading. First, the view that Jefferson's Qur'an was simply an interesting and largely unproblematic example of how, in Obama's words, "Islam has always been part of America's story," conveniently ignores disturbing facts about the West's engagement with Islam in

the eighteenth century. Such a view glosses over the sober-
ing reality that some of America's first Muslims were, in fact,
slaves brought to the New World against their will and, at
times, pressured to convert to Christianity. It also implies
that the act of translating Islam's holy book into English
was simply a project of scholarly interest or cultural curiosity without also serving Western economic and cultural
interests. To claim this about a translation made during a
period of active British expansion in India and Asia, as Sale's
translation was, is either misleading or naïve. Such a reading forgets that the modern linguistic and historical study
of "the East" by "the West" is not only a product of modern
European colonialism, but also is built directly upon premodern engagement with the foreign and "other" — Jews,
Muslims, and various other groups — as subjects of conversion or objects of polemical animosity.

Alternatively, Sale's text might be seen to reflect a rational
Enlightenment view of religion like that cultivated by Jefferson himself. In this view, which also seems to me to be a misreading, Sale can be seen to take stock of medieval polemical arguments against Islam without himself adopting them,
replacing them instead with a more scholarly and detached
view of Islam. Sale's restrained praise for Muhammad and
the Qur'an might seem to part ways with Juan Andrés's acer-
bic anti-Islamic polemic and Riccoldo's harsh condemnation of the Qur'an. Yet this interpretation gives in too readily to a facile narrative of the neutrality of Enlightenment
scholarship in contradistinction to the prejudice and hatred
of medieval and early modern polemics. Just as it is misleading to overlook the colonial and political interests of
early modern engagement with Arabic and Hebrew, so too
would it be an error to maintain that seventeenth-century
Enlightenment readers, including Thomas Jefferson, completely broke with precedent to achieve a more reasoned

and disinterested study of other cultures and other epochs. Such a reading ignores both Sale's reliance on medieval anti-Islamic sources and his endorsement of polemical views about the illegitimacy of Islam's claim to divine revelation. A third, slightly different, view — a variation of the second — might reject Sale as a reader while maintaining the myth of the Enlightenment intact. In this understanding, Sale is personally weighed down by his medieval sources, and his antagonistic engagement with the Qur'an and Islam is simply out of keeping with his rational and fair-minded age. However, such a view would still succumb to a caricatured narrative of the intolerant Middle Ages finally overcome by a tolerant and pluralistic modernity. One need only recall Dennis Prager's comments on Keith Ellison to see that polemical rhetoric over religion has yet to go out of style in our own enlightened day.

If we reject these readings of Jefferson's Qur'an — an overly positive one, an overly negative one, or an overly presentist and self-championing one — what options remain? Perhaps we can find guidance in the idea that the real misreading here is one that sees past historical periods — any historical periods, including our own — in overly simple terms. To view the past in black and white terms is to forget that medieval Christian polemics, for all their bile, are also at times ambivalent about other religions, displaying mixed opinions and pursuing mixed agendas. An apt lens for understanding these mixed intentions is the one that was proposed by Thomas Burman in his history of Christian Qur'an translation, from Robert of Ketton in the twelfth century to Juan Andrés in the sixteenth and George Sale in the eighteenth. As Burman explains, "Christian Qur'ān reading in this long period is characterized as much by what I will be calling philology — the laborious study of the meaning of Arabic words and grammar, of the historic Muslim understanding of the Qur'ān, and of its textual problems in both Arabic and Latin translation — as it is by polemic . . . these two modes of reading often existed side by side in the mind of the same reader." Jefferson's Qur'an, expressing both polemical rejection of Islam and also humanist admiration of the civilizations to which it gave rise, encapsulates this double intention, and it came to do so not because of its supposed modernity but, on the contrary, because it inherited this mode of maintaining two contrary things at once from the very medieval texts that strike us now as single mindedly polemical and vitriolic. As it has become caught in the modern polemical crossfire between Keith Ellison and Dennis Prager and all of its messy aftershocks, Jefferson's Qur'an is also a fitting embodiment of the mixed intentions and patent contradictions at the heart of our own modern engagement with the medieval past.

Further Reading

For Prager's comments, see his article "America, Not Keith Ellison, Decides What Book a Congressman Takes His Oath On," Townhall.com (November 28, 2006). On the Anti-Defamation League's response, see "ADL Statement on Dennis Prager's Attack on Muslim Congressman for Taking Oath of Office on Koran" (December 1, 2006), available at https://web.archive.org/web/20061230040601/https://www.adl.org/presrele/dirab_41/4934_41.htm. Ellison responded in "Choose Generosity, Not Exclusion," *The Washington Post* (January 4, 2007). On the claims about Obama's use of a Qur'an, see Angie D. Holan, "Obama Used a Koran? No, He Didn't," Politifact.com (December 20, 2007). Trump repeated his "medieval times" comment on numerous occasions, including in the second presidential debate (October 9, 2016), available from CQ Transcriptions and reprinted by the *New York Times*. For Trump's claim at a campaign rally that Obama "founded ISIS," see Nick Corsaniti, "Donald Trump Calls Obama 'Founder of ISIS'" (also in the *New York Times*). For his suggestion that his birth certificate possibly "says he is a Muslim," see Chris Moody and Kristen Holmes, "Donald Trump's History of Suggesting Obama Is a Muslim," available on CNN.com.

Thomas Jefferson's Qur'an was published as *The Koran: Commonly Called the Alcoran of Mohammed*, trans. George Sale, 2 vols. (London: L. Hawes, W. Clarke, R. Collins, and T. Wilcox, 1764), a reprint of Sale's first edition (London: C. Ackers for J. Wilcox, London, 1734). A history of Jefferson's Qur'an in the context of early American writing on religious freedom can be found in Denise A. Spellberg, *Thomas Jefferson's Qur'an: Islam and the Founders* (New York: Alfred A. Knopf, 2013). A study of Sale's translation in the context of other eighteenth-century writings about Islam is available in Ziad Elmarsafy, *The Enlightenment Qur'an: The Politics of Translation and the Construction of Islam* (Oxford: Oneworld, 2009). Two detailed overviews of medieval Christian polemics against Islam include Norman Daniel, *Islam and the West: The Making of an Image*, rev. ed. (Oxford: Oneworld, 2009), and John Tolan, *Saracens* (New York: Columbia University Press, 2002). A history of the earliest European translations of the Qur'an (into Latin) is Thomas E. Burman, *Reading the Qur'ān in Latin Christendom, 1140–1560* (Philadelphia: University of Pennsylvania Press, 2007).

My thanks to Kate Waggoner-Karchner for bringing Pfotenhauer's book to my attention. See her 2019 dissertation, "Europe, Islam, and the Role of the Church in the Afterlife of a Medieval Polemic, 1301–1543."

The Nazi Middle Ages

William J. Diebold

Figure 1 was widely circulated in the wake of the summer 2017 "Unite the Right" rally in Charlottesville, Virginia, in which a counter-protester, Heather Heyer, was killed. The photo got so much press because it shows, at its left edge, James Fields, Jr. Soon after the picture was taken, Fields killed Heyer by driving his car into a crowd. But I want to call attention to the man next to Fields; he holds a shield decorated with a complicated pattern. Shields generally evoke the Middle Ages, and the motif on this shield is, in fact, of medieval origin: It is taken from a type of sixth- and seventh-century CE metal jewelry made by the Alemanni, who lived in western Europe, in the upper valley of the Rhine River. This piece of neo-Nazi medievalism (the use of the medieval after the Middle Ages) is no singular exception; the motif on the Charlottesville shield also appeared on the cover of the manifesto written by the man who in 2019 killed 51 people in an attack on two mosques in Christchurch, New Zealand. The contemporary extreme right looks to the Middle Ages; this raises the question: If today's

Figure 1. Line-up of neo-Nazis with shields, including James Fields, from Charlottesville, Virginia, Unite the Right rally, 2017. Photo: Stephanie Keith.

neo-Nazis are fascinated by the Middle Ages, what did the original Nazis think about the period?

That question is not simply academic; the Middle Ages lay at the heart of the Nazis' self-conception. The very name of their regime evoked the medieval past because they believed their Third *Reich* ("Empire") was the rebirth of a first German Empire that originated in the tenth century. One sign of how important the Middle Ages were to the Nazis was how much time and money some leading Nazis put into medieval studies: Both Alfred Rosenberg, the Party's chief ideologist, and Heinrich Himmler, the head of the *Schutzstaffel* (the SS, the Nazi Party police and military) were devotees. This essay focuses on Himmler, but it is important to recognize that his was not the only Nazi Middle Ages. Although Nazi Germany was a totalitarian state, it did not have entirely consistent beliefs, even about party ideology. Nazi rule was much more chaotic and unstructured than the top-down view of totalitarianism familiar from a work like Orwell's 1984 because rule in Nazi Germany was split between a complete party *and* a complete state organization. The resulting competition often produced divisions, especially regarding so important a subject as the Middle Ages. This essay provides only one perspective and so would perhaps be more accurately entitled "A Nazi's Middle Ages."

Himmler, as head of the SS, had plenty on his hands, but he spent considerable time exploring scholarly and semi-scholarly questions. He created within the SS a research organization, the *Ahnenerbe* ("ancestral heritage"), to study what interested him. The *Ahnenerbe*'s name gives a good sense of what kinds of things those were. Like all Nazis — but to the extreme even for them — Himmler's worldview was racialized. He wanted to know about his ancestors, by which he meant not his spiritual or philosophical ancestors, but people he considered his blood relatives. For Himmler, no such "race" ancestor was more important than a Saxon duke named Heinrich (Henry), whom the Saxons elected as their king in 919. The Nazis, like many other German nationalists since the nineteenth century, considered Henry to have been the first king of Germany.

That claim is highly disputable because the distance between the medieval and modern worlds is so great. Henry's tenth-century realm did have some geographical overlap with twentieth-century Germany, but that hardly makes Henry, who lived centuries before the era of the modern nation-state, the first king of "Germany." Such historical scruples, however, were unlikely to stand in Himmler's way, especially since Henry I had other things going for him. Most of us, not entirely in thrall to racial thinking, would not put much genealogical stock in the fact that Henry I and Himmler shared a first name. Himmler did, and more; he went on to consider himself Henry's reincarnation.

Figure 2. Quedlinburg, Church of St. Servatius (twelfth and fourteenth centuries); interior as it was ca. 1900 (from Wilhelm Pinder, *Deutsche Dome des Mittelalters* [Leipzig: Langewiesche, 1910], pl. 5).

This meant that Himmler's illustrious "forebear" had to have a proper home. Henry I, after his death in 936, had been buried in a church at Quedlinburg in north-central Germany. In the twelfth century, a larger church dedicated to the Christian saint Servatius was built over the structure that housed Henry's tomb. Figures 2 and 3 are views of the twelfth-century church, looking east from its main body, the nave, into the choir, which is raised over the earlier church. Both photographs were taken from the same position, but at different times: Figure 2 around 1900 and Figure 3 in the second half of the 1930s, after the church at Quedlinburg had been radically transformed by Himmler and the SS to make it, in their view, a more fitting memorial for Henry. An examination of the transformation helps to make clear some aspects of Nazi thinking about the Middle Ages.

Figure 3. Quedlinburg, Church
of St. Servatius (twelfth and
fourteenth centuries); interior
in July 1940 (Landesamt
für Denkmalpflege und
Archäologie Sachsen-
Anhalt, Archiv der Bau- und
Kunstdenkmalpflege).

The most extensive and visually striking changes were
to the east end, where the altar sits and where the clergy
would be during Mass. At Quedlinburg, the choir had been
built in the Gothic style, distinguished by pointed arches
and large windows. The SS architects and historic "pres-
ervationists" ripped out the characteristic Gothic ribbed
vaulted ceiling and replaced it with a half dome. They also
masked the Gothic arches and windows by erecting in front
of them a new semi-circular wall. This was constructed in a
stripped-down version of the Romanesque, the medieval architectural style that chronologically preceded the Gothic;
Romanesque buildings are characterized by rounded arches
and a generally heavier appearance than the Gothic. This
neo-Romanesque wall at Quedlinburg was pierced with a
round window with stained glass showing an eagle hold-

ing a swastika in its talons. Why did the medieval Gothic choir at Quedlinburg have to give way to a modern version of the earlier Romanesque? The problem with the Gothic for Himmler and the SS was that they perceived it to be a "French" style (and the earliest Gothic buildings are, indeed, in what is modern-day France). For them, this made the Gothic totally inappropriate for a building housing the tomb of the first "German" king. The simplicity and strength of the Romanesque, by contrast, were perceived to be essentially German.

The changes made by the Nazis at Quedlinburg were numerous and affected things large and small. Himmler's men altered the building's name; it was now "King Henry's Hall" rather than the church of St. Servatius. The new name is inaccurate because the building was always a church, never a royal hall. The renaming, however, accorded well with the SS's strenuous insistence that Henry I prefigured their opposition to Christianity. (Like many Nazi organizations, the SS was hostile to the Christian churches, in part because they saw them as rival large-scale social groups that were not under Nazi Party control. For racial true believers such as Himmler, Jesus's Jewish birth was also not a point in Christianity's favor.) In support of his position that the thoroughly Christian Henry I was a proto-Nazi, Himmler cited a tenth-century historian who tells us that Henry, at his coronation, did not seek priestly anointing. For Himmler, this was proof that Henry thought that the Christian church should not meddle in politics. But this blatantly misreads the medieval source, which is explicit that Henry refused anointment not on political grounds, but because he did not believe himself worthy of the honor; he was, in other words, acting on the Judeo-Christian virtue of humility.

Many of the SS's changes at Quedlinburg expressed their neo-paganism and involved removing St. Servatius's liturgical furnishings, the things that made the building work as a church. This included the pulpit, visible between the columns on the right in Figure 2, from which the Lutheran minister would preach. Martin Luther's Protestant Reformation of the sixteenth century had its origins near Quedlinburg. For Protestants, preaching and hearing the Word are crucial to faith and the pulpit expresses their elevation of the Word; removing Quedlinburg's pulpit turned the church into a non-church. Also gone after the Nazi renovation were the altar, visible on the platform above the crypt in the earlier photograph, and the fixed pews that filled the nave, which were replaced by movable chairs. These new chairs were removed when Figure 3 was taken because that photograph was composed to emphasize the "purity" of Nazi Quedlinburg, but they are important: They were made at the concentration camp at Dachau.

The SS ran Dachau and they chose it as the source for the chairs because they knew they could get them for a good price there. This use of the modern economic logic of the cost-benefit analysis as part of a renovation that also reintroduced candles to spite electricity points to an important characteristic of Nazi medievalism: its inconsistency and contradictions. Many aspects of Himmler's project at Quedlinburg were frankly backward-looking; for example, the electric chandelier visible in the earlier Figure 2 is gone in Figure 3. SS Quedlinburg was lit by candles, a clear archaism, an attempt to go backward in time. But the acquisition of Quedlinburg's chairs from Dachau was just as clearly modern, driven by a concern for mass production and the bottom line. This uneasy mix of modern and pre-modern characterizes Nazi rule, including that rule's most horrible result: the Holocaust. The SS, of course, did not just rebuild Quedlinburg; they also spearheaded the murder of six million European Jews. Approximately half of these were killed in pre-modern fashion, shot one-by-one; the other half died in the thoroughly modern "factories of death" that were the Nazi extermination camps. We see here, on an infinitely larger and more horrific scale, the same combination of modern and pre-modern that governed the SS renovation of Quedlinburg.

Some of the changes instituted by the SS turned the church at Quedlinburg from a religious into a secular building; others made it a more useful Nazi building. The steps leading up to the choir were widened and the railings removed to improve access for SS processions (the movable chairs in the nave similarly served to clear possible impediments to marchers). The widened steps turned the Christian choir, the site of the altar, into a rostrum from which Himmler could address German pilgrims to Henry's new shrine.

On July 2, 1936, a millennium to the day after Henry I's death, Himmler entered the former church at Quedlinburg to give a speech. It was broadcast live, and residents of Quedlinburg and other German cities and towns were urged to place their radios facing out of their windows in order to transmit Himmler's words to the broadest possible audience (the ceremony itself was open to only the highest Nazi elite). As Himmler entered "King Henry's Hall," SS musicians played a fanfare on *lurs*, an early Scandinavian trumpet whose "Northern" pedigree made it the favored instrument of the most race-conscious Nazis. (This juxtaposition of the prehistoric *lur* and the modern radio again shows the self-contradictory character of Himmler's medievalism.) In his speech, Himmler had to skirt the embarrassing fact that no one knew where Henry I's remains actually were; they would be miraculously "discovered" by SS archeologists just in time for the following year's festivities. At the dedication, he got around their absence by relying on a characteristic Nazi way of thinking about history that was very much at work in the Quedlinburg transformation: the concept that all the best moments of the German past pointed directly toward the Nazi present.

In his speech, Himmler catalogued the ways in which he felt that Henry I prefigured the Nazis. Like them, the tenth-century king had been militarily efficient; he had expanded east into what is now Poland and Hungary; he had kept his distance from the church; and, finally and most importantly, he had created his German *Reich* with a speed and efficiency surpassed only by that of Hitler. This led Himmler to conclude that, despite the absence of any physical remains of Henry I, "we can best honor him for Germany . . . by giving our total loyalty to the man who, after a hiatus of a thousand years, has taken up King Henry's legacy: our *Führer* Adolf Hitler." This collapse of the distinction between past and present is typically fascist and is often seen as one of fascism's defining features. The logic underlying it is viciously circular because what determined the canon of "great" Germans of the past was precisely the degree to which their legacies could be shaped to mirror the Nazi present. But this circularity was part of the point; for the Nazis, German history took on shape and meaning only through Hitler's rule. It is ironic that this kind of understanding of history closely mirrors the medieval Christian interpretive technique known as typology, which reads the Hebrew Bible (the "Old" Testament) not on its own terms, but only with hindsight, for the way it is believed to prefigure Christ's life and Christian theology recorded in the New Testament.

This assimilation of past and present was expressed in Himmler's words; it was also expressed in the material fabric of the church at Quedlinburg. Indeed, such an assimilation is precisely what the renovation of Quedlinburg was meant to achieve. The new window in the apse placed the contemporary Nazi swastika directly above the (alleged) tomb of the early medieval king. Likewise, the strict symmetry and simplified forms of the choir — the wide steps with no railings leading to a speaking platform — made the restructured medieval church at Quedlinburg look just like the new Nazi state buildings that were being created in places like Munich and Nuremberg by architects such as Paul Ludwig Troost and Albert Speer. In these ways and others, the work at Quedlinburg was meant to mask the line between past and present.

Quedlinburg was far from the only medieval site in Germany to which Himmler devoted his attention and the resources of the SS. The medieval trading post at Haithabu, today a much-beloved tourist destination, was an SS excavation; at Braunschweig, Himmler undertook a church rebuilding very similar to that at Quedlinburg, this time to honor another of his medieval namesakes and alleged forebears, the twelfth-century duke Henry the Lion. But a final example of Himmler's medievalism brings us back to the Charlottesville shield-device.

In the early 1930s, Himmler purchased the seventeenth-century castle at Wewelsburg in north-central Germany and had it extensively renovated. As at Quedlinburg, slave labor was crucial for the project; the SS established a concentration camp at Wewelsburg to carry it out. Wewelsburg was never finished and much of the building and its records were destroyed on Himmler's orders at the end of World War II. We are thus not entirely certain what Himmler thought he was doing at the castle. This lack of certainty has made Wewelsburg a favorite site for the wildest projections about Nazis (for example, it would become Castle Wolfenstein), but Wewelsburg was undoubtedly some kind of a cult site dedicated to the SS itself. Its centerpiece was to be a set of elaborately outfitted rooms. One of these was reserved for the *Obergruppenführer*, the SS term for military generals (see Figure 4). This room's floor has — in inlaid stones — the

Figure 4. Wewelsburg Castle (seventeenth century and ca. 1940); interior of the *Obergruppenführersaal*. Photo: Dirk Vorderstraße, 2013, licensed under CC BY, 2.0.

same motif that was on display at Charlottesville in 2017. The Wewelsburg floor explains why neo-Nazis have adopted this particular pattern as their own. For Himmler and the SS, early medieval Alemannic jewelry underpinned and sanctioned this motif, but that source is of no importance for today's American Nazis. What matters to them about what they call the "Black Sun" (a name with no medieval sanction) is that it was used by the SS, the embodiment of all that the neo-Nazi wants to be. They could care less about the Alemanni.

Andrew Elliott has coined the term "banal medievalism" to refer to modern uses of the medieval that vaguely gesture to the Middle Ages but do not really engage with them. Himmler's evocation of Henry I at Quedlinburg was anything but banal: As we have seen, quite fine details of Henry's life and deeds were important to Himmler. But for today's neo-Nazis, the Black Sun is no longer even a banal *medievalism*; for them, the motif's history is significant, but that history goes back less than a century, only as far as Himmler's Wewelsburg. The bearer of the Charlottesville shield had no idea who the early medieval Alemanni were, nor the curiosity to find out.

Further Reading

The Nazi-era work at Quedlinburg is well documented in Klaus Voigtländer, *Die Stiftskirche Sankt Servatii zu Quedlinburg* (Berlin: Akademie Verlag, 1989). For an English-language treatment of the material, with special attention to transformations at Quedlinburg after World War II, when the town lay in the German Democratic Republic, see Annah Kellogg-Krieg, "Restored, Reassessed, Redeemed: The SS Past at the Collegiate Church of St. Servatius in Quedlinburg," in *Beyond Berlin: Twelve German Cities Confront the Nazi Past*, ed. Gavriel Rosenfeld and Paul Jaskot (Ann Arbor: University of Michigan Press, 2008), 209–27. Wewelsburg, its post-Nazi-era reception (including the "Black Sun"), and the SS are fully studied in the well-illustrated *Endtime Warriors: Ideology and Terror of the SS*, ed. Wulff E. Brebeck (Munich: Deutscher Kunstverlag, 2015). The National Socialist interest in the medieval has not been comprehensively studied, but a series of essays treating Nazi-era representations of the Middle Ages is *Mittelalterbilder im Nationalsozialismus*, ed. Maike Steinkamp and Bruno Reudenbach (Berlin: Akademie Verlag, 2013). Medievalism in social media and popular culture, including its use by right-wing groups, has been usefully studied by Andrew B. R. Elliott, *Medievalism, Politics and Mass Media: Appropriating the Middle Ages in the Twenty-First Century* (Cambridge: Boydell & Brewer, 2017).

What Would Benedict Do?

Lauren Mancia

Certain prominent American evangelical Christians are labeling our current moment as a "dark age." Foremost among them is Rod Dreher, a senior editor and blogger at *The American Conservative*, who anticipates in his 2017 book, *The Benedict Option*, that there are "people alive today who may live to see the effective death of Christianity within our civilization" (8). While Dreher's brand of Christianity is by no means universal, it is often upheld as one of the more thoughtful and intellectual examples practiced by evangelical Christians today. David Brooks called *The Benedict Option* "the most discussed and most important religious book of the decade," and even more liberal news outlets such as NPR and *The New Yorker* have sympathetically characterized Dreher as a welcome alternative to the ethnocentric right, noting his status as a former Brooklynite, or calling him a champion of "granola conservatism," "gun-loving organic farming," and "Birkenstock Burkeanism."

In *The Benedict Option*, Dreher argues that Christian values have been successfully defeated. According to Dreher, the rout began with William of Ockham's fourteenth-century nominalism and continued through Renaissance individualism, Reformation schisms, Enlightenment secularism, capitalist alienation, Marxist atheism, twentieth-century consumerism and sexual revolution, and LGBT activism. Dreher proclaims that American evangelicals particularly have been misguided in trusting Republican governments to steer culture on the path of righteousness. Dreher believes that, once the right to same-sex marriage was guaranteed by *Obergefell v. Hodges* in 2015, Christians hopelessly lost the battle to "save" (18) America. But Dreher has a medieval solution for this "dark" (77) moment: Christians should follow the model of the sixth-century Benedict of Nursia, whose monastic *Rule* prescribed a withdrawal from the world and created communities of Christian monks who could, in isolation, "withstand the chaos and decadence all around them" (15–16). Claiming that such Benedictine withdrawal "preserv[ed] Christian culture throughout the so-called Dark Ages" (4), Dreher believes that Benedict's *Rule* can be the guide for contemporary Christians living in the depravity of our time.

As a medievalist who studies Benedictine monasticism, and a twenty-first-century person, I empathize with parts of Dreher's position. I wholeheartedly embrace his concern that technology has disrupted basic human interaction and love his statement that "when the light in most people's faces comes from the glow of the laptop . . . we are living in a Dark Age" (71). Dreher's prescription for "digital fasting as ascetic practice" (226) is, in my opinion, a fabulous suggestion. Medieval monks of the early and central Middle Ages would also have appreciated many of Dreher's critiques. They would certainly have been shocked by Ockham's nominalist declarations against metaphysical realism and by Enlightenment secularism. And they would have agreed with Dreher that Christianity is not about "improving one's self-esteem and subjective happiness and getting along well with others" (10) or "mass consumer capitalism and liberal individualism" (11).

But Dreher's program is fundamentally based on an historical fiction. His romanticized picture of a monastic world filled with pure, wholly religious individuals is a fantasy that never existed. In Benedict's time and for many centuries thereafter, though monks tried not to be *of* the world, they were, in fact, very much still *in* it. Benedict's communities were not the perfect mono-cultural Christian oases Dreher desires, "ark[s]" in an otherwise "chaotic" and "barbarian" culture that had eroded the "civilization" of Rome (83). Benedictine monks both *did not* and *could not* wholly reject the world around them. At their best, monasteries were innovative cities on hills, exemplars that drew from and gave back to the diverse world around them in their quest to create and perpetuate medieval Christian rituals and ideals. Some medieval monks even saw their interaction with the temporal world as a chance to better their spiritual selves.

Dreher's depiction of medieval monastic culture is a homogeneous world of black-and-white morality, but, in fact, the medieval monastery was a heterogeneous world shaded in grey. A historically accurate "Benedictine option" becomes one that embraces diversity rather than homogeneity and engages symbiotically with the political, even using some values from non-monastic culture to strengthen the rigor of monastic faith. Much as Dreher might wish to imagine otherwise, the Middle Ages was innovative, diverse, and interdependent, much like our "dark" world is today.

What draws Dreher to the medieval landscape is his belief that medieval monks lived for eight hundred years in a kind of intentional spiritual seclusion, separate from the corruption of the uncivilized world. In Dreher's words, Benedictine monks saw themselves as members of an "ark floating atop tempestuous waters of destruction" (238), "respond[ing] to the collapse of Roman civilization" (2). But this could not be farther from the truth. In the *Rule of St. Benedict*, a monastery was not considered an ark, but a "tabernacle," a "dwelling place" for God (*RSB* prologue, lines 22–24, 39). The difference between an ark and a tabernacle is tremendous. An ark is a capsule, barred from interaction with the outside world, whose very existence hopes to preserve one culture while bearing witness to the destruction of others. A tabernacle is quite a different thing. In Exodus, the tabernacle was the portable tent that served as the earthly residence of God among his people, alongside the Israelites in the wilderness. By calling their monastery a tabernacle, Benedictine monks acknowledged themselves as dwelling places for God *in the midst* of worldly contagion. Benedictine monks believed that they were model citizens in God's earthly city, standing steadfast and inspiring onlookers with their vigor and their consistency. An ark is a fortress in a threatening and hopeless world; a tabernacle is an exemplar in a complex and heterogeneous one.

Dreher (following the antiquated account of historian Edward Gibbon) claims the sixth century was characterized by "wild, rapacious tribesmen rampaging through cities . . . neither know[ing] nor car[ing] a thing about what they [we]re annihilating" (17). But historians have long discredited Gibbon's ideas, problematizing the racist characterization that a "civilized" Rome fell prey to the "barbarity" and "chaos" of foreign invaders. Instead, we now understand, first, that Rome's internal problems, even at its peak, caused its transformation from a centralized empire to a more fragmented one; and, second, that European society is deeply indebted to the very cultures that Dreher dismisses as "barbarian." In fact, the Benedictine monks that Dreher prizes so dearly were *themselves* "barbarians," Germanic peoples who migrated into the lands of the former Empire. Prominent monks and nuns of the medieval world were not ethnically Roman, with names like Julius or Marcus, but were instead of "barbarian" derivation, with names like Alchion (a.k.a. Alcuin of York) and Rhotswitha (a.k.a. Hrotsvitha of Gandersheim).

Throughout the early and central Middle Ages, missionaries, themselves often monks, converted the "barbarian" Anglo-Saxons, Frisians, Visigoths, Saxons, and others to Christianity, setting up monastic outposts along the way. It was thus from a mosaic of diverse "barbarian" cultures that Benedictine monastic rituals and symbols were born. Here are just a few examples. The *Rule of Saint Benedict* required monks to cut their hair in a tonsure, a crown-shaped strip around the top of the head, setting them apart from the laity. Such a haircut was reminiscent of Christ's crown of thorns, but it was also an application of a "barbarian" value, which had long viewed the cutting of hair as an attack on a man's honor (hence the popular association of "barbarians" with long hair and beards). Monks, therefore, would have understood the act of cutting their hair as a supreme act of humility before God; the ritual gains meaning because of its contextualization in a "barbarian" culture. Similarly, as part of their pagan inheritance, monasteries around medieval Europe preserved Neolithic "thunderstones" in their church treasuries and in the rafters of their buildings well into the late Middle Ages; despite their Christian identities, medieval monks still believed the "barbarian" folklore that these flint arrowheads and axes had the magical power to protect their congregations from thunder and lightning. The *Rule* itself also drew from pagan Roman precedents: The seclusion and chastity required of monks and nuns, for instance, recalled Rome's Vestal Virgins, whose purity served to protect the Roman city. Medieval monks therefore did not repudiate their "barbaric" ancestry or isolate themselves from the influence of the pagan traditions around or before them, nor did they solely preserve Roman culture; instead, their rules and rituals reflected the diverse society of medieval Europe, "barbarian" and Roman both.

Moreover, Benedictine monks were never isolated from the world around them (no matter how vividly Dreher imagines this isolation). Indeed, in the words of renowned historian Peter Brown, monastic culture was highly influenced by the "constant mute pressure of lay expectations." In the Middle Ages, it was a monastery's association with the political world beyond its walls that allowed for monasticism to flourish at all. Charlemagne, Louis the Pious, William the Conqueror, and other political leaders understood that a stable, streamlined, prosperous realm relied on the presence of monastic houses, and their patronage in turn made the monastic livelihood a viable project. Monasteries thus became nodal points of power for entire regions, showcasing the piety of realms, providing economic prosperity and efficiency to whole constituencies, and helping to mobilize the local gentry for war. It was, in fact, the Carolingian emperor Charlemagne during the ninth century who made the *Rule of Saint Benedict* the standard for all monasteries in his realm and elevated Benedictine monasticism to its place of prominence, and it was the monastery of Cluny, founded by the wealthy duke William of Aquitaine, that regularized Benedictine monasticism further. Benedictine monks routinely prayed for their lay donors and kept extensive lists of patrons' names in books called martyrologies. Thanks to these lay patrons, monks and nuns became the collective owners of almost half of Europe's domestic properties.

One might expect that medieval monks were dismayed

by their reliance on secular patronage. This was not the case. Some monks welcomed the opportunity to advise popes, kings, and other leaders in the secular world; other monks even enjoyed their status because it made them (or their communities) fantastically wealthy. Certain monks even saw their interactions with the world as having a spiritual benefit. They relished both praying for and writing letters of spiritual advice to laypeople, believing that they could thereby impart to the secular world the spiritual rhythms of monastic communities. They believed that lay donations to monasteries rendered the landscape of the world more sacred, regenerating temporal things into spiritual ones. Some monks believed that, though the secular world was in some sense fallen, their interactions with that fallen world served to enrich their contemplative tasks. John of Fécamp, an eleventh-century monk from whose monastery William the Conqueror launched his ships toward England, believed that the chaos of the secular world created more genuine longing for God in a praying monk because it was through the contrast between secular and spiritual (and through the desire to escape the depravity of the secular) that God was found. Dreher insists that the life of an isolated Christian is superior to a life in the world, but medieval monks had a much more complex view: Interactions with the world enabled their livelihood, spread holiness, and ultimately sent them running back to prayerful isolation with vigor renewed.

Much of Dreher's mischaracterization of the monastic Middle Ages as a time that cherished a pure and isolated Christian homogeneity is understandable: His misrepresentations of the medieval past are bred from an anxiety about our current moment, an anxiety on the part of some conservative Christians that their values are under threat and their privilege is being undermined. It is this anxiety that causes him to simplify medieval monasticism to the point of misunderstanding it.

But, in addition to his simplification to the point of distortion, there are also some flagrant historical misappropriations in Rod Dreher's *The Benedict Option* that cannot go unmentioned. First, Dreher is vehemently against what he calls the "LGBT agenda" (9), which he believes stands in the way of American "religious liberty" (80). But medieval Christians before the twelfth century were actually relatively tolerant of homosexuality: In the pre-scholastic period, medieval Christians were no more opposed to homosexual intercourse than they were to extramarital heterosexual intercourse. Some historians have even gone so far as to identify particular medieval monks as champions of homosexual love (or at least of homosocial friendship): Indeed, thirteenth-century university theologians defined and cracked down on homosexual intercourse as "sodomy" in contrast with monastic precedent. Second, Dreher is appalled by the ways that American schools "normalize transgenderism" (156). Yet medieval Christian culture often required monks to playact as female biblical characters and adopt female voices in their prayers with an eye toward bettering their devotion — evidence that non-binary conceptions of gender have been around for centuries. Even more relevantly, monastic authorities frequently extolled religious women who "became" male, *viragos* conquering and negating their "innate" feminine weaknesses by becoming spiritual warriors, and thereby serving as perfected exemplars and intercessors for men around them. Third, Dreher believes that American education must privilege the history of "Western civilization — the civilization that is the father and mother of every citizen in the West, whether their ancestors immigrated from Africa or Asia" (155). The achievements of "Western civilization" however, would be nowhere without Middle Eastern, African, and Asian influences, and without the free labor that the West thought fit to seize in the early modern period (most of these ancestors did *not* "immigrate"!); moreover, Christian monasticism itself got its start in the deserts of the Middle East and with the help of Africans such as Augustine of Hippo. Finally, Dreher claims that "Christians in the emerging era will need to adapt to an era of hostility" (182) akin to the Jewish experience in the Middle Ages. But unless he can magically erase the privilege that Christians have enjoyed throughout the history of Europe and America and built into modern society, the "era of hostility" experienced by Jews in the Middle Ages will in no way be suffered by modern Christians.

At the end of the day, Dreher can only imagine a society in which white, heterosexual, male, and Christian history and culture remain dominant. To Dreher, an embrace of the "Benedict option" is required by Christianity's having "lost" the "public square" (9) in "chaotic" and "barbaric" contemporary America. But in no way has the public square been lost simply because the diversity of American society is slowly being actively acknowledged and *slightly* integrated into American curricula, culture, and law. Furthermore, we must remember that a society that publicly embraces Christian values does not always behave in a "civilized" manner. It was, after all, the medieval state that used Christianity to legitimize the barbaric violence waged in "holy" war during the crusades, in massacres of Jews, in the burning of "heretics," and in the persecution of homosexuals. Dreher's posture against LGBT rights, in particular, leaves one wondering how Dreher might respond if the Spanish Inquisition returned to the "public square" in the twenty-first-century United States.

Dreher is not the first to mischaracterize the medieval period — most famously, Enlightenment thinkers branded it an irrational time of "darkness and dense gloom" in order to promote their own moment as an age of reason, progress, and liberty. But lived history, as all lived experience, is never wholly one thing or another. The Middle Ages was not all dark, nor was the Enlightenment all light; the Benedictine monastery was neither reclusive nor was it mono-cultural. Monastic history was as complicated and contradictory as our current moment is, and it is our responsibility to our present, as well as to our past, to see our history in the gray-scale fullness of its complexity. Whatever our politics, religion, or ethnicity is, if we are to triumph over darkness, we must learn how history wrestled with and accommodated diversity, tension, and complication, rather than erase how it did.

Further Reading

To read the *Rule* for yourself, with an introduction and notes by a historian of medieval monasticism, see *The Rule of Saint Benedict*, edited and translated by Bruce L. Venarde (Cambridge: Harvard University Press, 2011).

On the Roman Empire's "fall" as a transitory period of "barbarian" accommodation (rather than a moment of "civilization's" destruction), and on the role that Christianity played in that transformation, see Peter Brown, *The Rise of Western Christendom*, 10th Anniversary Revised Edition (Malden, Mass.: Wiley-Blackwell, 2013).

For more on Benedictine culture, including its robust embrace of the *Rule* in the Carolingian period, and its political patrons and secular involvements, see James G. Clark, *The Benedictines in the Middle Ages* (Woodbridge, UK: The Boydell Press, 2011).

On homosexuality in the Middle Ages, see John Boswell, *Christianity, Social Tolerance, and Homosexuality*:

Gay People in Western Europe from the Beginning of the Christian Era to the Fourteenth Century (Chicago: University of Chicago Press, 1980). For a great bibliography on transgender people in the Middle Ages, see Karl Whittington's article "Medieval" in *Transgender Studies Quarterly* 1 (2014). For more on spiritual women *"viragos,"* see Barbara Newman, *From Virile Woman to WomanChrist: Studies in Medieval Religion and Literature* (Philadelphia: University of Pennsylvania Press, 1995), and Fiona Griffiths, *Nuns' Priests' Tales: Men and Salvation in Medieval Women's Monastic Life* (Philadelphia: University of Pennsylvania Press, 2018). On the ways that Christian culture in the medieval "public sphere" created a persecuting society as opposed to a uniformly moral one, see R. I. Moore, *The Formation of a Persecuting Society, 2nd Edition* (Malden, Mass.: Wiley-Blackwell, 2007).

Dreher has revisited and applied some of these ideas to the Catholic Church's recent child sex abuse scandal; see his *New York Times* opinion piece from August 15, 2018: "What Must Survive a Corrupt Catholic Church."

No, People in the Middle East Haven't Been Fighting Since the Beginning of Time

Stephennie Mulder

What is the deal with the endless violence in the Middle East? you might have asked yourself while watching the news one day. It seems that for as long as anyone can remember, the region was some version of a war zone. From conflicts in Israel and Palestine to Iraq, Yemen, Libya, Iran, and Afghanistan, most people associate the region with war. It's like an endless *Game of Thrones* episode — and the various overlapping and intersecting storylines seem nearly as complex to sort out. On the first day of a new semester, it's not unusual for one of my students to repeat something fatalistic along the lines of "Who knows? People have been fighting there since the beginning of time."

Pressed further, a series of common assumptions often emerges: that the Middle East, as birthplace of the world's three prominent monotheistic religions, is thus a place of religious fanaticism, and that a particularly intolerant and irrational form of faith and political life is evident there. Or that people in the region never properly "modernized" and are still attached to some kind of "medieval" mentality about faith, sect, and politics. In fact, this idea—that the Middle East is a place still irrationally, stubbornly embroiled in medieval conflicts and mentalities while the rest of the world has moved on—is probably the most common popular perception about the region among those outside it. But the truth is that this viewpoint tells us more about ourselves and our construction of the medieval past than it does about the history of the Middle East. In the actual medieval Middle East, most of the time, in most places, most people got along.

This is not to say there weren't conflicts. In modern times, the Middle East has been on the receiving end of violence imposed both internally and by external forces. The brutal logic of modern colonialism under the major European powers gave way to occupation by American forces in multiple conflicts. Indeed, current sectarian strife in Iraq and Syria is a new and surprisingly recent development, with origins in Saddam Hussein's Iraq and exacerbated by post-2003 American-influenced political landscapes. Premodern conflicts in the Middle East going back thousands of years were likewise a mixture of internal and external conflicts—from ancient Mesopotamia to the Roman Empire to the crusades, the region has certainly known its share of strife. But the same could be said about Europe, where, for example, Cambridge historian Mary Beard has referred to Roman expansion into modern Germany and France under the vaunted general Julius Caesar as a "genocide," and where medieval conflicts such as the Hundred Years' War raged for—well, more than a hundred years—eventually serving as the *actual* inspiration for *Game of Thrones*. This is not even taking into account that Europe is the location where the worst wars in modern history started. Nor do South or East Asia appear to have been any more or less fought-over than the Middle East. So why have we told *ourselves* that this region is particularly prone to war and conflict, and why do we assume it has always been that way?

In recent years, this perception has been frequently applied to Syria, where a peaceful demand for democratic reforms that began as part of the Arab Spring in 2011 was met with violent governmental suppression and spiraled, over the next years, into a brutal conflict between the Syrian government and various opposition factions. With the rise of the Islamic State group (ISIS) in 2014, the conflict took on an overt sectarian dimension that confirmed many peoples' perception that conflicts in the region are frequently rooted in strife between religious groups, and particularly between Islam's two main confessional communities, the Sunni and the Shi'a. When, on September 10, 2014, President Barack Obama announced a renewal of U.S. military action in Iraq and Syria in a nationally televised live speech, he justified his actions by noting that ISIS had "taken advantage of sectarian strife and Syria's civil war to gain territory on both sides of the Iraq-Syrian border." Today, the conflict in Syria is frequently presented by politicians and in the media through the lens of a competition between two, sectarian-defined nation states vying for geostrategic power: Sunni Saudi Arabia and Shi'a Iran. A headline in the *Jerusalem Post* on January 10, 2016 says it all: "Sunni vs. Shi'a: New Flare-up Rooted in Ancient Hatred: The roots of the crisis are to be found in the long-standing feud between Sunni and Shi'a, which dates from the very beginning of Islam." Sectarian conflict is thus often presented as though it has raged for 1,400 years, since the founding of Islam in the seventh century. This truism is usually accepted uncritically by the media, is common in popular discourse about the Islamic world, and, as we've seen in recent years, is also embraced by violent extremist groups such as al-Qaeda and ISIS, who use it to justify heinous acts of cruelty against minority groups.

But how true is this narrative? It's worth pausing for a moment to imagine how it would look if a similar storyline were applied elsewhere: if today's tensions between, say, Turkey and Europe were said to arise from a conflict between the eighth- to ninth-century Holy Roman Emperor Charlemagne and the Byzantine Empress Irene. Most of us would find the notion absurd. But attributing modern sectarian conflict in the Middle East to events that transpired during the foundation of Islam in the seventh century is every bit as nonsensical. So where does this narrative come from?

One reason for the pervasiveness of this narrative of unending conflict is that it's a tale frequently told in the medieval Arabic texts themselves. In the textual sources, the conflict was born in a dispute over the succession to the Prophet Muhammad. One group, who would go on to become the Sunnis, felt the succession should occur by consensus of the community. Another group, who would eventually become the Shi'a, felt the succession should go through the family of the Prophet, through the Prophet's cousin and son-in-law 'Ali ibn Abi Talib. The dispute culminated in 680 AD at the Battle of Karbala in today's Iraq, when proto-Sunnis martyred 'Ali's son and — in the Shi'a view — his successor, al-Husayn, and took his head and the members of his family in chains back to Damascus in Syria, capital of the Sunni Umayyad Caliphate (see Figure 1). Over the next centuries, the fortunes of both groups rose and fell, but eventually the Sunnis prevailed and the Shi'is became a minority devoted to the Prophet's family. A pivotal episode in this text-based narrative occurred in the medieval era, between the eleventh and thirteenth centuries. The Arabic sources call this the era of "Sunni Revival" because it saw the demise of the last Shi'i caliphate and the final entrenchment of Sunnism as the predominant sect in most regions of the Islamic world.

Now as we all know, history — particularly the history re-

Figure 1. Procession marking the martyrdom of al-Husayn in the Umayyad Mosque, Damascus, Syria, 2004. Photo: Author.

corded in texts — is often a tale told by the victors. But art and architectural historians don't rely on texts alone, and in this case, the history of architecture in Syria reveals a somewhat different tale. If we let the buildings speak, some vivid contradictions to the familiar narrative arise. For example, we learn that the period of "Sunni" Revival in Syria was, counterintuitively, the one in which the largest number of "Shi'i" shrines were built, some forty of which survive into the contemporary period. And we find that these "Shi'i" shrines were endowed, patronized, and visited by both Sunnis and Shi'is: in many cases, by some of Islam's most illustrious Sunni rulers. Far from being vanquished during the Sunni Revival, Shi'ism may well have been the dominant sect in northern Syria in the eleventh to thirteenth centuries. Although episodes of conflict are certainly part of the sectarian history of Islam, it would seem there's another tale,

Figure 2. The Mashhad al-Husayn, 1183–1260, Aleppo, Syria. Photo: Author.

too. Looking at architecture reveals an equally important past, marked by cooperation and accommodation.

Let's take one shrine in northern Syria and read it through the eyes of an architectural historian. The building in question is the Mashhad al-Husayn (Shrine of al-Husayn) (see Figure 2), a site of commemoration dedicated to the Prophet's martyred grandson, who, in addition to his pivotal role at the Battle of Karbala, was one of the Imams. The Imams are the religious leaders of the Shi'a, who believe them to be the perfect and infallible descendants of the Prophet. On aesthetic grounds alone, the Mashhad al-Husayn is one of the most spectacular buildings of the twelfth to thirteenth centuries, but despite its magnificence, it has rarely been studied. Imagine for a moment that the Cathedral of Notre-Dame in Paris had been largely ignored by European architectural historians, and you'll get a sense of how peculiar this is. The reason probably has something to do with the fact that the standard, conflict-driven narrative had no idea what to do with such a monumental "Shi'i" building constructed during the era of Sunni revival.

Let's start with the textual sources. There, the story of this shrine begins in the year 1177, when a shepherd sat on a high hill overlooking the ancient city of Aleppo in northern Syria (see Figure 3). His name was Abdallah and he was from a poor neighborhood of immigrants in the city. Abdallah had just returned from the noon prayer at the mosque, and, from his perch in the warm sun atop the mountain, he could see his sheep and hear their tinkling bells as they cropped the green shrubs and yellowing grass that grew down the hillside. On the horizon, inside the stout medieval walls newly rebuilt by the son of the great Saladin—the Sunni Muslim general who would soon recapture Jerusalem and evict the crusaders from the Holy Land—the towering mass of the ancient fortified Citadel shouldered its way toward the sky. Below the Citadel, the vast, labyrinthine *suq* (market) sprawled for miles in colorful, chaotic splendor under shady, vaulted-stone passageways, testimony to Aleppo's long history as a vibrant and cosmopolitan trade *entrepôt*, a key terminus of the Silk Route that linked China to the ports of the Mediterranean.

In the heat of the afternoon, Abdallah began to doze off. As he slipped into a dream, he had a strange vision. Nearby, a man emerged from a cleft in the rock and ordered in a commanding voice, "Tell the people of Aleppo to build a shrine here and call it the Mashhad al-Husayn!" Abdallah awoke, and, awestruck at the miraculous vision, dropped his shepherd's staff and ran to the *suq*, where he began recounting the miracle and exhorting the city's inhabitants to come build a shrine. Excited crowds quickly gathered and, inspired by the vision of the humble shepherd, organized

Figure 3. View over
Aleppo, with the
domes of the Mashhad
al-Husayn visible in
the foreground and the
Aleppo Citadel visible
on the horizon. Photo:
Author.

themselves for the task. Within days, groups of volunteers
were created, workdays were assigned, and soon, in an act
of medieval crowdfunding, the merchants of Aleppo had ar-
ranged a surcharge on their goods to provide money for the
project. Not long afterward, the shrine gained some more
illustrious patrons. The mayor of the city of Aleppo himself built an elaborate portal and, a few years later, in 1196,
that portal was torn down and replaced by an even more
spectacular one built by Aleppo's Sunni governor, al-Malik
al-Zahir, the son of Saladin (see Figure 4). Thus, if we read
carefully, even the Arabic textual sources reveal much that
complicates the narrative of perpetual conflict. We learn,

Figure 4. Detail, Portal of Mashhad al-Husayn, 1260, Aleppo. Photo: Author.

for example, that the shrine was an inter-sectarian project and that it was built by elites and commoners alike. What more can we deduce using the methods of an architectural historian?

We can begin by observing some formal elements of the building. When visually assessing the intent of a building's patron, important features include size, scale, and intricacy of surface ornamentation, which often attest directly to the dedication of time and money. And indeed, the portal built by al-Zahir was higher and taller than almost every other medieval architectural portal in Syria, and it was adorned with a particularly exquisite kind of ornament: a radiating, inlaid-stone interlace pattern on the outer face, married with a complex type of three-dimensional, interlocking, faceted stone ornament called *muqarnas* on the interior of the dome. The artisanal skill required for such a project is itself evidence of its significance. In other words, al-Zahir's portal was a monument meant to awe and astonish. But beyond the building's architectural features, the context of its construction is also an important clue: Recall that the Sunni ruler, al-Zahir, was proud to sponsor and build the Mashhad *alongside* the Shi'i residents of Aleppo. To confirm this, he emblazoned his name over the entrance on a large, square foundation plaque.

Furthermore, several other clues allow us to deduce that al-Zahir wanted to emphasize that the Mashhad al-Husayn was not a "Shi'i shrine," but rather a monument to pragmatic cooperation centered on a sentiment shared by both sects: generalized reverence for the Prophet's family. Indeed, in order to drive the point home, al-Zahir commissioned yet another inscription. This one wrapped around the portal's entrance façade and was located just above the heads of visitors entering the shrine (see Figure 5). It bore a remarkable message: It named the twelve Imams of the Shi'is alongside the four Rightly Guided Caliphs of the Sunnis. Indeed, the manner in which the inscriptions are juxtaposed forces the reader to begin with praise for the Imams of the Shi'is, then to pause and read the encomium for the Sunni Caliphs, and then to return to the final phrases of the tribute to the Imams. By using calligraphy of similar size and style and directly interlinking the two inscriptions, it visually equated the two groups of holy men and indicated their equal and complementary status in the eyes of the Sunni ruler.

The shrine in Aleppo did not stand alone. In fact, it is one of probably hundreds of such structures that were built in the medieval era throughout the eastern Mediterranean

Figure 5. Detail, inscription praising the twelve Shi'a Imams (*left*) and the final inscription praising the four Caliphs revered by the Sunnis (*right*), which includes a phrase blessing "all the companions of God's Prophet." Photos: Author.

and Iraq, supporting what would appear to be a strong Shi'a agenda during the period known as the "Sunni Revival." In Syria, at least forty of these medieval shrines still remain today, but, as with the Mashhad al-Husayn, each one was built, supported, and visited by both Sunni and Shi'a Muslims throughout their history. In other words, people have worshiped in them, side by side, for over a thousand years, and there is little evidence this posed a problem. These shrines were so numerous, in fact, that they formed a new sacred landscape, one that memorialized and inscribed the history of the family of the Prophet on the land, reiterating the memory of their lives and suffering through the footsteps of pilgrims over many centuries. In 2010, just before the war broke out, over a million visitors came to Syria from as far away as India and Iran to visit these shrines to the Prophet's family. All the while, just as they had been in the medieval era, they were visited by local people from all religious communities as well.

Though of course such shrines did not prevent periodic

episodes of conflict in the Middle East, their unceasing patronage and vibrant histories of visitation over the centuries invite us to re-think the ways we frame sectarian history in the Middle East. At the very least, it should make us nuance our medievalizing interpretive framing and consider more recent, colonial contexts as the source of current conflict in the region. At the Mashhad al-Husayn, at the end of al-Malik al-Zahir's inscription, he wrote an unambiguously worded entreaty: "May God be pleased with *all* the Companions of His Prophet." And with these words, al-Zahir carved in stone an incredibly flexible sentiment: the nuanced, negotiated sectarian history of Islam in Syria, a reality that until recent times, was mirrored throughout the Islamic world.

Further Reading

By discussing the histories of Iran and Afghanistan, this essay has used a wider geographical framing of the "Middle East" than is standard. However, the "Middle East" is itself a framing of European colonialism, so it may be worth considering the validity of the construct. Some scholars have begun to adopt the more geographically and historically neutral term "Western Asia" as a replacement.

The argument presented here is made in detail in Stephennie Mulder, *The Shrines of the 'Alids in Medieval Syria: Sunnis, Shi'is, and the Architecture of Coexistence* (Edinburgh: Edinburgh University Press, 2014). For an overview of Syria's rich architectural heritage, see Ross Burns, *Monuments of Syria: A Guide* (London and New York: I. B. Tauris, 2000) and his website, *Monuments of Syria*, which has a list of recently damaged monuments. A history of medieval Aleppo's architecture can be found in Yasser Tabbaa, *Constructions of Power and Piety in Medieval Aleppo* (University Park: Pennsylvania State University Press, 1997). Najam

Haidar, in *Shi'i Islam: An Introduction* (Cambridge: Cambridge University Press, 2014), provides a nuanced overview of the story of Shi'ism. For another look at medieval interactions between Sunnis and Shi'is, see Tariq al-Jamil, *Power and Knowledge in Medieval Islam: Shi'i and Sunni Encounters in Baghdad* (London and New York, I. B. Tauris, 2018).

A version of this essay appeared on notevenpast.org on September 1, 2014.

Ivory and the Ties That Bind

Sarah M. Guérin

On February 6, 2014, with the Eiffel Tower looming over-
head, the French government destroyed three tons of elephant ivory on the Parisian Champs de Mars (see Figure 1).
An industrial chipper rendered the coveted material into
dust, destined for the construction industry. Destroyed on
that day were 698 tusks and over 15,000 pieces of ivory,
carved into banal tourist souvenirs of tribal heads, statuettes
of laughing geishas, or bangles and beaded necklaces—all
objects seized since the signing of the Convention on International Trade in Endangered Species (CITES) by eighty
countries in 1989, an agreement that made the circulation
of elephant ivory illegal. The mass destruction of ivory
brought attention to the existence of contemporary terrorist groups using blood money from elephant poaching and
the ivory trade to buy arms. The market for elephant ivory
had thus been fueling the activities of terrorist groups in several central African countries: al-Shabaab in the Sudan; the
Janjaweed in the Democratic Republic of the Congo,

responsible for the Darfur genocide; and perhaps best known, Boko Haram in Nigeria and Niger.

The French actions on the Champs de Mars were in preparation for the London Conference on the Illegal Wildlife Trade in February 2014, a gathering that focused on the poaching of elephants for ivory, rhinoceros for their horns, and great wildcats for their skins, as well as on the escalating violence against rangers trying to protect these animals. The London Conference put forth a number of actions, including the eradication of the market for these illegal goods, targeting *both* supply and demand. Key among the action points is 15.II, the endorsement and encouragement of governments to destroy seized illegal wildlife products, particularly "high value items such as rhino horn and elephant ivory." It is beyond question that the goals of the conference were heroic — an attempt to staunch the ongoing bloody massacre of elephants and rhinos in Africa, a criminal endeavor whose profit margins sit closely behind those of human trafficking, illegal arms dealing, and narcotics. Yet the call for widespread pulverization of ivory objects could nonetheless lead precipitously to indiscriminate wreckage of important historical objects (see Figure 2). For example, days after the London Conference, the British national press reported that Prince William of England had, in a private conversation, called for "all the ivory owned by Buckingham Palace [to be] destroyed." A radical response indeed. In line with the London Conferences aims, the United States has stiffened wildlife trafficking laws: A comprehensive ban on the sale of elephant ivory has been in place since July 17, 2014, which includes a prohibition on the importation of antiques (defined as an object more than 100 years old), though these items can still be exported or resold across state borders. In addition to banning the importation of ivory,

Figures 1 and 2. Champs de Mars, Paris, February 6, 2014. The French government destroying three tons of seized illegal elephant ivory. Photo: Rockster Recycler.

new laws eliminate charitable tax deductions for all donated ivory works, regardless of whether they are of "antique" status. In the United Kingdom, debate has grown around a blanket ban on *all* ivory, modern or antique, including its exhibition in public institutions. The aim effectively would be to remove elephant ivory from the public sphere, stripping it of social value.

As well-intentioned as these policies are, imposing these regulations on historical art works—objects made at different times and in difference socio-economic circumstances than the present—itself might be considered to be unethical. More specifically, because the majority of the objects carved from ivory during the Middle Ages were crafted from elephant tusks hunted in Sub-Saharan Africa and transferred to Europe through caravan and maritime networks, banning such works from public museums or limiting their display in exhibitions would efface an important material trace of the African continent's involvement in world history in the Middle Ages. Like silks, spices, and incense, the use of ivory in medieval Europe is evidence of the fact that instead of being a self-sufficient, autonomous, and isolated society, Western Europe in the Middle Ages had extensive and profound connections to the wider world. I would even say that these ties are constitutive of medieval European self-identity. Furthermore, it is important to note the essential difference between medieval and contemporary ivory consumption. In the Middle Ages, the ivory trade was cooperative with the people who sourced it, rather than exploitative.

These dynamics of local political power construed through interregional connections can best be examined through an impressive group of ivory statuettes commissioned in Paris in the early 1260s. An extraordinarily large and beautiful group of three ivory statuettes depicting a central Virgin and Child flanked by two candle-bearing angels was commissioned for the Royal Abbey of Saint Denis, outside of Paris (see Figure 3). This monastery had long been closely associated with the Capetian royal house, the ruling family of France in the high Middle Ages, and was the burial place of French kings. The ornamentation of the

Figure 3. Glorification of the Virgin Group from the Royal Abbey of Saint Denis. Paris, early 1260s. Ivory with traces of polychromy. Virgin and Child, H: 34.8 cm. Taft Museum, Cincinnati, 1931.319. Two angels, H: 25.0 cm. Treasure of the Cathedral of Rouen. Photo: Archives du département des Objets d'Art, Musée du Louvre.

Saint-Denis ivory group register aristocratic tastes and fashions of the Parisian capital at the height of Capetian power. The Virgin wears a ring brooch on her cotte (her undergarment) and also originally had a larger brooch actually made of gold and gems attached to her surcot (the heavier outer dress). Her cloak was held in place by a doubled length of cord, twisting delicately along its length. A decorative tassel and an ornate lion's head catch the cord, stopping it from slipping through the eyelet of the mantle. Additionally, a fine girdle—a thin, jewelry-like belt with intricate buckles— cinches the waist of her dress, and it was originally highlighted with gold leaf and translucent colored glazes to emulate scintillating jewels. The Virgin is dressed like a modern noblewoman.

Beyond accessories, iconographic elements in the Saint-Denis ivory group bind the statuettes intimately with the ideals of the French royal court. While one of the Virgin Mary's hands supports the infant Jesus, the other grasps a flowering branch, originally starkly set off from the creamy white ivory by bright red and green colors. This iconography makes reference to the Virgin Mary's descent from the royal house of David, whose father, Jesse, was prophesied to be the stock from which the line of kings would follow. This line generated not just the kings of Israel, but indeed the Messiah: "And there shall come forth a rod out of the root of Jesse, and a flower shall rise up out of his root" (Isaiah 11:1). The flowering stem is thus proof of Mary's royal lineage — beliefs reinforced by the golden and bejeweled crown she wore on her head (the present silver one replaces the original described in inventories). In the understanding of the French monarchy in the thirteenth century, Mary and Jesus are members of the royal house of Israel, analogous to the royal house of Capet. A stained glass window depicting the Tree of Jesse, in the east end of the church of Saint-Denis, offers up the same message but in a different form (see Figure 4). Both window and ivory are visual arguments, likening the Capetian Royal Family to the Holy Family, bringing the French crown closer to the divine. Just as the beautiful and aristocratic Virgin bore a son who was the savior, so too the royal house of Capet bears a just king.

But if accoutrements and iconography bind the Saint-Denis ivory group to the aesthetics and political ideals of France, the material from which the figures are carved tether the ensemble firmly to Africa. The massive size of the three statuettes of the ivory group clearly indicates that it was made from at least three Savannah elephant tusks. The African savanna elephant (*Loxodonta africana*) has long been prized for its large tusks, which can grow to over 2.5

Figure 4. Tree of Jesse Window,
axial chapel, Royal Abbey of
Saint Denis, France, ca. 1140.
Photo: Painton Cowen.

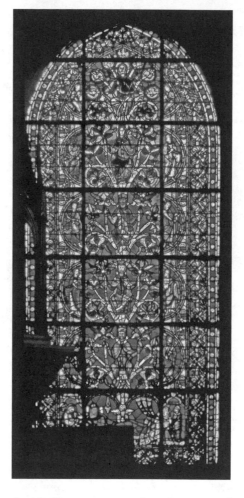

meters in length, and with diameters sometimes in excess of
15 centimeters. The central Virgin and Child of the Saint-
Denis group measures 35 centimeters high and uses the full
breadth of a tusk over 12 centimeters in diameter. The gentle
sway of the Virgin Mary holding the Christ Child on her hip
follows the natural curvature of the tusk. The two angels,

both approximately 25 centimeters high, are formed from slightly smaller ovoid tusks. The whole ensemble is a conspicuous use of the precious material imported from Africa. What difference does it make that this clear articulation of Capetian royal self-fashioning is made from material that was traded from as far afield as sub-Saharan Africa?

The trade routes that allowed such large-scale elephant tusks as those used in the Saint-Denis group changed dramatically over the course of the thirteenth century, perhaps surprisingly, in relation to the exigencies of the textile trade. For in what is today northern France and Belgium—the regions of Picardy, Flanders, Hainaut, and Brabant—the expanding textile trade precipitated the massive importation of the mineral fixative alum, a chemical necessary for preparing and dyeing wool. This coveted alum was available at several places in the middle of the Sahara. The Kawar oasis (today Bilma, Niger) had alum mines described by al-Idrisi, the Moroccan geographer resident at Roger II's court in twelfth-century Palermo, as "unequalled in quality." Another mine farther west, called Taghaza, produced equally excellent alum, but also edible rock salt. The latter is key, for the vast inland territories of West Africa required access to salt for both human and herd consumption—especially necessary in the high heat of the equatorial region. Peoples south of the Sahara were thus interested in trading their surplus goods—notably gold collected from the tributaries of the Senegal river—for biologically necessary salt. By the eighth and ninth centuries CE, these trans-Saharan exchanges became important caravan routes linking West Africa to the Mediterranean world. When merchants in the thirteenth century were looking for new sources of alum suitable for textile manufacture, they connected with the outlets of trans-Saharan caravan trade in North Africa in such places as Béjaia in modern Algeria, Gabès and Tunis in modern

Tunisia, and the Roman city of Tripoli in modern Libya. It is critical to recognize that without the access to African alum, celebrated innovations of medieval society would not have been possible. For the production of sumptuously dyed woolen textiles largely funded the building of the Gothic cathedrals, and the trade of northern European cloth across the Alps, and far beyond, established the framework for our modern monetary and banking systems.

The ties between Europe and Africa thus increased over the course of the thirteenth century, as European merchants enjoyed their improved access to Saharan resources. Although West African gold and Saharan alum were economically the most important, trans-Saharan caravans also brought a range of West African exports for sale to European merchants: exotic animal skins, leather, Grains of Paradise (a gingery spice), ebony, specialized shields made from oryx skins, ostrich eggs, parrots, indigo-dyed cotton, and, important for our consideration, savanna elephant ivory. During recent digs at Diouboye, a site on the savannas of eastern Senegal, among the gold-producing tributaries of the Senegal river, archaeologists have found evidence of a Mande community that specialized in hunting wild animals for the export market in leather, exotic skins, and ivory. The remains found at this site, dating from the eleventh through the fourteenth centuries, help conjure a particularly vivid scene of production and commerce at a West African center. Remains of leopards, jackals, crocodiles, and monitor lizards—none of which were important for the local diet— were found together with a surprisingly large number of bovid bones. The latter were eaten, but the numbers found at Diouboye exceeded local demand for meat, and the presence of large numbers of scraping tools and tanning pits on site points to industrial leather production. Moreover, among the remains of wild animals excavated at Diou-

boye are elephant bones—an extremely rare find at West
African archaeological sites. It suggests that the specialist
hunters of Diouboye were also felling savanna elephants for
their tusks.

We can hypothetically reconstruct the route an elephant
tusk might have taken in the late thirteenth century, transported from Diouboye all the way to Paris (see Figure 5). It
was likely Mande traders from the Empire of Mali who exchanged cloth, beads, metals, and salt with the community
of Diouboye for their export commodities—leather, leopard
skins, and ivory. These were transported across the savanna
to the Berber, or more correctly Amazigh, city of Oulata in
modern Mauritania. Oulata is located in the Sahel, which
means "shores" in Arabic, designating the transitional region
between the savanna and the desert. It was in the cities of the
Sahel that camel caravans were packed and from which they
departed across the Sahara. These caravans were led by the
Amazigh, the "free" people of the desert, whose knowledge
of survival in the arid landscape was built up over millennia and without whom no one, including modern explor-
ers, could navigate the inhospitable territories. Knowledge
of oasis sites along the way was critical. For example, the
Bir el Ksaib oasis sits some 465 kilometers north of Oulata,
across the most arid and desolate stretches of the Sahara, the
so-called el-Djouf or empty quarter. This most dangerous
part of the journey took a full ten days in the fourteenth
century, and there were no wells to replenish water supplies.
After resting in the Bir el Ksaib oasis, caravans likely next
stopped at Taghaza, the already-mentioned salt mines, and
Tabalbala in modern Algeria, before reaching the important
Saharan trade *entrepôt* of Sijilmasa (Morocco), situated in
the large Tafilalt oasis in the northern Sahara. From here,
caravans continued on toward the Mediterranean coast,
through the last of the desert, following dry river beds that

Figure 5. One of many trade routes active across the Sahara in the Middle Ages.

penetrate the Atlas mountains, which marks the edge of the Sahara. In such cities as Tlemcen (Algeria) or Ceuta (Morocco), arrangements were made with Italian merchants to exchange trans-Saharan products for European or Middle Eastern ones—woolen and silk textiles, ceramics and porcelain, timber and copper, among other goods. Ships loaded along the North African coast could, in the thirteenth century, sail all the way to the English Channel, unloading savanna goods at the docks of London, Calais, Bruges, or even Rouen on the mouth of the Seine. From these port towns and cities, merchandise was either carried by cart or by river barge to the Capetian capital, Paris.

This western trans-Saharan route, which connected the western savannas to Western Europe, was not, however, the only route active in the thirteenth and fourteenth centuries. There were viable paths at several junctures across the Sahara, all contributing to the economic systems that thrived in the Middle Ages. The complex inter-regional economic interactions spanned Mande, Amazigh, Arab, Italian, and French cultural and linguistic boundaries over some 5,600 kilometers, about one-seventh of the earth's circumference. The elephant tusks from which the ivory group from Saint Denis were carved had come a long way indeed.

Although the courtly demeanor and the creamy white color of the Virgin and Child, today housed at the Taft Museum in Cincinnati, Ohio, might seem to reference a hermetically sealed and self-sufficient Europe of the Middle Ages, it is, in fact, an object whose very existence is contingent upon a profoundly interconnected world. Whoever thought to create the group of ivory statuettes that celebrated the divinely ordained kingship of France, chose a material (at least implicitly) that was possible only thanks to involvement in a transregional system. That a symbol of Christian royal power was predicated upon trading relations, not only with the wider Islamic world at this time, but with territories far beyond the borders of known Christendom, reminds us, the modern historians, that the Middle Ages was a period as interconnected as our own—even if the power dynamics were radically different. The rich white color of the savanna elephant ivory may seem to indicate a discourse of whiteness, but reading that into the Gothic ivories may reflect more our modern concerns than those of the Middle Ages. (For different perspectives on this topic, see Patton and Young in this volume.) Understanding the trade routes that brought elephant ivory to Western Europe allows us to picture the actors involved, actively exchanging surpluses, even creating surpluses, to participate in interregional trade. From the banks of the Senegal River, traveling with Amazigh across the windswept Sahara, passing through the hands of Arab merchants in well-stocked funduks, onto the Italian ships that sailed from the Mediterranean almost to the North Sea—ivory traveled through many hands, hands of a vast array of shades. Should the display of these ivory statuettes ever be curtailed, we would lose—no, we would be suppressing—important witnesses to medieval Europe's dependence on the transregional interconnected web that constituted the world system.

Further Reading

The official document produced to prepare delegates for the discussion of the illegal ivory trade at the 2014 London conference was *Elephants in the Dust—The African Elephant Crisis: A Rapid Response Assessment* (2013, http://wedocs. unep.org/handle/20.500.11822/8539). The document describes the involvement of terrorist groups and their resulting profits and the increasing violence toward rangers, and also outlines suggestions for immediate response. For the trade in African ivory in the thirteenth and fourteenth centuries, see Sarah M. Guérin, "'Avorio d'ogni Ragione': The Supply of Elephant Ivory to Northern Europe in the Gothic Era," *Journal of Medieval History* 36 (2010): 156–74, which was written well before the astonishing analysis of the hunting site at Diouboye by Stephen A. Dueppen and Cameron Gokee: "Hunting on the margins of medieval West African states: A preliminary study of the zooarchaeological record at Diouboye, Senegal," *Azania: Archaeological Research in Africa* 49 (2014): 354–85. The route outlined for the journey across the Sahara is modeled upon that of the inveterate traveler Ibn Battuta, a scholar who traveled widely in the fourteenth century and joined a trans-Saharan caravan to West Africa in the 1350s. A lively and accessible account of his journeys can be found in Ross E. Dunn, *The Adventures of Ibn Battuta: A Muslim Traveller of the Fourteenth Century* (Berkeley and Los Angeles, 1986). Kathleen Bickford Berzock, ed. *Caravans of Gold, Fragments in Time: Art, Culture, and Exchange across Medieval Saharan Africa* (Princeton: Princeton University Press, 2019) examines the essential role the Sahara and its trade played during the European Middle Ages.

Blackness, Whiteness, and the Idea of Race in Medieval European Art

Pamela A. Patton

Perhaps nothing better illustrates the challenges of studying medieval concepts of race than the image type popularly referred to as the "Black Virgin," a loosely bounded category of sculptures, paintings, and more ephemeral modern representations—from votive candles and phone cases to tattoos—that depict the Virgin Mary with dark skin (see Figure 1). Although the medieval sculptures at the center of this tradition were once believed to have been dark-skinned when first made, recent analysis suggests that many were painted brown or black only toward or after the end of the Middle Ages; a few more may have darkened as a result of physical deterioration. When deliberate, these Virgins' retroactive darkening sometimes reflected a desire to demonstrate antiquity or to connect with Biblical passages, such as the description of the "black but beautiful" Bride in the Song of Songs, but later, in a colonialist Europe often obsessed with race, it was readily seen as promoting conversion among non-Europeans, especially in the Americas. Today, the raciality of such dark-skinned Virgins as the Mexican

Figure 1. Nuestra Señora de Montserrat, Abbey of Montserrat. Photo: Elisa A. Foster.

Señora de Guadalupe is often perceived to be integral to such figures' identities, as well as to that of the communities that venerate them. However, whether we can apply such an understanding of race retroactively to medieval images is a more complicated question.

Was blackness racial in the Middle Ages? What meanings did it hold for medieval viewers? As the example of the Black Virgin demonstrates, modern viewers of medieval art often assume an equivalency between skin color and racial or ethnic identity that mirrors their own contemporary thinking. Yet the medieval European view of the world differed sufficiently from the modern one that this assumption should be challenged. To do this, we must ask not only how medieval artists represented race, but how they and their viewers defined race in the first place.

Medieval people certainly thought about race, but neither the concept nor the words used to represent it were quite like those used today. The word "race" itself has a surprisingly limited medieval history: Its first use was in fifteenth-century Romance-language texts about animal breeding, and it evolved into a consistent classificatory term for people only during the eighteenth century. In the Middle Ages, as the historian Robert Bartlett has shown, writers tended instead to use words like *gens* and *natio* when classifying human groups. Neither term was used consistently, but most often, both words appear to have referred to self-constructed descent groups—that is, to "peoples" or communities that claimed both common ancestors and common habits, languages, and traditions. Such definitions may sound, and to some extent may have been, biological, but in practice the groupings that they describe were conceived predominantly on the basis of social traits such as language, religious practices, and even eating and hygiene habits. Although physical properties such as bodily appearance and family ancestry sometimes did figure into these groupings, they were not indispensable to them.

What more strongly unified the human classifications of the Middle Ages, as the literary scholar Geraldine Heng and others have suggested, was their potential not just to describe, but to delimit and essentialize specific groups of people in a way that accommodated them to a preexisting social hierarchy. People in medieval Europe were adept at classifying things, and they did not hesitate to use this talent to reinforce desired power relationships within a social structure in which they envisioned themselves at the top. The categories they created enabled them to assign status, control movement, and limit agency for groups that they identified as different from, and thus in their view inferior to, their own.

To classify outsiders as not just different but lesser had been a habit at least since ancient Greeks such as Hippo-

crates judged representatives of their own kind to be superior to the swarthy, enervated Africans and pale-skinned,
dull-witted northern Europeans whom they envisioned beyond their borders. To the Greeks, such peoples' bodily ex-
tremes, including the northerners' blond hair and too-white
skin, signaled moral and mental inferiority, even suitability
as slaves. In neither the ancient world nor in the medieval
one did the lack of a clear biological rationale for such thinking discourage preferential views and practices that modern
people might describe as racist. In this essay, I use the word
"race," despite its linguistic anachronism, to emphasize this
point.

Medieval ideas about skin color were nearly as complex.
Both actual and depicted skin color were understood by medieval beholders to bear a wide range of meanings that only
rarely related explicitly to racial identity. The brown, black,
blue, gray, and even purple hues chosen by artists to portray
dark-skinned figures more often signaled abstract social or
moral qualities understood as distinct from ethnicity. Among
the most common of these was evil or sinfulness, connotations traceable to early Christian theologians who saw blackness as a metaphor for sin and the devil. In their writings,
moral blackness became a metaphor so powerful that they
could describe the newly baptized as literally whitened by
the washing away of their sins. Similar thinking inspired monastic accounts of dramatic visionary temptations by black
"Ethiopian" demons that medieval artists sometimes por-
trayed as dark-skinned human figures that resembled, but in
truth had very little to do with, actual African people.

The strength of this skin-sin connection is confirmed,
rather paradoxically, by the few but important instances of
saintly figures whom medieval artists traditionally depicted
as black. These included the Biblical Queen of Sheba,
whose journey to hear King Solomon's wisdom was seen as

Figure 2. Portrait sculpture of Saint
Maurice, ca. 1240, Magdeburg
Cathedral. Photo: Hickey & Robertson,
Houston / The Menil Foundation.

a model for pagan conversion, and the medieval saint Maurice, the Theban soldier whose steadfast Christianity leg-
endarily earned him martyrdom (see Figure 2). Although
the depiction of these two figures with dark skin must have
been understood on one level as related to their foreign origin—Sheba in Ethiopia and Maurice in Egypt—a medieval
viewer steeped in Christian symbolic traditions also would
have understood it to suggest the moral limitations that these
figures overcame in pursuit of spiritual truth.

Dark-skinned foreigners such as Sheba and Maurice
illustrate a second medieval connotation of blackness: its
implication of geographical origins beyond the European
medieval world. This distance automatically implied a potential for enmity and danger, since the distant lands in

which such dark-skinned peoples were commonly thought to live, including India and Ethiopia, were also believed to be home to even more foreign and frightening beings, such as the Monstrous Races described there by ancient authors such as the ancient Roman naturalist and historian Pliny the Elder. The medieval authors influenced by Pliny associated these creatures' bodily peculiarities, from the single foot of the Sciapod to the chest-faces of headless Blemmyae, with negative moral traits, such as aggression, idolatry, and various other moral excesses, characteristics that compounded the sinfulness already assigned to their dark-skinned human neighbors.

Such syllogistic reasoning, and the dark color that came with it, could also extend to other groups perceived as foreign or threatening to those living in Europe. From the twelfth century onward, for example, medieval European artists increasingly chose to depict Muslims as dark-skinned figures despite the fact that most Muslims they encountered would have been medium- to light-complexioned. The Muslim cavalryman shown fighting a Christian knight in the fourteenth-century Luttrell Psalter offers a case in point (see Figure 3). Like many of the marginal images in this luxurious prayer book, the scene does not directly illustrate the adjacent psalm text (Psalm 41); instead, it portrays a knight who is often identified as the twelfth-century Muslim leader Saladin facing the English crusader king Richard I. The figure's fantastically blue skin, sneering expression, and ludicrous helmet lend him an air of the monstrous, while the African head points to his "foreign" origins. That the Muslims who held the Holy Land at the time when this image was made were primarily light-skinned Mamluks seems to have concerned the Psalter's artist and viewers very little: For them, Saladin's dark skin operated on other symbolic fronts, suggesting religious antagonism, geographical distance, and

Figure 3. Jousting scene, Luttrell Psalter, 1325–35. London, British Library, Add. MS 42130, fol. 82r.

the potential for violence that continued to be associated with Muslims by fourteenth-century Christians captivated by the concept of crusading.

Depicted dark skin also could signal low social status, including servitude or slavery. This visual convention had roots in ancient Roman art, where dark skin was often combined with stereotyped African features to create such stock figures as the black bath attendant or black camel driver. While these types had, to some extent, reflected the actual practice of owning black slaves in parts of the Roman empire, such slavery became far less common in Europe for most of the Middle Ages. In medieval art, the figure of the black slave instead became an abstract stereotype capable of representing all manner of subordinates, from executioners and infantrymen to musicians and household servants. In many such images, the implication of low status overlapped with other well-established connotations of dark skin, such as foreignness or religious difference. In a historiated initial in the ca. 1300 law code known as the *Vidal Mayor* or *Fuero de Aragón*, the dark skin of the two runaway slaves presented to the king thus would have been understood by their Spanish Christian viewers as reflecting both their subordinate status and their religious identity (see Figure 4).

As noted, the readiness with which medieval artists envisioned slaves to be dark-skinned belied medieval reality for most of the Middle Ages. In contrast to the Islamic world, to which trans-Saharan trade imported black slaves in some numbers, relatively few slaves held in Europe were black until the mid-fifteenth century, when Portuguese exploration of the African coast initiated the regular importation of enslaved Africans. Before that time, Europe's demand for slaves generally was met either through the subordination of local captives after military conquests or through trade with the east, especially the Balkan region; in either case, such slaves were usually light-skinned. The convention of the black African slave in European medieval imagery, then, remained primarily a figment derived from Roman artistic traditions, fed by the negative connotations linked with dark skin in medieval culture, and possibly bolstered by a dim awareness of slavery practices in the Islamic world.

The one context in which medieval artists do seem to have linked skin color with actual physical appearance was in the portrayal of individuals from geographical regions that those in Europe either knew or believed to be inhabited by black people, chiefly Egypt, Ethiopia, and other parts of Africa. Depictions of such figures often combine dark skin with quasi-racializing features, such as curly hair or full lips, as in the portrait of the famous king of Mali, Mansa Musa (reigned ca. 1312–ca. 1337), in the world map of the so-called

Figure 4. Initial Q
depicting Muslim slaves
apprehended, Vidal Mayor
("Fuero de Aragon"), ca.
1300. Los Angeles, The
J. Paul Getty Museum,
MS Ludwig XIV 6, fol.
244r. Photo: Courtesy of
the Getty's Open Content
Program.

Catalan Atlas (see Figure 5). Produced in Mallorca around
1375 by the Jewish cartographer Abraham Cresques, the
Atlas contains cosmological texts and a world map partly
based on navigational charts. In the section representing
Africa, the Malian king, described in a nearby inscription
as "Musse Melly . . . sovereign of the land of the negroes
in Gineva (Ghana)," sits on a cushioned throne, wearing a
Gothic-style crown and holding a scepter and golden orb in
reference to his royal power and the gold mines he famously
controlled. His skin is medium brown, lightly modeled with
gray and outlined in black; his hair and beard are tightly
curled; and his profile includes the low-bridged nose and
full lips common in European stereotypes of Africans. Since
Musa had died in Mali half a century before the Aragonese
map was produced, his likeness must be a fabrication, but it
convincingly links his dark skin and Africanized stereotype
with a specific geographical locus and, by extension, with
his *gens*, or "people."

Figure 5. Portrait of Mansa Musa in the Catalan Atlas of Abraham Cresques, 1375. Paris, Bibliothèque Nationale de France, MS Esp. 30, Fol. III.

The examples discussed here illustrate how few of the meanings borne by skin color in medieval art were clearly related to race, at least as modern viewers would define it. Except in cases such as Mansa Musa or other figures from certain African regions, medieval artists did not consistently associate dark skin color with specific cultural or ethnic groups. Instead, and more important in understanding the visual traditions that would follow, is that they consistently imputed a set of negative values—sinfulness, foreignness, violence, and social inferiority—to the possessors of dark skin. This allowed skin color to function, then, not as a specifically racial marker but as an implement of racist thinking.

This strategy is also attested by the ways in which medieval artists in Europe handled the opposite of blackness: whiteness. By the later Middle Ages, the idealized, pale-skinned features of Gothic figures could serve as shorthand signs for moral purity, social elevation, and political authority. Paralleling the snowy-white princesses of medieval romance literature (themselves forerunners of our modern Snow White and similar heroines), such figures combined starkly whitened skin with other positive social markers, such as attenuated proportions, graceful gestures, and costly clothing, that asserted their superior status. Although medieval artists' treatment of blackness and whiteness in such cases cannot be described as racial in the strictest modern sense, their stark alignment of skin color with the moral, social, and personal values of their day stands uncomfortably close to the racism and colorism of the modern world.

For medieval artists, it would seem, dark skin was both less and more racial than we might expect it to be. While its power to signal race *qua* race remained relatively weak, it inflected medieval imagery with social, religious, and moral connotations that foreshadowed modern racial thinking in ways easily missed, or misconstrued, by modern viewers. Dark skin could be racial in the Middle Ages, but much more often it was not; either way, it facilitated the organization of culture in ways that many would describe as racist. To pause and consider this paradox serves real purpose for a modern world still grappling with its own embedded yet shifting conceptions of racial identity. Like the Black Virgin itself, the complex significance of skin color in medieval art counters the self-reinforcing assumption that medieval people's values simply mirrored our own. Instead, it reveals and challenges the mechanisms beneath both medieval and modern notions of race, difference, and self.

Further Reading

Robert Bartlett's discussion of the linguistic and conceptual differences that complicate modern understanding of medieval ideas about race, updating work in his earlier publications, appears in "Medieval and Modern Concepts of Race and Ethnicity," *Journal of Medieval and Early Modern Studies* 31, no. 1 (2001): 39–56. A broad-ranging argument that racial thinking and practices, based on a variety of bodily and cultural factors, already existed in the Middle Ages is made by Geraldine Heng, *The Invention of Race in the European Middle Ages* (Cambridge: Cambridge University Press, 2018). For analysis of the ways in which medieval artists signaled both human and monstrous difference, see the influential study by Debra Higgs Strickland, *Saracens, Demons, and Jews: Making Monsters in Medieval Art* (Princeton, N.J.: Princeton University Press, 2003). An important resource for the study of dark skin in medieval art is David Bindman, Henry Louis Gates, and Karen C. C. Dalton, eds., *The Image of the Black in Western Art* (Cambridge, Mass.: Belknap Press, 2010); originally published between 1976–89, this work has been updated in the new edition with the addition of several new essays. On the variable connotations of blackness in the artistic genre known as the "Black Virgin" and a brief discussion of when such sculptures acquired their color, see Elisa A. Foster, "The Black Madonna of Montserrat: An Exception to Concepts of Dark Skin in Medieval and Early Modern Iberia?" in *Envisioning Others: Race, Color, and the Visual in Iberia and Latin America*, edited by Pamela A. Patton (Leiden: Brill, 2016): 18–50.

England Between Empire and Nation in "The Battle of Brunanburh"

Elizabeth M. Tyler

English nationalism often takes the historical unity of England for granted and lacks an interest in the other constituent countries of the United Kingdom. This dynamic is most recently and most acutely apparent in Brexit, the intended withdrawal of the United Kingdom from the European Union (EU) after a highly divisive referendum in 2016. As a nationalist movement, Brexit has not only radically changed the relationship of the United Kingdom to the rest of Europe, but it has also destabilized the relationship between the constituent parts of the UK: England, Scotland, Wales, and Northern Ireland. This is not least because Northern Ireland and Scotland voted to remain in the EU, while it was only in England and Wales that majorities voted to leave. England's apparent ability to dictate policy to the rest of the United Kingdom brings to mind the tendency of some English (and North American) people to elide England and Britain. The complexity of identity in the modern UK includes this elision of England and Britain (without regard to Scotland, Wales, and Northern Ireland), internal divisions within the UK constituent countries themselves (such as between northern and southern England or between Highland and Lowland Scotland), and constant movement of populations between these different regions of the UK as well as across borders with the Republic of Ireland and the rest of Europe. Contrary to myths of pure national origins, this mixing — this diversity — was always a feature of Britain and Ireland, as the early medieval literature of England makes clear.

This piece aims to use a reading of one mid-tenth-century Old English poem, "The Battle of Brunanburh," to open up the political complexity of Britain and Ireland in the early Middle Ages. In so doing, it challenges traditional literary criticism, which has tended to find straightforward (or even inevitable) expressions of unified Englishness in Old English poetry. Early medieval Britain was divided between many different kingdoms, including several under the control of rulers who traced their lineage back to Germanic incomers of the fifth century. We usually refer to these kingdoms as Anglo-Saxon and call their language Old English. "Brunanburh" celebrates the victory of two of these Anglo-Saxon kingdoms (Wessex with Mercia) over their adversaries in 937, an event that will be explained more fully in the text that follows. An analysis of "Brunanburh"'s poetic style will reveal that the poem celebrates the internal diversity and wider connections of Britain in order to glorify the efforts of one kingdom and one dynasty (that of Wessex) to exert dominion over their neighbors. English literature did not begin within nationalizing horizons but within imperial horizons. "Brunanburh" not only reveals the imperial origins of the writing that has come to constitute "national" English literature, but it also invites us to recognize the connections between the nationalism of Brexit and the ways we read Old English literature.

The association of Old English poetry and national identity has its roots in the practice of literary criticism itself. From its birth in the nineteenth century up to the present day, literary criticism often projects modern national identities back onto the kingdoms of medieval Europe. This teleological move is often explicitly nationalist. Within this nationalizing mode of literary history, writing in Old English, which flourished unusually early compared to German and French, for example, is often seen to reflect an early sense of Englishness, dating back even to the eighth century. Recent historical, archaeological, and linguistic work demands, however, that we rethink such Anglocentric approaches to the literature of medieval Britain. In the study of early medieval English literature and culture, postcolonial criticism has productively exposed the imperial dimensions of the initial introduction of literacy into England as part of Christianization by the Roman Church. Postcolonial critics of Old English have been less interested in the imperial designs of later English elites themselves, however, in particular the campaigns of the West Saxon kings of one small kingdom in southwest England to dominate their neighbors in the rest of England, Scotland, Wales, and even Ireland. Scholars of Old English have tended to accept, rather than dissect and analyze, West Saxon rhetoric about England as a nation.

Nevertheless, the imperial designs of the West Saxon kingdom, located in southwest England and only one of the many small kingdoms in Britain at the time, were fundamental for the creation of a single state in Anglo-Saxon England (that is, England from the arrival of Germanic-speaking settlers in the mid-fifth century to the Norman Conquest of 1066). The unification of the "English" under the West Saxons in a kingdom called England was far from preordained; rather, it has a specific history. We can identify key moments in that history. According to the written record that survives from the Middle Ages, it was Pope Gregory I, a sixth-century Roman, who first called the Germanic inhabitants of Britain the English. The context was his decision to send missionaries out to convert these people; he did this without realizing the political and ethnic complexity of the island and that both Britons and Irish were already at work evangelizing these incomers. Bede, writing a religious history in the eighth century, influentially developed Gregory's idea of an English people; his work *The Ecclesiastical History of the English People* was read widely in Britain and Ireland and in continental Europe. The creation of a political union to mirror the ecclesiastical structure (that is the creation of an English national, rather than simply religious, identity) only occurred as the consequence of many other developments, both before and after Pope Gregory's naming of the English. These developments began with the subsuming of an indigenous Romano-British population (that is, the Britons) by an Anglo-Saxon elite across the fifth, sixth, and seventh centuries. (Contrary to the Anglo-Saxon migration myth, the Britons were not all slaughtered or pushed into Wales.) Already in the eighth century, the West Saxons had begun to take over other English kingdoms, gaining, in the ninth century, the dominance previously held by Northumbria and Mercia. The ninth and tenth century also saw the West Saxon assimilation of the Scandinavians (Vikings) who settled in eastern and northern England. Ultimately, the West Saxons formulated an imperial vision of the relationship between the English and the other peoples of Britain and Ireland — including the Strathclyde Welsh living in what is now southwest Scotland, the Welsh, and the Cornish (all three were descendants of the Romano-British); the Scots; and the Hiberno-Norse, who were a mixed population of Irish and Scandinavians (Vikings) who settled in and around Dublin.

By imperial, I simply mean rule that extends over multiple peoples who had separate political identities. In the case of Britain, these peoples were ruled over by separate kings, who became, to different degrees, subjected to the West Saxon kings. Englishness is not a pre-existing natural identity but rather the outcome of a well-documented process whereby elites consolidated and extended their power through the creation of ethnic identity.

"The Battle of Brunanburh" constitutes the entry in the *Anglo-Saxon Chronicle* for the year 937 AD that celebrates the victory of one West Saxon king, Athelstan, over the Scots, Hiberno-Norse, and Strathclyde Welsh. "Brunanburh" is the first poem to be included in the *Chronicle* and as such it stands out in high relief from the surrounding prose. Before turning to focus on this poem, it will be useful to consider the inception of the *Chronicle*. Despite its modern name, the *Chronicle* was not an account of all of Anglo-Saxon England, but rather the history of the West Saxon ruling dynasty, which came to rule all of England: It is dynastic rather than national history. The *Anglo-Saxon Chronicle* was begun in the 890s in the court of Alfred the Great, and it was one result of his policy to promote written Old English (rather than Latin) as part of the creation of an English identity. This view is very clear in the preface, written in his name, to a translation of Pope Gregory's *Pastoral Care*. Alfred wrote of English as the language that "we" the *Angelcynn* ("the English") all understand. But an imperial vision underpins this vision of the use of writing in the vernacular; when Alfred goes on to survey the state of learning among the English, he ranges north and south of the River Humber, well beyond his own kingdom located south of the River Thames. Moreover, he presents written English as a successor to the prestigious languages of the ancient world:

> Then I remembered how scripture was first found
> in the Hebrew language, and afterwards, when the
> Greeks learned it, they turned it completely into
> their own language, and also all other books. After-
> wards the Latin people in the same way, when they
> learned it, they turned it all, through wise translators,
> into their own language.

In writing in their own language, the English would be following on from the Romans.

With the political and literary context in place, we can
now turn to "Brunanburh" itself. A translation of the poem
appears at the end of this chapter. The poem describes how
King Athelstan (924–39) and his brother Edmund (939–46)
secured victory at Brunanburh, an unknown location in
the North of England. Drawing on the support of the West
Saxons and Mercians, they defeated the combined forces of
the Hiberno-Norse and the Scots. The Hiberno-Norse King
Olaf Guthfrithson had recently reclaimed York and the area
around it, and King Constantine of the Scots was consolidating his powerbase among the Anglo-Saxon kingdom of
the Northumbrians and the Strathclyde Welsh. Athelstan
was the first king to be styled, in royal documents known
as charters as "king of the English" (*rex Anglorum*), and the
poem offers us a unique opportunity to show how English
literature negotiated the complex identities of early medieval Britain. Other charters reveal an imperial dimension to
Athelstan's status as king of the English in the use of a Greek
word for king (*basileos*) and his assertion of rule over all of
Britain; he is "king of the English and equally governor of
all of Britain" (*basileos Anglorum et eque totius Britanniæ
orbis gubernator*). Most striking in this regard is a charter
for 935, made at a meeting in Cirencester, which the scribe

describes taking place "in the city at one time constructed by the Romans" (*in civitate a Romanis olim constructa*). It was here that Athelstan routinely required the kings of Wales to pay taxes to him. This charter is witnessed by five kings of Britain, who are derogatorily called *subreguli*, that is, sub-kings or sub-kinglets: These men were Constantine, king of Scotland; Owain, king of the Strathclyde Welsh; and three Welsh kings, Hywel of Deheubarth, Idwal of Gwynnedd, and Morgan of Gwent. Athelstan is presented as an emperor both in his rule of England *and* in his rule of Britain.

In "The Battle of Brunanburh," Alfred's imperial English language becomes the basis for a new imperial poetic style that entangles Old English, Old Norse, and Carolingian Latin poetic styles in recognition of Athelstan's imperial kingship over Britain. The poem resists an English identity: Nowhere is Alfred's *Angelcynn* mentioned, but rather Athelstan and Edmund lead the separate peoples of Wessex and Mercia. After the battle, Athelstan and Edmund returned to their homeland, Wessex. The boast that five kings fell at Brunanburh portrays the battle as one for dominion over Britain, not England. The closing lines, in which the poet triumphantly harkens back to the fifth-century Germanic invasion of Britain, drive home the same sense of British conquest. In terms of its geographical horizons, the poem maps out a wide space: The defeated Constantine returns to the North and Olaf to Dublin, underscored as in Ireland. This West Saxon imperial vision is sanctioned furthermore by God. Wordplay on *æþel* ("noble") ties together the name of "*Æthel*stan" ("noble-stone") (line 1 of the translation), Edmund's title of "*æþel*ing" (Old English for "prince") (line 3) and the sun, said to be God's "*æþele* gesceaft" ("noble creation") (line 16). Athelstan's empire was divinely sanctioned.

The poem's style draws from literatures in several languages and associates the poem's imperial vision with both

Anglo-Saxon tradition and the international court surrounding Athelstan, which included both Scandinavian speakers of Norse and clerics, noblemen, and princes from the Carolingian realms in mainland Europe (where Athelstan was a power broker). "Brunanburh"'s traditionalism is evident in its Old English alliterative poetic form, in its distinctive archaic vocabulary, and in such well-attested Old English motifs as the beasts of battle, who gruesomely feast on the bodies of dead warriors (lines 61–65). "Brunanburh" powerfully and innovatively deploys this traditionalism in support of West Saxon imperial ambition. But "Brunanburh" draws from Old Norse and Carolingian poetry in Latin to innovate as well. It is the earliest surviving poem to use heroic verse to praise a contemporary Anglo-Saxon ruler, rather than to recount, as *Beowulf* does, the deeds of legendary heroes. In this it reveals a debt to both Old Norse skaldic verse (praise poetry whose taste for violence and triumphalism is unparalleled in Old English poems before "Brunanburh"), and Latin poetry in praise of Carolingian emperors. Both kinds of poetry were appreciated in Athelstan's court, from which "Brunanburh" may have emerged. There skalds rubbed shoulders with Latin poets as they all competed to praise the king, and Norse and English poetic styles were shaped in dialogue and in conflict with each other and with Latin.

The wordplay of "Brunanburh" on *æþel* discussed in the preceding text, which hints at divine approval for Athelstan's victory, is reminiscent of Latin poetry written for Carolingian princes in the rest of Europe, in which punning was an important stylistic feature. One Latin poem written for Athelstan, "Carta dirige gressus" (Letter, direct your steps) puns repeatedly on the Latin word *saxum* for "stone," which recalls both Athelstan's "Saxon" ancestry and the second element of his name — "stan" — which means "stone" in Old English. Meanwhile, the poet of "Brunanburh" also signals

his debt to skaldic verse by adopting Old Norse words, such
as "cnear" for "warship" (line 35) and kennings (compressed
metaphors), such as "wæpengewrixel" for "exchange of
weapons" (line 51). In the process, his Old English poem
comes to imitate skaldic verse's ostentatious obscurity. This
appropriation of the poetic style of the enemy signals on a
generic and stylistic level that the areas of Britain settled and
ruled by Scandinavians since the ninth century had become
part of Athelstan's realm. At the same time, it signals that the
English identity that Athelstan was building up was not homogenous, but one that brought together different peoples
under one rule. The way that "Brunanburh" situates itself
between Latin and Old Norse poetry underpins its sparkling
imperial style and cuts away any simple equation between
English language and English identity.

English identity does become a feature of the *Anglo-
Saxon Chronicle* later in the tenth century. England, then
established as a kingdom, was under threat from renewed
Scandinavian attacks, whose end result was the conquest of
England by Cnut, the king of Denmark. These later entries
articulate Englishness in the context of external threat,
rather than a period of kingdom-building. The transition
from "Brunanburh"'s celebration of West Saxon dominion
over Britain to the defense of England implies that empire preceded nation: There could be no England without
there first being a hegemonic Wessex. This sequence left
its mark on Old English poetry and entries in the *Anglo-
Saxon Chronicle* written after "Brunanburh." A reading of
"Brunanburh," which attends to its imperial, rather than national, horizons, looks past these retroactive declarations of
Englishness. It brings forward the diversity of Britain, even if
we see that diversity yielding to English dominion.

Looking at the portrayal of the Welsh in "Brunanburh"
points to the importance of reading texts beyond those writ-

ten in English or by the English, if we are to see the diversity of early medieval Britain. The absence of the Welsh from alongside the Scots and Hiberno-Norse in "Brunanburh" requires explanation. Partly, this is because Brunanburh was a battle for the North, in which the Welsh of Wales, still loyal to Athelstan, did not participate. Owain, king of the Strathclyde Welsh, was there and possibly the poet subsumes the Strathclyde Welsh into Constantine's forces because they were allied. But the reasons for the Welsh absence probably lie elsewhere. In the closing lines, the poet declares that the Welsh had already been conquered centuries earlier when the Angles and Saxon arrived from the continent. "Brunanburh" insists on the subjugation of the Welsh and, like Bede's *Ecclesiastical History*, it seeks to efface the earlier Britons from history.

Although represented as already conquered, the Welsh remained a strong threat to the Anglo-Saxons. They were well aware of the specifically imperial ambitions of the West Saxon kings and that England was being created at the expense of the Welsh kingdoms. The Welsh poem "Armes Prydein Vawr" ("The Great Prophecy of Britain"), most likely written in the years just after the battle at Brunanburh, imagines a broad insular coalition, drawn from across the present-day Wales, Ireland, Man, Scotland, and including Norse as well as Bretons, driving the foreign Saxons into exile. Just like "Brunanburh," it sees the current conflict as beginning with the arrival of the Angles and Saxons on British shores in the fifth century (line 32). Led into battle by the Welsh, these combined forces will leave the defeated Saxons as "food for wild beasts" (*a mal bwyt balaon*) (line 60)—as "Brunanburh" boasted was the fate of those opposed to Athelstan. The poem rails against subjection to a "Great King" (*mechteyrn*) (Athelstan) (line 100) who through his agents in Cirencester (line 69) imposes taxes on the people of Britain. Where "Brunanburh" ended by recalling the coming of the Angles and the Saxons, "proud war-smiths" (*wlance wigsmiþas*) (line 72) from across the sea to Britain, *Armes Prydein* ends with the Saxons heading into exile "at anchor on the sea" (*wrth agor ar vor*) (line 191). "Brunanburh" and "Armes Prydein" are both poems that insist on the diversity of the peoples of Britain in the early Middle Ages; listening to "Armes Prydein" can jolt us out of troubling and impoverished nationalizing readings of Old English poetry that would reduce these peoples to the English and their enemies.

"Brunanburh" insists that we not turn to the Anglo-Saxon past in search of a stable English identity but rather that we recognize that Englishness was forged for political ends, bringing together people who spoke different dialects (as in Northern England) and different languages: Celtic ones (like British and Irish) and Old Norse. The poem's clear emphasis on the West Saxons' imperial designs on all the peoples of Britain and its delight in violence points to the messy origins of a polity that only later became "English" in anything like the modern sense. Its engagement with Old Norse and Carolingian Latin poetry exposes the awareness on the part of its author and its first audiences of the West Saxons' place in a wider world of intellectual and political exchange. When read alongside Athelstan's charters and "Armes Prydein Vawr," "Brunanburh" brings both the diversity of Britain and the hegemony of England into full view. As ethical readers of medieval texts, we shouldn't fail to see both this diversity and this hegemony. Postcolonial theory has transformatively challenged the way we read modern English literature: demanding that we step outside the imperialist position, seeing what was lost in the face of empire, the centrality of imperialism to English identity and, critically, that we engage with colonial and postcolonial literary cultures. These theoretical and political imperatives apply equally to medieval literature.

The Battle of Brunanburh

In this year, King Athelstan, the lord of warriors,
the ring-giver of men, and his brother too,
ætheling Edmund, won life-long glory
in the conflict of swords' edges
around Brunanburh. They cleaved the   5
   shield-wall,
hewed battle-linden with the remnants
   of hammers,
sons of Edward, as was inborn in them
from their forebearers, that they in battle
against every enemy, should protect their land,
treasure and homes. Hated ones perished,   10
people of the Scots and shipmen,
doomed, fell. The field grew dark
with the blood of men, when the sun,
in the morning, the famous star,
glided up over the ground, the bright candle   15
   of God,
the eternal Lord, until the noble creation
sank as it set. There many men lay,
gutted by spears, northern men,
shot, over their shields, and the Scots,
lay weary, sated with war. The West Saxons   20
   onwards
the whole day, in choice troops
pursued the loathed peoples,
hewed down the fleeing soldiers, harshly from
   behind
with mill-sharp swords. The Mercians did not
   withhold

hard handplay from any men,   25
who with Olaf, in the hold of a ship,
over the surge of the sea, had sought the land,
doomed in battle. Five lay dead
on the battlefield, young kings,
put to sleep by the sword, likewise also seven   30
of Olaf's warriors, a countless host,
of both seamen and Scots. Then was put
    to flight
the lord of the northmen, driven by need,
into the prow of a ship, with a little troop;
the warship pressed ahead in the water, the   35
    king set out
on the fallow sea, saved his life.
Likewise there also the wise one came in flight
to his native land in the north, Constantine,
hoary old warrior, had no cause to exult
at the meeting of swords; he was sheared of   40
    kinsmen,
deprived of friends in the homestead,
slain in conflict, and his son left behind
in the place of slaughter, destroyed by wounds,
inexperienced in war. The grey-haired man
had no cause to boast of the clashing of swords, 45
the old enemy, any more than Olaf did;
with the remnants of their army, they had no
    cause to rejoice
that they were better in warlike deeds,
on the battle field, in the clashing of banners,
in the meeting of spears, in the coming   50
    together of men,
in the exchange of weapons, when on the
    slaughter-field they
played with the sons of Edward.

Then the northmen departed in nailed warships,
wretched remnant of spears, on Dingesmere
over deep water, seeking Dublin,   55
back to Ireland, ashamed.
Likewise, the brothers both together,
king and ætheling, sought their home,
the land of the West Saxons, rejoicing in war.
They left behind them, to share out the bodies, 60
to enjoy the food, the dark-coated one,
the black raven, horny-beaked,
and the dusty-coated one, the white-tailed eagle,
greedy war-hawk, and the grey beast,
the wolf in the woods. No greater slaughter   65
    of people
had ever yet been carried out
on this island before this
with sword-edges, as the books tell us,
old learned men, since from the east,
the Angles and Saxons, rose up   70
over the broad sea, sought out Britain,
proud war-smiths, overcame the Welsh,
the glory-bold warriors got a homeland.

Further Reading

Texts and translations of "The Battle of Brunanburh," "Carta dirige gressus," and "Armes Prydein Vawr" are all available in *The Battle of Brunanburh: A Casebook*, ed. Michael Livingston (Exeter: Exeter University Press, 2011). This volume contains many other texts useful for study of "Brunanburh" along with historical, literary, and linguistic commentary. The multilingual style of "Brunanburh" is wonderfully analyzed by Samantha Zacher in "Multilingualism at the Court of King Æthelstan: Latin Praise Poetry and *The Battle of*

Brunanburh" in Elizabeth M. Tyler, ed. *Conceptualizing Multilingualism in England, c. 800–c. 1250* (Turnhout: Brepols, 2011). Zacher's article contains references to key work on the Latin and Old Norse poetry of Athelstan's reign. Pauline Stafford's article, "The Anglo-Saxon Chronicles, Identity and the Making of England" (*Haskins Society Journal: Studies in Medieval History* 19 (2008): 28–50) opens up the complexity of the identities, regnal and regional, negotiated in the different versions of the *Anglo-Saxon Chronicle*, distancing it from preoccupations with "Englishness." Sarah Foot's "Where English Becomes British: Rethinking the Contexts for *Brunanburh*" (in Julia Barrow and Andrew Wareham, eds., *Myth, Rulership, Church and Charters: Essays in Honour of Nicholas Brooks* [Aldershot: Ashgate, 2008], 127–44) argues for the British rather than English horizons of the poem. Thomas Charles-Edwards's *Wales and the Britons, 350–1064* (Oxford: Oxford University Press, 2013) looks at early medieval Britain from Wales and includes discussion of "Armes Prydein Vawr." See especially Chapter 16, "The Britons and the Empire of Britain." For an influential discussion of Anglo-Saxon literature from a postcolonial perspective, which sees England's relation to Rome, but not English imperialism within Britain, see Nicholas Howe's chapter, "Englalond and the Postcolonial Void" in his *Writing the Map of Anglo-Saxon England: Essays in Cultural Geography* (New Haven: Yale University Press, 2007).

The research for this article was supported by the Centre for Medieval Literature, funded by the Danish National Research Foundation, and located at the University of Southern Denmark and the University of York (project number DNRF102).

Whose Spain Is It, Anyway?

David A. Wacks

When nations write their histories, ethnic and religious minorities, people displaced by migrations, and other marginalized groups do not tend to feature in them until they are able to organize and make an outcry. In the United States in the 1950s and '60s, Native Americans, African Americans, and Chicanos, all of whom had been present since the nation's origins, organized to claim their political power, and as part of the process lobbied to have their voices included in school and university curricula. In Spain, the task of acknowledging voices silenced by history is much more difficult. Absent any significant Muslim or Jewish bloc in Spain, the question becomes an interior monologue: What do Spanish Islam and Judaism mean to *Catholic* Spain? And even more problematically, given the history of massive conversion from Judaism and Islam to Catholicism, Catholic Spaniards ask themselves, where do *they* (Jews and Muslims) end and *we* (Catholics) begin? Spain's identity as a modern nation-state depends on non-Islam and non-Judaism. It is well-known that many Spaniards descend from

Jewish and/or Muslim ancestors and many aspects of Spanish culture are indebted to the medieval Jewish and Muslim communities in Iberia. Yet our capacity to understand these cultural contributions has been fundamentally clouded by the bloody process by which these elements of the Spanish past were appropriated by modern Spanish culture. What do medieval Iberia and its violent past tell us about race relations today?

Jews in Spain have a history going back to (at least) the Romanization of the Peninsula. By the 1492 Edict of Expulsion, Jews had lived on the Peninsula since at least the fourth century CE. Muslims first came to the Peninsula in 710, and the great majority of the Peninsula would soon come under Muslim rule, to stay so until the beginning of the eleventh century, when northern Christian principalities began to make significant incursions into al-Andalus (Muslim-ruled Spain and Portugal). During the early centuries of Muslim rule, many Iberian Christians converted to Islam. Even after the tide turned in favor of Christian rule in the thirteenth century, the Kingdom of Granada remained under Muslim rule until 1492.

The story one reads in Spanish textbooks is that with the defeat of Granada and the expulsion of the Jews and subsequent conversion of Muslims beginning in 1502, Spain was now a Christian land. However, the majority of Andalusi Muslims (Muslims from al-Andalus) were, in fact, descended from Christians already living in Iberia when al-Andalus was established, which puts the idea of an "Islamic invasion" into question. In any event, because the Catholic Church had declared crusades to conquer Iberia, Spanish nobility implied a legacy of crusade. Conquistadors carried this mindset to the New World: that conquest and conversion of non-Christians was an inherently Spanish concern and central to their emerging national identity. The country's patron saint James (Santiago, Christ's disciple who according to tradition preached the gospel in Roman Hispania) is nicknamed "Muslim Slayer" (*Matamoros*), and eventually gave his name to the Mexican city just across the border from Brownsville, Texas.

Muslim and Jewish Iberians *loved* their country (al-Andalus in Arabic or Sefarad in Hebrew), and sang its glories unapologetically. Around the year 1200, the Seville-based poet Ismail ibn Muhammad al-Shaqundi proudly declared, "I praise God that I was born in al-Andalus and that he has given me the good fortune to be one of her sons. . . . To exalt North Africa over al-Andalus is to prefer left to right, or to say the night is lighter than the day. Ridiculous!" At about the same time in Toledo, Judah al-Harizi, writing in Hebrew, described his homeland as "a delight to the eyes. Her light was as the sun in the midst of heaven. The perfume of her dust was as myrrh to the nostrils and the taste of her delicious fruits was as honey to the palate." In 1615, Miguel de Cervantes gave voice to the pain of displacement many Moriscos (the last Spanish Muslims) felt in the lines of *Don Quixote* only two years after their final expulsion: "We did not know our good fortune until we lost it, and the greatest desire in almost all of us is to return to Spain; most of those, and there are many of them, who know the language as well as I do, abandon their wives and children and return, so great is the love they have for Spain; and now I know and feel the truth of the saying that it is sweet to love one's country." Spanish Jewish exiles looked back at Sefarad with similar nostalgia, though it was mixed with bitterness over their own persecution and expulsion.

Though in recent years Spain and Portugal have offered citizenship to descendants of the Jews they expelled in 1492 and 1497 respectively, they have not extended the same courtesy to descendants of Andalusi Muslims, who are still considered strangers in their ancestral lands, "Eastern" or "Oriental" intruders in the Christian West. "Maghreb," the

Arabic name for the Kingdom of Morocco, essentially means
"west." The Iberian Peninsula is just as far west as Morocco.
So, whose West is it anyway? Jews had been there in the
West since Hispania belonged to the Roman Empire (which
is still considered "the West" even though it included places
such as Syria and Egypt that are not typically considered
"Western" today), to when al-Andalus was in the Western
reaches of the Arab world.

Andalusi monuments have long been considered part
of Spain's national patrimony. Today's Spaniards are the
guardians of some of the most amazing monuments in the
Arab world, including the Alhambra fortress of Granada,
the Giralda (ex-minaret, current bell tower) of the Cathedral of Seville, the Mosque of Córdoba, and the Alcázar or
Fortress of Seville, to name a few. The question has always
been whether the Spanish were curating the monuments
of a subject colonial culture, as were the British in Egypt
or India, or whether the Alhambra was, in fact, part of their
own national cultural legacy.

The appropriation of Muslim and Jewish monuments in
Spain followed a complicated series of events in which the
Christians sometimes tolerated, sometimes persecuted, but
finally expelled the Muslim and Jewish populations. King
Ferdinand III of Castile (1230–52), earned sainthood for conquering the important Andalusi cities of Qurtuba (Córdova)
and Ishbilya (Sevilla). Fernando's son Alfonso X (1252–84)
took a very different approach to religious coexistence. He
established a school of Arabic studies in Seville and proposed the translation of the Qur'an, the Torah, the Talmud,
and the *Zohar* (the foundational text of Jewish mysticism,
written in Spain in the thirteenth century) into Castilian,
the dialect of vernacular Latin that would eventually become known as Spanish. While he did maintain policies
that by today's standards seem harshly anti-Semitic (for ex-

ample, he legislated distinctive dress codes for Jews and forbade them to leave their houses during Holy Week), Alfonso
was far more tolerant in his treatment of Jews and Muslims
than other Christian monarchs.

Nonetheless, a rising tide of popular anti-Semitism over
the course of the fourteenth century culminated in a wave
of violent pogroms that swept Spain in the summer of 1391.
Over the course of the fifteenth century, the situation grew
worse so that by the second half of the century, the Pope
would celebrate Queen Isabella and King Ferdinand as
"The Catholic Monarchs" in recognition of their conquest
of Muslim-ruled Granada and subsequent Expulsion of the
Jews (1492) and forced baptism of Muslims (1502). Thus,
Spain began to imagine itself as a wholly Christian society,
inoculated against its Jewish and Muslim past by its zeal in
eradicating these creeds from its midst.

All of this means that Spain and Portugal, since 1502 and
until quite recently, have had virtually no officially Jewish or
Muslim population. Subsequently, social prestige in Spain
was largely a function of how actively not-Jewish or not-
Muslim one was, or perhaps by how many Muslims your
family killed on the battlefield. At the end of the fifteenth
century, the Castilian poet Jorge Manrique (a high-ranking
noble) could state quite plainly in a now-famous poem of his
that "the good priests and monks earn salvation by praying
and crying out to God / and famous knights by suffering
in struggle against the Muslims." A steady stream of official
letters of crusade from Rome reinforced this attitude with
economic and spiritual support for those Iberian Christians
who fought against Muslim-ruled Granada. This wedding of
respectability with overt anti-Semitism persists, in modified
forms, even today. Popular anti-Jewish violence historically
swelled during Holy Week, when those faithful remembering the death of Jesus would visit local Jewish communities

with violence in what they imagined was revenge for his death. In the city of León during Holy Week, it is traditional to drink wine mixed with lemonade, a practice still referred to as "killing jews" (*matar judíos*). By the same token, a town in Castile was, until 2015, named Castrillo Mata Judíos (*Camp Kill Jews*) — it's now named Castrillo Mota de Judíos (*Jew Hill Camp*).

Given all this, it's no surprise that the Hebrew and Arabic literature of the territory currently known as Spain and Portugal didn't make it into the required reading lists of today's Spanish school children and university students. In fact, despite the massive outpouring of very high-quality Arabic poetry produced on the Peninsula, you'd be hard pressed to walk into a popular bookstore in Madrid and find an anthology of Andalusi poets in Spanish translation.

However, despite centuries of Inquisition, expulsions, and cultural policing, Iberia remained a place where Jewish and Islamic culture continued to survive in different ways. The Expulsion of the Jews — and conversion to Christianity of those who chose to remain in 1492 — transformed Spain from being the most important center of Hebrew learning in the Jewish world to being the most important center of Hebrew learning in the Latin Christian world. Many learned rabbis became Christians, entering the Church. Thus, Spain's humanist universities excelled in Hebrew scriptural studies, and a team of scholars at the University of Alcalá de Henares published the first polyglot Bible (including the Hebrew, Latin, Greek, and Aramaic texts) in Europe in 1517. However, one could also get into trouble studying Hebrew the *wrong* way. A few decades later, a Hebrew professor at the University of Salamanca, Friar Luis of León — a *converso* or descendant of Jews converted to Christianity — was jailed by the Inquisition from 1572–76 for translating the Song of Songs directly from Hebrew into Spanish (translations of

Holy Scripture into the vernacular were technically prohibited at this time).

The study of Arabic and Hebrew had long been one way in which Christian Iberian monarchs sought to dominate Muslim and Jewish minorities. Back in the thirteenth century, King Alfonso X of Castile and the friar Ramon Llull both opened schools of Arabic for Christian clerics to learn the language of the Qur'an. For them, the study of Arabic had two distinct goals: On the one hand, if you could understand the Qur'an, you had a better chance of converting Muslims; on the other, Castilian-speaking Christians stood to learn a great deal from Arabic books of science and astronomy.

Despite this early Christian Iberian interest in the superior material and scientific culture of al-Andalus, many Spaniards still do not consider Iberian Muslims and Jews and their cultural legacy as part of their own cultural identity. Why is this? The question of race may have something to do with it. Though modern sources often represent Andalusi Muslims with stereotyped African features and as dark-skinned (and to be sure there were some dark-skinned Africans among Andalusi Muslims), as far as we know the Muslims of the Peninsula were not, in general, physically distinguishable from their Christian neighbors: For example, sources describe the Caliph Abd al-Rahman III as having red hair and a red beard, which he dyed brown in order to appear more authentically Arab. Religious difference, which fulfilled a social function similar to that of what we like to call "race" today, was instead marked by clothing, hairstyle, food, and (sometimes) language. Some sources, such as the thirteenth-century *Cantigas de Santa Maria* of Alfonso X, depict Jews with stereotyped Semitic features that "normalize" after baptism (for example, exaggerated noses become smaller), which suggests that these depictions were not meant to be physically accurate but rather to represent the spiritual transformation of Christian baptism.

Mass conversions of Jews in 1391 and 1492, and then of Muslims in 1502, created substantial populations of Christians who had once been practicing Jews or Muslims, or who had descended from practicing Jews and Muslims. These converts (*conversos*), who as Christians, did not face the same social restrictions as when they were Jews or Muslims, were now free to occupy powerful positions in Church, at court, and in local administration. One such convert, Pedro de la Cavallería, who after his conversion rose to power at the court of Alfonso IV of Aragon, was accused by the Inquisition of continuing to practice Judaism secretly. In his defense, he testified that his conversion (sincere or otherwise) unlocked tremendous social advancement for him. Inquisition records report him having said, "Could I as a Jew, ever have risen higher than a rabbinical post? But now, see, I am one of the chief councilors of the city. For the sake of the little man who was hanged [Jesus], I am accorded every honor, and I issue orders and decrees to the whole city of Saragossa." The rapid rise of such converts was a threat to Old Christians' sense of superiority; they sought a way to make the New Christians second-class citizens, as they had been as Jews. The answer was in the blood. Baptism, they argued, could not wash away the stain of Judaism from the blood of the *converso*, and if a Jew, by virtue of her stained blood, could not make a legitimate Christian, they should not enjoy the benefits accorded to other Christians whose blood was "pure."

In the middle of the fifteenth century, the state began to issue Blood Purity Laws (*estatutos de limpieza de sangre*), similar to the Nazi Nuremberg laws, restricting the rights and freedoms of New Christians. These were meant to keep New Christians as second-class citizens, limit their professional and economic prospects, and reduce their social influence. These laws were backed by considerable force. Starting in 1478, the Spanish Inquisition, nothing less than a massively international secret police (the *Santa Hermandad* or Holy Brotherhood), with relatively unlimited powers and resources, violently policed the borders of Spain's Christian identity. Charged with rooting out heresy in Spain's Christian community, the Inquisition ruthlessly targeted New Christians, incentivizing Spanish subjects to denounce their friends, neighbors, and family members for Judaizing, or practicing Judaism in secret. In some cases, they were authorized to persecute unconverted Jews as well. This very powerful institution soon became a very rich one as well: They were empowered to confiscate the property of their prisoners, with a cut going to the Crown. The incentives proved irresistible, and the Inquisition established offices all throughout Spain, the Americas, and the Philippines.

Despite the threat of incarceration or even execution, many New Christians continued to practice Judaism and Islam clandestinely. Moriscos (literally "Muslim-ish"), as converts from Islam were derisively called, created an underground literature, written in Spanish with Arabic characters: *aljamiado* (from the Arabic word *ajamiyya* or non-Arabic language). Over the sixteenth century, the Spanish Crown issued a series of edicts meant to strip the Moriscos of their culture. They banned the use of the Arabic language in books and in daily speech, along with banning the traditional food, dress, music, and even communal baths used in Morisco communities. This increasing repression led to a bloody civil war in which Morisco forces, often viewed by Old Christians as a fifth column of Spain's rival Mediterranean superpower, the Ottoman Empire, rose up in the Alpujarra mountain range south of Granada and held off royal troops for three years before being brutally put down. Despite this decisive military defeat, at least some Moriscos

continued to practice their culture and religion until their
expulsion from Spain in the beginning of the seventeenth
century. It is a little-known fact that less than a decade before
the Mayflower reached Plymouth Rock, Spanish Muslims
were continuing to live a legacy of Islam with nearly nine
centuries of history, and Spanish Jews, some of whom had
been educated at Catholic universities, plotted their escape
to Amsterdam and Italy where they could live openly as Jews.
Like it or not, for all the Inquisition's efforts over more than
a century, Spain was still the land of the Three Cultures.

Further Reading

Students looking to learn more about Spain's Muslim and
Jewish heritage should read the engaging and thought-
provoking *The Ornament of the World*, by María Rosa
Menocal (Boston: Little Brown, 2002), which is a standard
work in the field. For focused studies of Muslim and Jewish
history, respectively, see Brian Catlos, *Kingdoms of Faith:
A New History of Islamic Spain* (New York: Basic Books,
2018), and Jane S. Gerber, *The Jews of Spain: A History of
the Sephardic Experience* (New York: The Free Press, 1992).
Matthew Carr tells part of the later story of the Muslim expulsion in *Blood and Faith: The Purging of Muslim Spain*
(New York: New Press, 2009).

James T. Monroe's *Hispano-Arabic Poetry: A Student
Anthology*, 2nd ed. (Piscataway, N.J.: Gorgias Press, 2004)
offers a highly accessible collection of some of the most im-
portant Arabic poets of medieval Iberia, while Peter Cole's
*The Dream of the Poem: Hebrew Poetry from Muslim and
Christian Spain*, 950–1492 (Princeton: Princeton University
Press, 2007) introduces readers to some of the rich corpus of
Hebrew poems from the Peninsula.

PART III
#Hashtags

A little learning is a dangerous thing
Drink deep, or taste not the Pierian spring
There shallow draughts intoxicate the brain
And drinking largely sobers us again
　　—ALEXANDER POPE, "AN ESSAY ON CRITICISM" (1709)

Alexander Pope's warning about the dangers of shallow or fleeting engagement with the sources of knowledge (often misquoted and paraphrased as "a little knowledge is a dangerous thing") could easily be applied to the Internet age. In the era of widespread digital publication, streaming video, and social media, most communications are indeed "little": They come in small packages, designed to fit screens that are no larger than our hands. In this compressed format, a wry joke, a funny or striking juxtaposition of an image with a few words, or a short burst of video can go viral, gaining an enormous, global audience in only a few moments. Competing for this coveted viral status with images, video loops, and pointed memes, ideas are reduced to a headline or a few snippets of text. Immediacy and impact are everything.

How do the Middle Ages feature in this world of rapid-fire communications, hot takes, and hashtags? How do they fare? It would seem, for one thing, that as media has changed, the Middle Ages have come to the fore as a surprisingly potent resource for effective and provocative themes and images. This is particularly true if we compare the ubiquitous and comparatively bland references to the Middle Ages in, say, the architecture and branding of American White Castle fast food restaurants with the violent, threatening imagery built on images of knights in the online discussion forums of the American far right. As the essays in this section demonstrate, the Middle Ages are currently invoked to make arguments about masculinity, ethnic identity, gender roles, race and ethnicity, and religion. In all of this summoning up of the medieval past, the Middle Ages are seen to be popular, accessible, and a source of much humor and creativity. As with so much else in the mainstream of digital culture, however, the unanchored and decontextualized images and ideas meant to point to the Middle Ages often invite only the shallowest of readings, and encourage just about anyone to weigh in and provide their own imaginative interpretations. The rising frequency of encounters by a broader audience with the Middle Ages brings with it a need for more conversations about the sources of our memes and shorthand expressions, a need for experts to engage with the public and for the public themselves to engage actively with what they see. As in Pope's words of warning, much is sacrificed when we choose only "shallow draughts" of knowledge about the past in place of the more complete sources of information that nurture fuller understanding.

The section opens with two chapters dealing in the purest stuff of the viral social media phenomenon: compact units

of information referring to the Middle Ages that are striking
and funny, quickly consumed, and instantly passed along.
For Marian Bleeke, the memes and macros that we see on
the Internet share with medieval marginalia the frequent use
of humor with the intention of offering political and social
critique. Where the creators of today's memes mainly use
medieval images to uphold what they consider "traditional"
gender roles and social attitudes, the images in medieval
marginalia were, in fact, often used to challenge dominant gender norms. Andrew Reeves invites us to consider a
widely reproduced and digitally shared flowchart of medieval sexuality. This chart, originally created in the context of
an academic study of law and sex in medieval Christian Europe, is now used as an object lesson in either the cold and
improbably puritanical nature of medieval sexuality or as an
example of the incoherence of medieval law. Reeves suggests not only that we return the laws to their proper context
(medieval attitudes to the body) but also that we consider
whether these laws are any more or less coherent than attitudes toward sexuality in contemporary faith communities.
When we encounter a medieval meme, Bleeke and Reeves
both ask, is this fragment of the Middle Ages trying to reas-
sure us about who we are as modern people?

Racial identity and its articulation around images redolent of the medieval past are the subject of the following
two essays by Maggie M. Williams and Helen Young. Both
Williams and Young address the expectations that certain
images grounded in the Middle Ages should belong exclusively to white Europeans. Williams explores the history of
the so-called "Celtic Cross," a cross inscribed in a circle,
which in fact predates Christianity and appears in contexts
far removed from Ireland. The range of meanings that this
symbol has come to embody since the later nineteenth and
early twentieth centuries has little to do with its medieval

manifestations. Williams relates how this symbol became a sign of Irish Catholic and then Irish-American identity, as Irish communities in America were struggling to establish their claims to the privileges of whiteness. The twentieth century also saw the deployment of the symbol by Nazis during the Second World War, by white supremacist prison gangs since the 1960s, and by contemporary neo-Nazis. Young explains why it has been so difficult for white authors, filmmakers, and audiences to countenance the casting of non-white actors either in medieval historical dramas or in medievalizing fantasy narratives like *Game of Thrones*. Like Williams, Young finds the origins of the assumed link between "medieval" and "white" in the Enlightenment and post-Enlightenment nationalist period when Americans and Europeans were eager to ground their ethnic origins in a safely homogenous "white" medieval past.

Among the medieval motifs persistently replicated and shared on social media are those associated not only with race, but also with gender and religion. While Will Cerbone's essay takes on the image of the medieval Scandinavian warrior — the Viking — as the epitome of masculine strength "who lives by his fists and his axe," Adam M. Bishop explores the use of crusading imagery and the crusade-inspired hashtag #deusvult by white supremacists and those advocating racial, ethnic, and religious conflict against non-whites and non-Christians. These essays argue that the Viking and crusader histories to which these motifs refer were more complicated than what their memeification implies. Both Cerbone and Bishop also suggest that in offering to complicate and enrich discussions of the historical sources of our popular culture, we must not absolve the subjects of our study from scrutiny as manifestations of a kind of toxic masculinity (in the case of the Vikings) and racist hatred (in the case of the crusaders).

J. Patrick Hornbeck II's essay responds to a demand that a modern community (progressive Catholics) recognize themselves as the manifestation of a medieval category (heretics). What does it mean for a modern conservative Catholic to insist that those who disagree with certain current doctrinal teaching to "own" or recognize their position as one of actual heresy? As Hornbeck explains, the history of heresy within the Catholic tradition makes the accusation a very serious and inflammatory one. At the same time, his essay shows how theological debate, disagreement, and personal choice (the root concept behind the word "heresy") were always a feature of medieval religious history. Like Bishop and Cerbone, Hornbeck does not believe that it is necessary either to give in to stereotypes about the Middle Ages as a time of terror and violence or to apologize for medieval attitudes for us to understand that using the hashtag #ownyourheresy confuses and shuts down the continuous dialogue that modern media, complete with memes and hashtags, can so greatly facilitate.

Modern Knights, Medieval Snails, and Naughty Nuns

Marian Bleeke

From the alt-right protestors at Charlottesville on August 12, 2017, to online macros and memes, twenty-first-century appropriations of the Middle Ages frequently feature a construction of masculinity that is premised on an ideal of knighthood and so grounded in violence. Photographs of the Charlottesville protestors show young men carrying shields and banners emblazoned with various medieval-style symbols, from Norse runes to the black eagle of the Holy Roman Empire. Likewise, multiple online macros — assemblages of images and texts — combine the image of a knight in armor, identified as a crusader by the cross on his chest, helmet, and/or shield, with texts calling for violence against Muslims. One reads, "There doesn't have to be a Muslim ban if there are no Muslims," while another proclaims "I'll see your jihad and I'll raise you one crusade." The medieval references of the alt-right protestors and of online content come together in videos and macros based on a photograph of Kyle Chapman, also known as "Based Stickman," assaulting a counter-protestor during a March

2017 rally in Berkeley. This image forms the basis for multiple others that cast him as a so-called "alt-knight." One example places Chapman alongside a crusader and praises him with the text, "Hero of our times, the Alt-Knight rises, thank you Based Stickman."

This chapter will first examine constructions of gender, both masculinity and femininity, that appear in the alt-right movement and in online macros that make use of materials from the European Middle Ages. As will become clear, the medieval past is frequently used to legitimate narrow and restrictive forms of both masculinity and femininity, often by suggesting that gender has always been — and so should continue to be — construed in these specific ways. In order to contest this use of medieval materials, I next introduce a type of imagery known as *marginalia*, defined as images that appear around the edges of medieval artworks. While marginalia can be difficult to understand, the specific examples discussed here reference constructions of gender similar to those visible in the contemporary alt-right and online materials, but do so in order to undermine them: Here knights cower in fear before snails, and nuns pick penises off of a tree for their own use. These images demonstrate that constructions of gender have always been open to contestation and so the medieval past cannot be used to legitimate any specific forms of masculinity or femininity.

Constructions of femininity are much less visible in materials stemming from the contemporary alt-right — deliberately so. In a post on her blog, *Wife with a Purpose*, entitled "Women's Roles in the Movement," Ayla Stewart gives her reasons for backing out of an agreement to speak at Charlottesville and then deciding not to attend the protest. She explains that, as the event grew in scale, she came to feel "out of place" speaking there, because she saw speaking as a role for leaders and not for a mother. This explanation implicitly genders leadership, identifying it as a masculine role by opposing it to her identity as a mother. She then adds that the expectation of violence at the event convinced her security team that it would not be safe for her to attend. This comment identifies femininity with vulnerability because there was a concern for her safety, but apparently not that of male protestors. Next, she lists the actions she will be taking in the future, identifying them as proper "women's roles": speaking only at private events targeted to women or in public with her husband present, learning first aid, stockpiling emergency supplies, and offering moral support to the men in the movement. These comments identify femininity for the alt-right with the private sphere and with caretaking roles enacted there. Other women in the movement have faced hostility from their male counterparts for taking on public rather than private and supportive roles. For example, in a series of tweets from December 3, 2017, Tara McCarthy described women in the movement as being "constantly harassed by low status anonymous trolls" apparently in order to "bully us off the internet." Ironically, these tweets have since been deleted.

Similar constructions of femininity appear in online macros that make use of medieval materials. The eleventh-century textile known as the Bayeux Embroidery (commonly and improperly referred to as the Bayeux Tapestry) has formed the basis for a large number of macros that include multiple images featuring a woman named Aelfgyva (see Figure 1). In two of these, an enthroned male figure with a sword in his lap points toward Aelfgyva and the accompanying text orders her back into the kitchen: One reads simply, "Woman this is not thy kitchen," while the other exclaims, "Returneth thineself unto the kitchen yon wench! Maidens have not a place upon thy internet!" These are medieval-styled versions of a common misogynist meme that again identifies femininity with the private or domestic sphere

Figure 1. Aelfgyva and a cleric from the Bayeux Embroidery. England, ca. 1070. Photo: Erich Lessing / Art Resource.

and denies women a public voice online. The addition of the sword in these medievalized versions adds an implied threat of violence aimed at keeping women "in their place." In the first example, the projection of this meme back into the Middle Ages may be intended to create an impression of continuity in gendered norms over time and so to give these ideas added legitimacy in the present. In the second example, however, the reference to the internet introduces an anachronism that is likely meant to be funny. Here we may be meant to laugh at this version of femininity as "medieval" in the sense of being old-fashioned or backwards. If so, this specific macro may, in fact, present a critique of this set of ideas about gender.

Other Bayeux Embroidery–based macros present Aelfgyva as the focus of sexual attention from men and so make women's sexual availability a defining characteristic of femininity. Two combine Aelfgyva with a pointing male figure and a text that demands access to her breasts. They read: "Bosoms or be gone with thee" and "Bare thy bosoms or make a hasty egress." These macros rely on a contrast between Aelfgyva's heavily draped form and the texts that call out specific, invisible, body parts. This contrast may again be intended to be humorous. However, the demand that Aelfgyva expose her breasts or disappear turns that potential humor into hostility against her. These are also medievalized versions of a common misogynist meme, one that is used on certain online discussion forums — notably 4chan and its associated boards — to demand that any participants who identify themselves as women post photographs of their bodies or stop participating. As in the first Aelfgyva example discussed, the projection of this meme back into the Middle Ages may be intended to suggest that the male demand for sexual access to women's bodies is a constant in gendered norms and so may be intended to legitimize it.

The macros based on the Bayeux Embroidery were generated using the "Historic Tale Construction Kit." On this website, figures from the embroidery can be dragged and dropped into place, and text can be typed in to accompany them. The fact that this site is the immediate source for these macros means that their producers were not necessarily familiar with the original Bayeux Embroidery and so may not have been directly inspired by its depiction of Aelfgyva. However, the macros do recall Aelfgyva's situation in the original — to a degree. In the Embroidery too, Aelfgyva is paired with an aggressive male figure who lunges toward her. Here, however, she is offered some protection by a structure that surrounds her and the fact that the man's movement crosses into that structure lends his action a sense of violation. Also unlike the macros, the text in the original leaves the exact nature of the figures' interaction open to question, as it states simply "Where a cleric and Aelfgyva" and does not complete that sentence. Finally, in the lower margin of the textile, a naked male figure with enlarged genitalia squats underneath one of the enclosure's support posts and repeats in reverse the cleric's reach toward Aelfgyva. This figure clarifies the sexual nature of the cleric's approach to her and characterizes it as illicit. Thus, where the last two macros discussed appear to endorse a sexualized approach to Aelfgyva, that is not the case in the medieval original. In the Embroidery, the cleric's action is delegitimized in a variety of ways and most emphatically by the marginal figure who shows it to be grotesque.

The squatting figure beneath the Aelfgyva scene is one in a series of images that appear on the edges of the Bayeux Embroidery and seem to comment on the action that takes place in its central field. These images are an early example of marginalia, images that appear on the edges of a wide variety of medieval works of art and relate in various ways to the pictures and texts that occupy their centers. Marginalia are especially common in manuscript books made in England and northern France in the thirteenth and fourteenth centuries. The texts in these books vary from the biblical Book of Psalms to the story of Sir Lancelot, and their marginal imagery ranges even more widely. Marginalia frequently come as a surprise to modern viewers as they include sexual and scatological subjects as well as grotesque and hybrid creatures. Scholars have struggled to understand the significance of these images and it has become clear that no single explanation can account for all of them. As a genre, marginalia are as varied as the macros discussed previously and are likewise capable of both endorsing and undermining social norms. Some of these images present parodies or critiques of constructions of gender and sexuality that are similar to the alt-right notions discussed at the beginning of this essay. These medieval images make clear that these narrow conceptions of gender and sexuality have always been contested and so undermine the use of references to the medieval past to le-

Figure 2. Knight and Snail, detail from the Smithfield Decretals, ca.
1300–1340. London, The British Library, Royal MS 10 E 4, fol. 107r. Photo:
The British Library Board.

gitimate their perpetuation in the present. Medieval marginalia can mock the conception of the armored knight as an
embodiment of ideal masculinity and suggest female agency
rather than invisibility and sexual availability.

One fairly common motif in late medieval marginalia
is the fight between an armored knight and a snail. One
example comes from the Smithfield Decretals, an early
fourteenth-century copy of a collection of church laws
made in southern France with marginal imagery added in
England (see Figure 2). The images in this manuscript's
margins range from scenes about the production and use
of the Decretals themselves, to biblical tales and miracle
stories, to scenes involving knights, including the combat
with the snail. Here the snail is a giant that attacks the knight
by projecting itself off of a hill and into the air so that one
of its antennae connects with the knight's shield. The shield
carries a profile face that glares back at the snail. The knight
himself, however, shrinks away from the creature. He bran-
dishes a club instead of his sword, while its scabbard extends
out behind him, like a tail tucked between his legs.

Two additional examples come from a copy of the Book
of Psalms known as the Gorleston Psalter, made in England
in the early fourteenth century (see Figure 3). Its images include multiple initial letters that contain representations of
Christian figures along with extensive marginalia. The snail

Figure 3. Knight and Snail, detail from the Gorelston Psalter, ca. 1310–1324. London, The British Museum, Add. MS 49622, fol. 193v. Photo: The British Library Board.

in these images is smaller than in the Smithfield Decretals example, but assumes a position of power above the kneeling knight. In one, the knight elevates his sword and shield to defend against the snail and the face on his shield aggressively sticks out its tongue. In the other, however, the battle appears to be lost as the chevalier has already laid down his sword and raises his hands, as if begging the snail for mercy.

The apparent defeat of the knight by the snail in these and other images has been interpreted most convincingly as a representation of cowardice. That interpretation can be extended by understanding the knight-snail motif as a critique of knightly standards for masculinity. The knight as an ideal male is supposed to be brave rather than cowardly, as well as powerful and strong. However, those purported virtues are largely a product of his equipment: the horse that elevates him, the shield and armor that allow him to block blows from others, and the sword that allows him to counterattack. In these images, the knight's dependency on equipment is turned against him. Instead of being raised up by horses, these warriors are minimized through juxtaposition with the normally diminutive snails. Their shields, in turn, are braver than they are, as the shields' faces directly confront the snails, while the men themselves shrink behind them. Finally, the knights' armor is subtly related to the snails' shells through their coloring and details. In the image from the Smithfield Decretals, the snail's blue shell recalls the knight's blue tunic, and in the images from the Gorleston Psalter, the snails' blue-green shells recall the interior of one knight's shield and the exposed interiors of both knights' tunics. In all three, finally, the linear details of the snails' shells recall those in the mail that covers knights' arms and legs. To extend this visual analogy, if the knight's armor is like a snail's shell, then his body inside of that armor must be like the snail itself: soft and vulnerable.

Other types of marginal imagery similarly challenge the constructions of femininity discussed previously. We might expect medieval nuns in their closed convents to exemplify ideal femininity as invisible and voiceless. Yet nuns appear frequently in manuscript marginalia and are represented there in some surprising ways. In one example from a Book of Hours (a type of private prayer book) made in northern France in the fourteenth century, the nun's distinctive wimpled and black-veiled head is attached to an animal's hind end and then to a tail that becomes a gloved hand, which makes a blessing gesture (see Figure 4). On the page, this nun-hybrid is shown to be an object of considerable attention as a female head in a nearby initial letter looks toward it and the corner of her letter's golden frame extends toward it and then expands into a red leaf form. This nun is no shrinking female: Instead, she struts around the page, shaking her blessed and blessing rear in the face of reader-viewers.

A series of marginal images featuring nuns in another manuscript, moreover, challenges the construction of femininity through aggressive male sexuality in the Aelfgyva

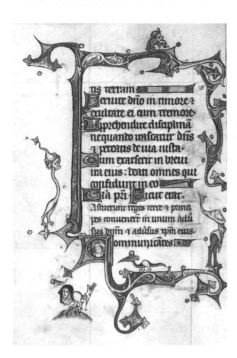

Figure 4. Nun-hybrid, female viewer, and other marginalia, detail from a Book of Hours, fourteenth century. Baltimore, The Walters Art Museum, MS 90, fol. 108v.

macros by showing these women exercising their own sexual agency. These images appear in a copy of the *Roman de la Rose* that was made in Paris ca. 1325–53 and at least partly illuminated by a woman, Jeanne de Montbaston. In the margins of this manuscript, nuns initiate sex with men and handle male genitalia. In one vignette, a nun first leads a man by a string attached to his penis and then directs him to climb a ladder to reach her at the top of a tower, and in another, a man kneels in prayer before a nun, both figures remove their garments, and they have intercourse. Two images in the manuscript feature a tree on which penises grow as fruit: In one a nun picks penises from the tree and then embraces a man, and in the other two nuns pick penises from the tree while a man hands over his penis to a third

Figure 5. Nuns at the penis tree and a man hands his penis to a nun, detail from a *Roman de la Rose* manuscript, 1325–1353. Paris, Bibliothèque nationale de France, MS fr. 25526, fol. 160r.

sister (see Figure 5). The penis tree images are particularly striking in that they suggest an autonomous female sexuality, one that may be satisfied by a male organ, but does not require a man. These nuns can take care of themselves.

Because manuscript books were made for elite owners and reader-viewers, these images would originally have had a limited audience, a condition that would have restricted the force of their critique of gendered norms. Their placement in the margins may likewise have restricted the power of their commentary because they could be understood as afterthoughts and so easily dismissed. However, today the internet has the capacity to make such images available to a broad audience — both the snail-knight motif and the nun–penis tree images have received some attention online, although mostly in circles interested in medieval manuscripts. What has yet to happen is a deliberate use of these and similar images to challenge contemporary medievalizing constructions of gender, such as those discussed at the beginning of this essay. I want to challenge the readers of this essay to do just that. Go to the "Historic Tale Construction Kit" and make your own macros that present Aelfgyva as a fighter, able to fend off aggressive men, or that critique knightly masculinity using other images from the Bayeux Embroidery. You might also upload examples of manuscript marginalia to another meme generator and use them as the basis for your own macros. Share them widely online so that we can occupy the public space of the internet with images that challenge the use of the medieval past to legitimate restrictive and destructive constructions of masculinity and femininity.

Further Reading

Michael Camille's *Image on the Edge: The Margins of Medieval Art* (Cambridge: Harvard University Press, 1992) provides an overview of different types of medieval marginalia and their potential meanings. The use of medieval materials in contemporary online culture is discussed in Andrew B. R. Elliott, *Medievalism, Politics, and Mass Media: Appropriating the Middle Ages in the Twenty-First Century* (Woodbridge: D. S. Brewer, 2017). Ryan M. Milner provides an analysis of memes in *The World Made Meme: Public Conversations and Participatory Media* (Boston: MIT Press, 2016). Kathleen M. Blee's *Inside Organized Racism: Women in the Hate Movement* (Berkeley: University of California Press, 2002) examines gender and women's roles in the racist movements of the 1990s, and a recent report from the Anti-Defamation League, *When Women Are the Enemy: The Intersection of Misogyny and White Supremacy* (https:// www.adl.org/resources/reports/when-women-are-the-enemy -the-intersection-of-misogyny-and-white-supremacy) brings that analysis up-to-date for the contemporary alt-right.

Charting Sexuality and Stopping Sin

Andrew Reeves

The flowchart in Figure 1 began its life as an illustration in historian James Brundage's *Law, Sex, and Christian Society in Medieval Europe* and has gone on to achieve its place as a meme, surfacing now and again on social media. Sometimes it appears with credit for its source, but sometimes it just appears as something mildly amusing about medieval Christianity and sex. We are likely to enjoy a titillated chuckle as we imagine a churchman thinking in detail about the many possible ways one can (but should not) have sex. We chuckle because we can't imagine going into this level of thought about what forms of sex are permissible. When James Hamblin reproduced it in *The Atlantic*, he noted that it explains why "sex is still a weird thing." We might further think that it tells us that prior to the mid-twentieth century, there was no sex apart from heterosexual missionary position with the lights off. Some who read and share this chart self-identify as radical traditionalists ("rad-trads" as the term often appears online) or as "integralists" (those who believe that the ideal social order is a union of Catholic Church and State).

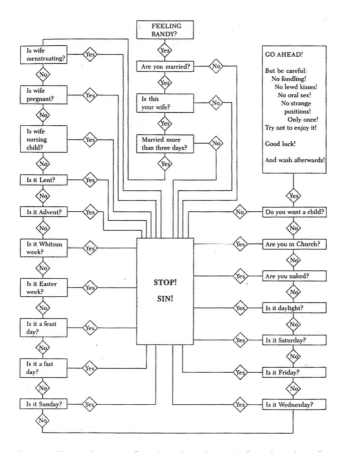

Figure 1. The medieval sex flowchart. From James A. Brundage, *Law, Sex, and Christian Society in Medieval Europe* (Chicago: University of Chicago Press, 1990).

These readers may look at this chart and imagine a time when people had a more wholesome and balanced view of sexuality.

Stripped of its context and reduced to a meme, this chart obscures as much as it tells us about how medieval

Christians understood sexuality and the body and how the strictures of the Church as an institution did or did not find fulfillment among laypeople. When we add these questions, what appears as a chart showing that medieval people thought that sex was bad quickly becomes much more complicated. Who wrote these rules? Why did they write them? And did anyone actually follow them? All of these questions reveal a medieval theology of the body and sexuality that is not only far removed from even that of modern conservative Christians but which also sat uneasily with a laity that at best gave only half-hearted acquiescence to its doctrines and teachings.

The chart's sources bring us to a key question in the history of sexuality. Sexual relations are one of the most private acts that people can engage in — so how can we get a window onto these acts centuries in the past? One answer is in the process of confession. Ever since the beginnings of the Christian religion, churchmen had wrestled with what to do if a Christian, whose sins were forgiven at baptism, sinned again. How was this problem — Christians have their sins forgiven, but then sin again — resolved? In the early years of the Church, the answer is somewhat murky. We encounter scattered decrees of regional councils that certain severe sins could lead to the expulsion of the believer from the company of the faithful with a gradual readmission allowed only after a set of gestures to demonstrate remorse for the sin. Such gestures included acts such as standing outside of the entrance of the church in sackcloth and ashes (as St. Ambrose of Milan specified in the fourth century). But most of these instances of expulsion and reconciliation were for sins committed in public or widely known. We are on much shakier ground when it comes to those sins committed in private.

We begin to see light thrown onto private sin and its reconciliation in the so-called penitentials, documents drawn

up for Irish monks in the sixth century. These would pre-
scribe a private penance — that is, a regimen of prayer and
self-denial — for the monk who had sinned privately and
confessed it to his superior. But these quickly came to be
applied to Christian laypeople who would be associated with
a monastery, either as the dependent peasants who worked
on lands the monasteries owned (monks might be required
to be individually poor, but the monastery could collectively
own large amounts of land) or as laymen or women who
wanted to take a more active part in religious life. As Irish
monks established monasteries on the Continent over the
seventh century, these penitentials came into use throughout Western Europe. Although in 829 the Council of Sois-
sons ordered that penances be more standardized, even the
standardized penances still tended to follow the Irish model.
As the chart notes, the requirements of what was and was
not allowed even in (heterosexual) marriage were particularly restrictive. Moreover, they often had very rigorous and
set penances, such as a period of fasting that might run for
many years. It would seem that what this chart conveys as
a meme is accurate. But if we look more closely at our evidence, it gets more complicated.

Medieval moral theologians organized sins by severity —
for example in lists of the so-called seven deadly sins. These
sins had been held to be the root of all other sins since at
least the time of Pope Gregory the Great (reigned 590–604).
Of these sins, the one that we often refer to as lust — a better translation would be lechery — referred to acts that con-
travened the Church's teachings on sexuality. Churchmen
held it to be the least severe of the capital vices: The worst
sin, pride, came from a distortion of the spiritual nature of
humanity, but lechery was a distortion of a God-given faculty, the sex drive. Both modern conservative Christians and
their detractors often assert that a theologically and socially

conservative Christianity regards sexual sins as the worst sins. In the famous (or infamous, depending on one's politics) *Left Behind* series of novels written to promote evangelical protestant Christianity, we see this thinking distilled when the character of Chloe — one of the heroes who is meant to serve as a model to the readers — refers to the rules for Christian life as "morality and sex and all of that." This thinking, however, does not accurately represent the medieval hierarchy of sins. This emphasis on sexuality comes out of the social changes of the last century and responses to those social changes.

Indeed, theologically and socially conservative Christians might be the most surprised of anyone by medieval theologies of sexuality. James Dobson (b. 1936) advocates against all forms of sexuality outside of heterosexual monogamous marriage. When consulting with worried parents of adolescents, however, he acknowledges that if their children are masturbating this is a relatively modest vice. A medieval moral theologian would say nearly the opposite, namely that masturbation is even more unnatural than Dobson would say that same sex relations are. To masturbate was to be at once the active and the passive partner, to take on both male and female roles, and to thus disorder nature. The thirteenth-century moral theologian Robert of Sorbonne wrote that a confessor (the priest hearing a confession) was to tell the penitent that someone who masturbated had "sinned more gravely than knowing [their] own mother."

The modern Catholic Church distinguishes between contraceptive and abortion, and most evangelicals do the same. Medieval medicine and moral theology, however, made no distinction between abortifacient and contraceptive. All were "poisons [or potions, since the Latin word *potiones* is the same] of sterility," and all were forbidden. But in those areas where modern conservative Christians make no distinctions, medieval moral theologians did. Medieval canonists and physicians generally held that an embryo developed a soul at around forty days and so abortion before that forty-day mark — although very much a sin — was not as severe as an abortion after "ensoulment."

A word is in order on same-sex relations. Medieval Catholic moral theology forbade same sex relations, although the manuals of moral theology primarily locate the sin in "intercourse outside the place designed for that purpose." Their writers regarded heterosexual oral or anal sex to be just as much a "vice against nature" as same-sex intercourse. Indeed, modern historians disagree among themselves as to whether medieval people recognized the existence of homosexual people as a category at all or whether they recognized only homosexual acts as part of a broader category of "unnatural" sex.

Our reading of medieval churchmen on sexuality becomes murkier still when we look at how guides to confession and penance changed in the Central Middle Ages (that is, the eleventh and twelfth centuries). Some penances in the later documents are still remarkably harsh (for example, fasting every Wednesday and Friday for seven years), but then others are remarkably lenient. Sins for murderers, for example, could range from a perpetual fast from meat for a parricide to a seven-year fast for a murder with no other aggravating circumstances. When listing the penances for bestiality, the canonist Ivo of Chartres (1040–1115) noted that some churchmen suggested ten years, some suggested seven, and some suggested a year, but some suggested a mere hundred days. He leaves the penance up to the judgment of the priest. By the end of the twelfth century, manuals for clergy hearing confessions gave suggested penances, but counseled confessors to use their best judgment. So when Richard Poore, bishop of Salisbury from 1217 to 1228, suggested penance for adultery, he was careful to allow a woman to do penance in a way that could conceal it from her husband lest she incur his wrath. In a word, those writing for people hearing a confession had strict standards, but realistic expectations. By the years after the twelfth century, even harsh penances were more intended to deter the penitent from future sin than to punish. When the Fourth Lateran Council of 1215 required that all Christians, lay or clerical, go to confession at least once a year, it was this more humane system of assigning penances that became the standard.

Both learned debates and manuals of penances came from the pens of educated churchmen. We ought to ask, then as now, who listened. When this moral theology encountered the experience of laypeople, what seems like a rigid and unbending set of prohibitions acquires even more nuance. We first need to note that these normative requirements often represented an ideal. After all, Charlemagne sought to dig a canal between the Danube and Rhine rivers (a distance of some 600 miles)—a failure that historian Alexander Murray used to illustrate the gap between medieval ambition and fulfillment.

We know that theory and practice often differed because churchmen frequently complained about both clergy and laypeople behaving quite differently from what moral theologians and canonists prescribed. Bishops throughout Western Europe consistently exhorted their priests to tell laypeople that sex without marriage was a mortal sin (that is, a premeditated disobedience of God, which meant a sinner would go to hell if it were not forgiven through confession)—and that this was the case even if both parties intended to eventually get married. Such decrees are a fairly clear indication that whatever standard a work of moral theology might set, laypeople were happy to get most of the way there. Even ordained priests flouted the rules: After the Church required that all ordained priests be celibate, moral theologians such as Thomas of Chobham (who wrote at the beginning of the thirteenth century) complained that priests kept wives — and that married priests would hear the confession of each other's wives.

This is not simply a matter of laypeople and parish priests being too ignorant to understand the Church's teachings. Canon law and medieval church court records are some of our best sources on medieval sexuality because they show us a laity that understood canon law well enough to make fairly sophisticated arguments in an attempt to "game the system," as it were.

The teaching of canonists and moral theologians, for example, was that marriage was indissoluble. "What God has joined let no man put asunder," as the saying based on Matthew 19:6 went. Canonists also held, though, that there were circumstances under which a marriage, although performed, was not canonically valid. Such a marriage could (and can) be declared not to have taken place through a declaration called an *annulment*. Not every marriage will be a happy one: This was as true for the Middle Ages as for the present. Those in an unhappy (or politically inconvenient) marriage saw the system of annulment as a way of escaping their condition, searching for a set of circumstances that might render their marriage invalid. Canon law, for example, held that a marriage between a child's godfather and godmother was invalid because it was incestuous — "spiritual incest" as the canonists and moral theologians described it. This led to the practice of couples in a marriage they sought escape from agreeing to be a child's godfather and godmother in order to invalidate the marriage. This tactic was tried at all levels of society, and drew enough attention that Pope Alexander III (reigned 1159–81) had to decree that it did not work that way: A godfather and godmother could not contract a marriage,

but a husband and wife standing as godfather and godmother would not invalidate an already-existing marriage.
Subsequent bishops' decrees in the thirteenth century indicate that this remained an ongoing concern.

Attempted annulments were not the only way that laypeople could dynamically negotiate a seemingly strict set
of requirements that confined sexuality to sacramental marriage. If laypeople were not always clear on what made a
marriage invalid, they knew what made a valid one. Canon
law stipulated words of promise in the present tense ("I
marry you") and consent by both parties followed by con-
summation. This was one of two sacraments — baptism was
the other — that needed (and need) no involvement by an
ordained priest. Words of marriage followed by sex would
make a couple married in the eyes of God and canon law.

As a result, one of the more common instances in which
we see laypeople of lower social rank appearing in the
records of church courts is when two people had a sexual
encounter and the words exchanged before sex came into
dispute. An "I will [eventually] marry you" said in the heat
of the moment when sex is on offer carried an entirely different set of legal consequences from "I marry you." The
consequences would often be monumental because if the
words of marriage and consent were exchanged and sex followed, then two people were bound in wedlock even if they
were the only ones who had been present at the wedding.
This sort of a marriage carried out in nobody else's sight was
called a clandestine marriage.

A clandestine marriage could be a way of using canon
law's requirements as a way of marrying outside of requirements set by a family (which was the case when contracted
by elites). As a rule, even though canon law required consent, most couples married by the arrangement and with
the permission of families. This was truer the further up one
rose on the social ladder.

If, however, a couple could exchange the words of promise and have sex, then their marriage was valid and insoluble.

For all of these reasons, the canon law of the Church forbade clandestine marriage. A clandestine marriage was nevertheless still valid. Although as modern commentators have noted, this represents a contradiction at the heart of the Church's doctrines on marriage, it shows that in spite of canonists' attempts to bring some order to the often confused and chaotic domain of human sexuality, it was fundamentally difficult to control. Clandestine marriage could represent an effort by laypeople to put control of marriage and sexuality into their own hands.

So what does Brundage's flowchart tell us? It tells us that in some circumstances, very few forms of sexual relations were allowed by the Church. But those same prohibitions existed in a theology of sexuality and the body that, while in many ways drastically different from our own, had its own internal consistencies. And these rules existed against a backdrop of laypeople who often creatively responded to and dealt with them rather than simply obeying what they saw as the teachings of the Church. Perhaps when we chuckle at a meme, we are illustrating not so much an understanding of medieval sexuality, but are instead reflecting what we think we have left behind (or lost) in the modern world. We would do more justice to medievals to understand them, for better or worse, however illiberal, on their own terms.

Further Reading

One of the best introductions to sexuality in the Middle Ages is, of course, the source of the flowchart, James Brundage's *Law, Sex, and Christian Society in Medieval Europe* (Chicago: University of Chicago Press, 1987). For more detail on how medieval guides to sin and confession evolved over the Middle Ages and how their treatment of sexuality evolved with them, the best sources to consult are three books by the late Pierre Payer: *Sex and the Penitentials: The Development of a Sexual Code, 550–1150* (Toronto: University of Toronto Press, 1984); *Sex and the New Medieval Literature of Confession, 1150–1300* (Toronto: Pontifical Institute of Mediaeval Studies, 2009); and *The Bridling of Desire: Views of Sex in the Later Middle Ages* (Toronto: University of Toronto Press, 1993). The best source for information on how confession in the Middle Ages shifted from public penances to rigorously prescribed private penances and then finally to penances based on the judgment of the priest is Rob Meens's *Penance in Medieval Europe, 600–1200* (Cambridge: Cambridge University Press, 2014).

Sadly, most of the actual manuals to confession have not been translated. The main English language translations are to be found in John T. McNeill and Helena M. Gamer's *Medieval Handbooks of Penance: A Translation of the Principal "Libri poeniteniales" and Selections from Related Documents* (New York: Columbia University Press, 1938). When consulting these documents, some caution is in order. They mostly date from the early Middle Ages and the assigned penances contained in them were often exceedingly harsh to the extent that modern scholars doubt how often (if ever) the full penances were assigned to laypeople. We are on more solid ground with the guides to penance written from the late twelfth century and later, but most of these are in Latin.

A shorter late-medieval guide to penance (that of Alexander of Stavensby) can be found in the primary source reader *Medieval Popular Religion*, edited by John Shinners (Toronto: University of Toronto Press, 2009), 19–24. Alexander of Stavensby's *On Penance* presents a useful example of the sort of guide that a parish priest of the later Middle Ages would have used in both hearing a confession and assigning penances.

Finally, the issue of same-sex relations in the Christian Middle Ages is vexed. The late John Boswell opened up this field of study with his groundbreaking *Christianity, Social Tolerance, and Homosexuality: Gay People in Western Europe from the Beginning of the Christian Era to the Fourteenth Century* (Chicago: University of Chicago Press, 1980). Boswell suggested that earlier medieval Christianity had shown greater tolerance of same-sex relations than later medieval Christianity, and it touched off a vigorous scholarly debate. The current consensus is that Boswell's reading of the evidence was selective and paid too little attention to the manuals of moral theology that are the foundation of this chapter.

"Celtic" Crosses and the Myth of Whiteness

Maggie M. Williams

> Because we can't use the [Nazi] swastika is
> why we use the Celtic Cross. It symbolizes
> Christendom and Christianity and also the white,
> pre-Christian tribes in Europe.
> — POST TO A DISCUSSION GROUP ON THE WHITE
> NATIONALIST WEBSITE STORMFRONT (USERNAME:
> LUFTWAFFE TROOPER, POSTED APRIL 4, 2010)

This post from the white nationalist website Stormfront illustrates the contemporary function of the so-called "Celtic"
cross as a racist dog whistle. The phrase "Celtic cross" is
used to describe a variety of cross-in-circle designs, and
while it is an ancient symbol, its modern manifestations often muddy the distinctions among ancient, medieval, and
modern cultures in Europe and America. More insidiously,
the term "Celtic" in this context brings a long, post-medieval
history of nationalism and white supremacism to bear on the
image. Here, I use Irish examples — and the history of tension between Irish and African Americans specifically — to

offer a critical perspective on the use of the word "Celtic" to describe medieval and modern ringed crosses. My aim is to contribute to dismantling the white supremacist narrative that seeks to oversimplify the history of medieval Irish images and ultimately weaponizes the past against people of color and Jewish people in the modern world.

The visual image described in the Stormfront post consists of a white, equal-armed cross, outlined in black and set within a black circle. Stormfront's version of the cross includes the slogan "White Pride World Wide" around the ring. In the ancient world, such designs appeared in Scandinavia, central Europe, Ireland, and elsewhere, but they are pre-Christian in date and therefore did not originally symbolize "Christendom and Christianity," as Luftwaffe Trooper would have it. This willful conflation of pre-Christian and Christian cultures is already troubling, but when the poster goes on to equate the design with the "white, pre-Christian tribes of Europe," they engage in a broader and more harmful construction of Christian whiteness as something that transcends the specifics of time and place. Indeed, white supremacists often fantasize about a pre-national Europe, where they envision a blended culture of pale-skinned people — Celts, Vikings, Anglo-Saxons — whom they can classify as "white." In reality, each of these groups was already more diverse than they imagine, and each also had demonstrable contact with non-European people of color. What is more, medieval people had a very different conception of race, one that did not include a notion of "whiteness." In white supremacist internet forums, however, Scandinavian symbols such as runes frequently appear alongside "Celtic" ones, and usernames like "Vikingcelt" are quite popular.

So, if the earliest historical examples of the ringed cross in Europe are neither "Celtic" nor "Christian," what are they and how have they been misunderstood or appropri-

ated by some of their champions today? In the case of the
Bronze Age petroglyphs in Kivic, Sweden (see Figure 1),
equal-armed crosses within circles symbolize multiple concepts: They clearly represent chariot wheels on the central
stone, but appear to be standalone symbols on the right.
White nationalists sometimes call this image "Odin's" cross,
although there is no evidence connecting the design with
the Norse god Odin. Conflating a pre-Christian deity with
the Christian notion of a cross in this way serves to construct
an indefinite sense of "white" Christian culture that fuses
very different contexts into a single, convenient narrative
and symbol of dominance.

Additional Bronze Age examples of objects with ringed
cross and/or wheel designs include several gold items
thought to be pendants, which were found in Switzerland
(see Figure 2). It may be surprising to learn that Switzerland, areas of eastern Europe, and even the Middle East,
provide material evidence (including DNA) that points to
the ethnic and cultural origins of the historical Celts in those
regions. An ethnolinguistic group of peoples who were moving around northern Europe from the Iron Age to the early
Middle Ages (ca. 2500 BCE–500 CE), the Celts were not na-

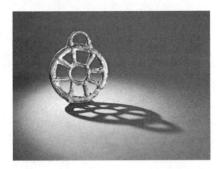

Figure 2. Bronze pendant from Les Bains du Crêt, Neuchâtel, late Bronze Age (ca. 1000–900 BCE). Photo: Y. André / Laténium, 2010, licensed under CC BY 3.0.

tive to Ireland, although they undoubtedly had a strong impact there. While their art uses cross-in-circle designs from time to time, the Celts were not Christian either. The scanty evidence we have suggests that Celtic religion was polytheistic, and crosses in that context would not refer to Christ, the Crucifixion, or Christian salvation. Actually, for some historians, Ireland's early conversion to Christianity — around the fifth century — constitutes the moment when ancient Celtic culture was eclipsed. Nevertheless, the term "Celtic" became associated with Ireland beginning in the eighteenth century, both in academic references to the "Celtic" church and in moments of political nationalism. In fact, as far as we know, the historical Celts did not play a prominent role in erecting the medieval Irish stone crosses, but their apparent preference for curved forms may have influenced the monuments' ringed shape.

From approximately the seventh to the twelfth century, hundreds of ringed Latin crosses made of stone were erected across Ireland. (A "Latin" cross has a tall vertical piece as opposed to a cross with vertical and horizontal arms of equal length.) Some scholars have suggested that the ringed Irish cross may have been inspired by imported African and Middle Eastern works of art. In particular, a textile from

Coptic (Christian) Egypt and a Christian manuscript from Syria have been proposed as possible sources. The surviving Irish crosses measure anywhere from about seven to twenty feet in height, they are carved from a variety of materials like sandstone and granite, and most of them are decorated with shallow, three-dimensional images known as *reliefs*. Some have elaborate narrative programs (mostly scenes from the Bible), and others are covered in intricate interlace designs. Scholars have studied the figural scenes extensively in an effort to understand the ways in which medieval audiences might have "read" the imagery. Archaeologists have excavated many of the sites where the crosses were erected, finding that some may have been associated with burial grounds, but the form did not become commonly used as an individual grave marker until as late as the eighteenth century.

We have very little written evidence about the crosses' meanings in their original settings. A few brief mentions of them in the historical documents known as *annals* describe them as "high" (*ard*), and several crosses have inscriptions that name people whom we can trace to the annals for the purposes of dating the sculptures. Despite the lack of related textual evidence, one cross that has attracted the attention of scholars is the richly adorned tenth-century *Cross of the Scriptures* at Clonmacnois, a monastic settlement founded in the sixth century by Saint Ciarán (see Figure 3). Clonmacnois was built at the place where the main east-west road across Ireland intersected with the primary north-south waterway, the Shannon River. This central location allowed the small monastery to develop a sizeable lay village nearby, and both archaeological and historical evidence suggests that Clonmacnois was a bustling center of religious and economic activity in the Middle Ages. By the early tenth century, Clonmacnois had become a popular burial place for local kings, and the community had the resources to erect

Figure 3. The Cross of the Scriptures at Clonmacnois. Photo: Author.

monumental carved stone crosses within its walls. There are three surviving medieval crosses at Clonmacnois, as well as fragments from additional sculptures.

Carved from sandstone, the *Cross of the Scriptures* at Clonmacnois measures 3.9 meters in height and is decorated all around with figural scenes and interlace designs. It also has two fragmentary inscriptions in Old Irish that have been reconstructed and roughly translated as: "A prayer for King Fland, pray for the king of Ireland," and "A prayer for Colman who (?erected) the cross with King Fland." Historians have connected the Fland and Colman named in the inscriptions with a king who ruled that part of Ireland in the early tenth century, and a contemporary abbot of Clonmacnois. They have used these names, as well as stylistic analysis of the carvings, to date the cross to circa 900. The images on the cross include many stories from the Bible and a few scenes that have been more challenging to identify. One scene appears to depict King Fland and Abbot Colman working together to refurbish the monastery in the early tenth century (see Figure 4). Many of the stone buildings on the site were erected at that time, and it seems that the crosses may have resulted from that campaign of construction. The image may simultaneously refer to the founding saint establishing the monastery in the sixth century because medieval images can often be understood to have multiple meanings.

For medieval audiences, a sculpture like the *Cross of the Scriptures* served several purposes. For one thing, it could have marked the location of the monastery in the landscape. The crosses are large and visible from quite far away. More specifically, the *Cross of the Scriptures* may have been intended to demarcate the holiest part of the site, as archaeological excavations have revealed several elite burials near the cross. For the monks, aristocratic laypeople, and pilgrims who were permitted into the inner sanctum near the cross, it probably also served as a devotional object. The inscriptions and some of the politically important scenes are located near the base of the cross, close to an adult's field of vision when kneeling before the sculpture. For local villagers or others passing through, the cross probably served as more of a landmark than a devotional object per se.

Overall, a monument like the *Cross of the Scriptures* marked the community of Clonmacnois for its many different constituents. It gave them a symbol of local pride, something like the Statue of Liberty. At the level of the images depicted on the cross, it illustrated sacred text and reinforced important political relationships. For example, the image of King Fland and Abbot Colman working together allowed both ecclesiastics and powerful laypeople to see themselves as contributing members of a Clonmacnois community. At the same time, the imagery on the cross

Figure 4. King Fland and Abbot Coman, detail from The Cross of the Scriptures at Clonmacnois. Photo: Author.

linked those local relationships to the overarching religious theme of Christian salvation. From the start, the *Cross of the Scriptures* was designed to articulate complex, layered symbolism that referred to local, regional, and even international ideas. It was more than just a cross.

That sophisticated medieval symbolism was eventually flattened in the service of politics as the term "Celtic" began to be applied to these objects, particularly during the nineteenth-century "Celtic Revival." It was during this period that Irish (and Scottish) cultures were defined as "Celtic" to contrast them with the English. In both literature and the visual arts, the Celtic Revival operated in an atmosphere of cultural nostalgia that often directly invoked political nationalism as Ireland attempted to extricate itself from British rule.

For centuries, Irish Catholics had been facing brutal con-

ditions of oppression, and they had even been categorized
as a race distinct from (and lesser than) the English. For this
and other reasons, there were instances where the oppression of the Irish in North America was likened to that of
enslaved Africans. In turn, some Irish leaders such as Daniel
O'Connell (1775–1847), spoke passionately in favor of the abolition of slavery in the United States, emphasizing the long
antislavery tradition in Ireland and the connections he saw
between the oppression of Catholics at home and the plight
of others abroad. In Boston in January of 1842, O'Connell
presented a statement against slavery that had been signed
by thousands of Irish immigrants. Unfortunately, this vocal
opposition to the brutal American practice was not well received in all arenas. Some Irish Americans felt that any foreign voices on the matter were inappropriate, while others
reacted more strongly, to the point of suggesting that abolition was a British plot to weaken the United States. And ultimately, O'Connell's focus was on conditions in Ireland. He
had dedicated his life to emancipating Irish Catholics and to
achieving repeal of the Acts of Union (1800) with the goal of
self-governance in Ireland. More than that, O'Connell and
his Repeal Association sought full Catholic participation in
government, something that had only been made possible
by the 1829 Act of Emancipation. There were American
chapters of the Repeal Association as well, and often they
were supported financially by wealthy Irish Americans,
among whom were Southern slave owners. O'Connell felt
he needed the financing of those slave owning Irish Americans, and so he backed off from his abolitionist rhetoric.

While O'Connell and other prominent Irish Americans
were debating abolition in the political sphere, millions of
impoverished Irish people were arriving in the United States.
When they entered the labor market, they were thrown into
direct contact and competition with other ethnic groups,

many equally desperate for work and social stability. Only their skin tone differentiated them from freed African slaves, and they clung to that advantage at every turn. In reality, for many Irish immigrants to the United States, abolition was at best uncomfortable: It allowed freed slaves into the workforce to compete for jobs. For, as Noel Ignatiev demonstrates in his 1995 book, *How the Irish Became White*, the agendas of the abolitionist movement, the American labor movement, and the political struggles in Ireland sometimes conflicted, increasing tensions among Irish and African Americans specifically. But labor competition alone cannot account for the sullied history of race riots in Philadelphia, for instance, where there is ample evidence of Irish people actively attacking black people, including women and children. As Ignatiev argues, "Slavery in the United States was part of a bipolar system of color caste, in which even the lowliest of 'whites' [that is, the Irish] enjoyed a status superior in crucial respects to that of the most exalted of 'blacks.'" Later, he summarizes as follows:

> Because blackness was the badge of the slave in
> America, people from Ireland who went there
> entered the free labor system, which made them part
> of the dominant race. As unskilled workers, they oc-
> cupied the lowest place within it. Ethnicity marked
> the spot.

Ethnicity, here, means being Irish, specifically. Fair skin tone, on the other hand, is what allowed the Irish to become "part of the dominant race." It was during this same period, in the decades around the year 1900, that the image of the "Celtic" cross really began to catch on, particularly as a grave marker or small decorative replica. The World's Fairs in Chicago (1893) and St. Louis (1904) included Irish pavilions with full-scale plaster casts of high crosses on view as well as smaller souvenirs available for purchase. Americans could even buy a "Celtic Cross" tombstone from the 1910 Sears Catalog. For better or for worse, this kind of visibility allowed the symbol of the "Celtic" cross to become firmly associated with an Irish American identity, which was too often equated with a generalized notion of "whiteness."

During the twentieth century, such imagery began to be deployed more actively in racist contexts. One of the oldest white-supremacist organizations in the United States — the Ku Klux Klan — has used a version of a cross-in-circle design known as the "blood cross" since around 1900. In Europe after World War II, white nationalist groups such as the L'Oeuvre Française and the British National Socialist Movement began using a ringed cross symbol like the one that appeared on the Stormfront website. The early years of the twenty-first century have been marked by a rise in white-nationalist movements, and the equal-armed version of the "Celtic" cross frequently appears as their symbol. The same design often appears as a tattoo as well. For instance, the white-supremacist character "Skinhead Helen" on the popular show *Orange Is the New Black* has a white pride "Celtic" cross tattooed behind her right ear.

This modern, explicitly racist version of the "Celtic" cross operates as a symbolic strategy that alludes to the distant past, falsely promoting the idea that "white" culture is universal and normative. Although the people who built the ringed Irish crosses were not Celts, the association of the term "Celtic" with the image developed during a period of strident Irish nationalism. Oppressed Irish Catholics developed a passionate connection to the image, out of a sense of nostalgia and pride in their own history. That passion mutated in negative ways once the Irish in America were put into direct competition with freed slaves, as demonstrated by historical accounts of physical violence against black Americans. As

Irish immigrants gained power in the United States — often pushing black people down to do so — they shifted into a position of privilege. There are certainly modern instances when the ringed Irish cross appears in seemingly innocent contexts, such as among neo-pagans; however, institutional racism is so pervasive in American culture that we must question even those "non-racist" scenarios. As Ignatiev and others have illustrated, American conceptions of whiteness, among the Irish as well as other groups, developed in direct opposition to concepts of blackness. Whiteness came to be defined in terms of a constructed hierarchy in which pale skin color was equated to superior social standing. In the contemporary world, images of the simplified "Celtic" cross abound among white-supremacist and neo-fascist groups. We must be cautious about the contexts in which it appears; even more so, we must approach the term "Celtic" with a critical eye, as it is often used as a thinly veiled reference to white-supremacist ideologies.

Further Reading

This essay was inspired by Sierra Lomuto's 2016 blog post on *In the Middle*: "White Nationalism and the Ethics of Medieval Studies," www.inthemedievalmiddle.com/2016 /12/white-nationalism-and-ethics-of.html. Peter Harbison wrote the most extensive catalog of the medieval crosses: *The High Crosses of Ireland* (Bonn: Römisch-Germanisches Zentralmuseum. Forchunginstitut für Vor- und Früh-geschichte in. Verbindung mit der Royal Irish Academy, 1992). Jeanne Sheehy provides a comprehensive study of the Celtic Revival in art in *The Rediscovery of Ireland's Past: The Celtic Revival, 1830–1930* (London: Thames and Hudson, 1980). More information on the history of the actively racist "Celtic" cross can be found on the websites of the

Anti-Defamation League (https://www.adl.org/education /references/hate-symbols/celtic-cross) and the Southern Poverty Law Center (https://www.splcenter.org/fighting-hate /intelligence-report/2006/look-racist-skinhead-symbols-and -tattoos). Noel Ignatiev's *How the Irish Became White* (New York: Routledge, 1995) describes the development of Irish racial attitudes in nineteenth-century America. For more on how racist symbols and language function in American politics, see Ian Haney Lopez, *Dog Whistle Politics: How Coded Racial Appeals Have Reinvented Racism and Wrecked the Middle Class* (New York: Oxford University Press, 2014).

Whitewashing the "Real" Middle Ages in Popular Media

Helen Young

Recreating the European Middle Ages in popular culture can be politically fraught, particularly (although not exclusively) when it comes to representing people of color. The video-game *Kingdom Come: Deliverance* (2018), set in Bohemia in 1403, sparked international debate over whether "historical accuracy" justified the choice not to include characters of color in the game and whether that exclusion was racist. It was not a new controversy. During the game's successful 2014 Kickstarter campaign, Tumblr-user @medievalpoc was the target of violent threats: The blogger had showed that the "realistic" game could include racially and culturally diverse characters, providing historical and academic evidence on the site "People of Color in European Art History." The notion of "historical accuracy" has also been used to justify excluding people of color from, or to criticize their inclusion in, medievalist fantasy settings — that is, settings that are inspired by the European Middle Ages that include magic or similar unreal elements.

George R. R. Martin, for example, invoked historical accuracy in a LiveJournal post to justify not including Asian characters in his *A Song of Ice and Fire* novels. Conversely, inclusion of characters of color in the medievalist worlds of HBO's *Game of Thrones* and Bioware's *Dragon Age* game franchise drew hostile responses from some fans, as did the casting of the Black British actor Idris Elba as Heimdall in Marvel's *Thor* franchise. That zombie dragons, magic and mages, and superheroes and aliens are all present in these various examples makes it clear that a demand for "realistic" elements in these fictional worlds is not the heart of the issue. It is contemporary feelings, not historical facts, that underlie this demand and negative response to the mere idea that people of color might have lived in Europe during the medieval period. This essay asks why modern audiences typically expect to see only white characters represented in medievalist worlds, whether those worlds are said to be "historical" or "fantasy." Why do some respond in negative, even violent, ways when that expectation is not met?

We can work toward answering these questions by turning first to the medieval period itself. People of color were present in Europe during the Middle Ages, as academic research increasingly demonstrates. The establishment of kingdoms by African Muslims in the Iberian Peninsula during the eighth century is just one of the more well-known examples of mass migration and fusion of cultures in medieval Europe. Medieval people, wherever they were from, often traveled more widely than we tend to assume now, for trade, on pilgrimages, and as invaders and conquerors. As @medieval-poc's Tumblr shows, from at least the thirteenth century on, numerous medieval works of art from across Europe depict figures with features that can be identified with sub-Saharan Africans, strongly suggesting that the artists were familiar with people from that region in real life. A thirteenth-century representation of Saint Maurice in Magdeburg Cathedral is just one example (described in detail by Pamela Patton in "Blackness, Whiteness, and the Idea of Race in Medieval European Art" in this volume). Inclusion of people of color and others whom we now do not recognize as European in medievalist fictions, whatever their medium, is thus not historically inaccurate.

Because negative claims about the historical inaccuracy of representing medieval people of color are made about fantasy texts as often as they are made about texts that aim for high levels of historical verisimilitude, a straightforward desire for realism — a reflection of the historical world as it likely would have been — cannot be at the heart of the problem. We might instead consider whether what audiences and creators desire is authenticity instead of accuracy — that is, whether they want their "historical" world and its narratives to *feel real* more than they want them to *be factual*. When even professional historians have only a limited sense of what any part of Europe actually looked and sounded and smelled and felt like at any point of the Middle Ages, how can we as audience members claim to recognize what is "accurate" or not about these fictional worlds? Rather, what we tend to be invested in when it comes to medievalist fictions in any medium is what we think we know about the Middle Ages, and whether what we see aligns with our expectations of a medievalist European (or Europe-like) setting.

Why, then, do we expect the people of "medieval Europe" to be white? Like many other modern notions about the medieval period, the idea that Europe in the Middle Ages was racially homogeneous and "pure" white developed during the eighteenth and nineteenth centuries. From about the sixteenth century to the mid-eighteenth century, classical Greece and Rome had provided models for emulation for much of European culture and society, while the

Middle Ages were typically seen as a barbarous period of
little interest or value. In the last decades of the eighteenth
century, however, there was a major shift in focus from classical to medieval narratives of origin, a shift strongly linked
to new ideas about race that developed out of new scientific
methods that arose during the period we often call the Enlightenment. In eighteenth-century Europe and in its colonies, newly emerging scientific discourses and methods were
used to categorize humanity into races and subsequently to
try to explain differences between the categories of people
thus created. This way of thinking held that "races" had fixed
characteristics, such as skin and hair color, intelligence, and
capacity for artistic expression, that were inherited and persisted unchanged over centuries. Culture, especially language and literature, was held to be the outward expression
of the inner characteristics of a race. Thanks to this outlook,
the Middle Ages became the period of history that all the
nations, peoples, and cultures of Europe could take up as
common cultural inheritance because, unlike the cultures
of classical Greece and Rome, all Europeans could claim
descent from medieval people. The Middle Ages also came
to be understood as a period that had occurred only in Europe, with the corollary and erroneous belief that only white
people had ancestors in the Middle Ages. The idea of a racially pure Middle Ages thus became crucial to constructing
whiteness as an inherent difference between European and
all other racial identities. This is not to say that race and
whiteness were not legible concepts in medieval Europe
and throughout the early modern period; Geraldine Heng's
book, listed in the "Further Reading" section at the end of
this chapter, shows that they were. Rather, race and whiteness took on new dimensions in the eighteenth century in
response to the scientific thought of the Enlightenment, and
they gained greater power when they were used to justify
European colonialism and imperialism on the false grounds

that whites were inherently different from and superior to all other peoples of the world.

From the late eighteenth century onward, ethno-nationalist interest in the Middle Ages was present in Europe, its colonies, and its former colonies like the USA and Australia in almost every aspect of culture, from architecture and art to literature and politics. Thomas Jefferson, for example, was an avid amateur medievalist who believed strongly in the facticity of racial character and the descent of white Americans from medieval Anglo-Saxons. He unsuccessfully advocated for the seal of the United States to feature the legendary Saxons Hengist and Horsa on their first landing in England. In fact, nineteenth-century culture shaped a great deal of what we now think of and recognize as "medieval." It was during this era that fictionalized versions of the European Middle Ages became very popular, not least through Gothic novels such as *The Castle of Otranto* (1764) by Horace Walpole and the later historical fictions of Sir Walter Scott, most famously his novel *Ivanhoe* (1819), which were very widely read across the English-speaking world, including in the United States and Australia. We can trace the distinction between the "accurate" and the "authentic" at least as far back as Scott. In an introductory letter at the start of *Ivanhoe*, possibly his most well-known and influential work, Scott wrote that it was not necessary to provide a "precise imitation" of the past as long as the general "character and costume of the age . . . remain inviolate," and admitted to having "confused the manner of two or three centuries" in the novel. What's more, Scott's novels and many others like them typically represented the nations of Europe inaccurately as a "whites only" space and engaged directly with the race theory of the time. *Ivanhoe* thus opens with a discussion of race in medieval England, which suggests that the Normans and Anglo-Saxons had become a single people by the end of the Middle Ages.

Centuries-old habits, however, are not the only factors that shape audience expectations in the twenty-first century. Another reason so many of us expect to see only white people populating Europe in the Middle Ages, with perhaps the occasional person of color as an exotic outsider, is that we have seen it before many times over since childhood in films, television, video games, and more. Western popular culture typically represents white people at much higher rates than are proportional to national populations: A 2016 survey from the University of Southern California, for example, found that only 7 percent of Hollywood movies had a cast that represented national averages, with less than 30 percent of characters with dialogue from racially and ethnically diverse backgrounds, compared to 40 percent of the U.S. population. When people of color do appear onscreen in medievalist narratives, their characters tend to be transient, isolated figures or invading enemies with narrative justification for their (usually temporary) presence that stands in stark contrast to the seemingly natural and narratively unremarked presence of white bodies in "medieval European" spaces. Morgan Freemans's character Azeem in *Robin Hood: Prince of Thieves* (1991), for example, travels from the Middle East to England with Robin (played by Kevin Costner) for the sole purpose of repaying him for saving his life. More recently, for the first six seasons of HBO's *Game of Thrones*, Daenerys Targaryen, the white-skinned, blond-haired last scion of the former ruling house of Westeros, is exiled to the continent of Essos. In Season 7, she arrives in Westeros to reclaim her family's throne with an invading army of brown-skinned Unsullied and Dothraki. The references used to construct their cultures clearly derive from aspects of the real world outside Europe: The Dothraki are nomadic horse-herders who mix cultural references to the Mongols, Huns, and Native American peoples, while the

Unsullied are an army of slaves comparable to the Jannis-saries of the Ottoman Empire. These characters of color need a narrative reason — following Daenerys — to travel to fantasy-Europe, while Daenerys needs a narrative reason to be outside it. The presence of these characters of color in medievalist European settings did not draw any particular criticism; contrast this to the furor that arose around Idris Elba's casting in the *Thor* franchise mentioned previously. The difference is that Heimdall, a figure inspired by Norse mythology, is understood as belonging to Europe and is therefore expected to be white, while invading armies from outside (fantasy) Europe are not.

Although most popular culture now does not seem to en-gage directly with ideas about race, it often inherits and re-transmits racist ideas written into popular representations of the Middle Ages of the nineteenth century, precisely when it does not recognize or challenge them. J. R. R. Tolkien's *The Lord of the Rings* (1954–55) and the film and video game franchise (2001–present) developed from his trilogy are good examples of how popular culture can transmit outdated concepts of race and the supposed whiteness of the Middle Ages into contemporary culture over decades of production. In Middle-earth, the "good" races — elves, dwarves, and humans — are constructed through references to European cultures and peoples; the Riders of Rohan, for example, strongly reference Anglo-Saxon English culture. Tolkien described orcs, the foot-soldiers of evil, in racial terms in his letters, calling them "degraded and repulsive versions of the (to Europeans) least lovely Mongol-types," and they have racialized characteristics such as black skin in his books. The stories of the different peoples of Middle-earth reflect nineteenth-century theories of polygenesis, the idea that different races were created by God at different times: In Tolkien's world, elves, humans, and dwarves are all created at different times and in different places. *The Lord of the Rings* also reflects nineteenth-century attributions of the downfall of civilizations to essential human differences and racial mixing. While these notions were being questioned by the time Tolkien was writing, and have since been conclusively disproven by genetic studies and modern science, they were still prevalent and are reflected in the medieval-inspired world of Tolkien's novels. Nineteenth-century ideas about race were written into the fabric of Tolkien's world, only to be repeated and amplified through contemporary forms of racist representation in our latter day adaptations. Orcs in Peter Jackson's films are racialized; the Uruk-hai embody anti-Black stereotypes with their height, black skin, and hair that resembles dreadlocks. The more than twenty video games, which are now part of the Warner Brothers franchise based on Jackson's films, repeat these same negative stereotypes through the re-use of visual aesthetics and footage from the films as well as by taking up the racialized structures of Middle-earth as Tolkien first created it.

Some works of popular culture, however, actively resist re-iterating the imagined whiteness of medieval Europe. Frank Yerby, the first best-selling African American author, challenges the very idea of medieval racial purity in the prologue to his novel *An Odor of Sanctity* (1965), set in ninth-century Spain. There, Yerby describes more than a millennium of migrations of peoples from continental Europe and North Africa into the region, saying they poured "their blood, their speech, their habits of thoughts into the caldron" and emphasizing the diversity of medieval Spain. Casting actors of color in films or including characters of color in video games also resists racist conventions, even when producers do not specifically articulate a political purpose or deny having one. These examples are relatively few compared to those which reproduce entrenched racialized histories, however; the habit of thinking of the European Middle Ages as a "whites only" space is hard to break. Examples like those just mentioned, and others such as casting Angel Coulby as Gwen (Guinevere) in the BBC's *Merlin* (2008–2012) or Sophie Okonedo as Margaret of Anjou, the wife of English King Henry VI, in the BBC's *The Hollow Crown: The War of the Roses* (2016) have all been met with some degree of resistance. Yet their increasing number may be a sign that contemporary culture is actively moving away from passive repetition of racist conventions, tropes, and expectations in medievalist media.

Popular culture shapes what we think we know about history in part because we encounter it long before we enter a history classroom, if we ever do. It both reflects and reproduces widely held ideas that often have centuries-old foundations. Understanding audience responses when those ideas are challenged, for example by the inclusion of characters of color in medievalist Europe-inspired popular culture settings, requires an understanding of those deep foundations. Approaching the European Middle Ages and their reception through the lens of critical race studies reveals that ideas about race in the present depend on the past being represented in particular ways. When popular culture versions of medieval Europe represent people of color as belonging, their presence troubles some of the very foundations of contemporary white racial identities. This is why some audiences — even those who may not think of themselves as actively invested in white identity or racial politics — may find representation of people of color in medievalist texts disturbing and objectionable.

Further Reading

Geraldine Heng's book *The Invention of Race in the European Middle Ages* (Cambridge: Cambridge University Press, 2018) is a useful entry point to critical race theory and to ideas about modernity and the medieval, putting medieval studies and race studies in dialogue. The book explores European medieval formations of race, and its fourth chapter includes discussion of evidence for the presence of people from sub-Saharan Africa in Europe during the Middle Ages. Patrick Geary's *The Myth of Nations: The Medieval Origins of Europe* (Princeton: Princeton University Press, 2002) shows that Europe's medievalist nationalisms emerged during the nineteenth century and challenges the concept of racial and cultural purity on which they depend. Cord Whitaker's article "Race-ing the Dragon: The Middle Ages, Race, and Trippin' into the Future," published in *postmedieval* 6, no. 1 (Spring 2015): 3–11, includes a personal account of an African American medievalist scholar, his experiences of being racially "othered" to the European Middle Ages, and his resistance to being positioned that way. Kathryn Wymer explores some ways that casting people of color in medievalist film and television challenges the imagined whiteness of the European Middle Ages and interrogates historical and contemporary racial power structures in her article "A Quest for the Black Knight: Casting People of Colour in Arthurian Film and Television" in *The Year's Work in Medievalism* 24 (2012). The first two chapters of Helen Young's *Race and Popular Fantasy Literature: Habits of Whiteness* (New York: Routledge, 2016) demonstrate how nineteenth-century concepts of race and racial medievalisms became entrenched in popular culture in the twentieth century and remain there in the twenty-first, focusing on the fantasy genre. The third chapter further explores the connections of race, authenticity, and medievalism in twenty-first-century popular culture.

Real Men of the Viking Age

Will Cerbone

Picture the Viking of heavy metal, video games, and Marvel comics: the stoic loner with a flowing mane of golden or fiery red hair and a beard to match, bulging arms hefting a preposterous battle-axe that has split the heads of many foes. Intense eyes beam out from beneath a horned helmet stained with the blood of his enemies, one that hides his scarred, craggy face. At a sidelong glance from a stranger, he will fly into a rage in defense of his honor. He lives by his fists and his axe, terrorizing the God-fearing peoples of Europe with death and pillaging for the glory of his heathen gods. In battle, an amulet in the shape of Thor's hammer wards him against the magic of trolls, and he cries out for the blessing of Odin. When he dies, his body burns in his longboat while his spirit rides off to Valhalla on the aurora-borealis horse of a buxom Valkyrie in a chainmail bikini.

On some level, we're all aware that this Viking is a cartoon (see Figure 1). Casual historians know that only some Viking expeditions intended to raid or conquer territory, and that "Viking" was a word used to describe traders, ex-

Figure 1. Cover to the album *Hail to England* by Manowar (1984). Illustration by Ken Landgraf. Note the incongruity of the Viking bearing a Union Jack, which was adopted in the 1600s to represent a nation that claims descent from a number of kingdoms that were terrorized, vassalized, and subjugated at various points by various Scandinavians.

plorers, mercenaries, whale hunters, and frontier farmers. Those who have read up on Leif Eriksson's voyages to North America will know that women as well as men funded and even led Viking expeditions. Fun-fact listicles have long informed the public that horned hats don't appear in the archaeological record (at least not before Richard Wagner), and how they'd be terrible to fight in anyway (the horns are big handles for an opponent to grab). Vikings were cosmopolitan! The image of the burning-boat funeral comes not from a European observer but an Abassid Muslim (and Ibn Fadlan's account—dramatized though not by much in Michael Crichton's 1976 novel *Eaters of the Dead*—is well worth seeking out).

Nonetheless, the cartoon Viking remains the center of an aesthetic and a site for imagination, artistic expression, and play. Every jeweler at the Renaissance Fair sells their own take on a Thor's hammer amulet, and the symbol in pewter or tattoo ink is worn by fans of the Marvel movies, neo-pagans, metalheads, tabletop RPGers, professional medievalists, and—as the others must grapple with—white supremacists. (Witness Faroese folk metal band Týr's attempt to distance themselves from neo-Nazi fans in 2011's *The Shadow of the Swastika*.) Even though they are drawn by a fantasy, fans seek out historical authenticity to bring themselves closer to the exotic past that inspires them. Those jewelers proudly take design cues from archaeological prototypes. Metal bands adapt medieval myths and folk songs. Fans teach themselves a few words of Old Norse or learn to decipher runes, and they seek out the eddas and the sagas because they want to know what Vikings really thought about the world. These sources are full of violence and aggression (and their consequences), but what was it like to live in such a violent time and place? What was the nature of the honor that Vikings fought, pillaged, and killed for? And how can we know?

Norse literature and mythology come to us largely through manuscripts written or copied in Iceland after the end of the Viking period (in the eleventh century and following). The historicity of each poem and saga (whether its text depicts actual events or religious beliefs) is subject to debate, but it is enough here to say that this literature preserves general attitudes about the world, and the *Islendingasögur* (the sagas that depict events in Iceland) seem to present the social framework of the island, if roughly and with artistic license. Beginning in the seventeenth century, European nationalists looked to these texts (among others) for origin stories that might unify the newly forming nation-states and patched them together with texts from many other times and places into a "Germanic" literature. Adolph Hitler followed them in co-opting this literature in his attempt to fabricate a historical justification for his vile ideas about the supremacy of the Aryan race. Through motivated reading, he and his propagandists found brave conquerors who ruled the world through unchecked aggression, rapacious desire for plunder and territory, and love of violence: qualities that fascist states encourage their citizens to emulate.

The Icelanders who wrote these stories down, however, were not violent fascists, and they recognized that in order for one person to plunder, another must be plundered. The sagas absolutely do contain strongmen who need no friends or allies and take what they want without regard for the consequences, but these qualities mostly adhere to tragic misanthropes, awful neighbors, and primitive monsters. (Some sagas, such as *Fóstbrœðrasaga*, are redemption stories shaped by the heroes' transformation away from this precise stereotype.) The misguided emulation of the bad guys from Norse literature continues down to the present day, but an informed reading of the sources — the sagas, the law codes, and the archaeological record, which grows in size and sophistication every year — shows a deep ambivalence about hypermasculine, violent behavior, even back into the Viking Age. By the historical period, the Sagas of the Icelanders, in particular, depict a reverence for the law as a program to control the violent, antisocial expression of masculinity for which the cartoon-Viking is revered.

Direct witnesses to the Viking Age are rare, fragmentary, and difficult to interpret. Our knowledge comes mostly from grave excavations, enigmatic runestones, and details preserved in literary sources centuries younger than the events they depict. One window onto Viking-Age attitudes toward violence is the literary treatment of the *berserkr* (plural: *berserkir*). The *berserkr* (meaning, perhaps, "wearing a bear skin" or "bare with respect to his shirt [i.e. unarmored]") is a fearsome warrior who enters a frenzy (biting his shield to control spasms of rage) and leaps into battle heedless of his own protection. The *berserkr* is devoted to the god Óðinn (Odin), the king of Asgard and master of war and magic — he who will lead the armies of the gods against Loki and the forces of destruction at the battle at the end of days, the *Ragnarǫkr*. Odin blesses the *berserkr* with invulnerability to the sword and the heat of the flame. Mastery of Odin's magical techniques can allow a warrior to take on the form of a wolf or a bear in combat. Ravens (so they say) even carry medicinal herbs to a *berserkr* in the heat of battle.

It is easy to see the *berserkr* as the Viking *par excellence*, but the popular imagination has it exactly backward: The *berserkr* is a figure reviled for his antisocial behavior. In the legendary sagas (semi-mythological, looking back to prehistory), Kings often retain the services of both *berserkir* and *úlfhéðnar*—Odinnic spear-wielding wolf-people — but only so that the real heroes can beat them up. Just as King Arthur's knights civilize the land by slaying bestial giants, King Hrolf kráki's warriors arrive at the king's hall, suffer insults from his *berserkir*, and then drive them off to take their places. In other stories, a *berserkr* might live alone in the woods, occupying some grove without any explicit motivation to do so, seemingly waiting to briefly impede a protagonist. *Beowulf*'s swamp-dwelling monster Grendel is a *berserkr* at heart, and Grendel in turn shares many qualities with the protagonists of the Icelandic outlaws' sagas, especially Grettir Ásmundarson, a figure despised even as he is respected for his martial prowess.

Such a negative view of the invincible, chosen champions of the king of the warrior gods might surprise the modern reader, but unambiguous reverence for Odin is itself an anachronism. In the Norse religion as we have been able to reconstruct it (and this is painstaking work that has taken many wrong turns), Odin is violence personified. In this role, he is undoubtedly powerful, but his blessings are capricious and double-edged. Odin (like battle itself) can turn on his champion in an instant — after all, Odin blesses warriors so that they become great, but Odin needs great warriors to

die in battle so that they can come dwell in Valhalla to await
the *Ragnarǫkr*. Even worse, to the Viking mind, Odin is a
shape-changer, willing to take on the form of a woman when
it wins him some advantage. Above all, he is the master prac-
titioner of magic, and magic is very dangerous: When males
do magic — even if they are gods — they attract *ergi*.

Ergi can be translated as "effeminacy" or even "gender-
bending" (from which some scholars have inferred that the
practice of magic involved wearing the clothes of — and
thereby becoming — the opposite sex). But it is a vivid,
multivalent term for shame of a distinctly sexual character,
and it is central to the social worldview of the Vikings. *Ergi*
is tied up with some of the strongest taboos in Viking-age
society — around homosexuality, incest, and gender roles —
and the preoccupation with manliness as *ergi*'s antidote
was a major social driver from the Viking period well into
the Christianized era of the Sagas of the Icelanders. Entire
books have been written teasing out the precise relationship
between magic and *ergi* (and one is listed in the "Further
Reading" section at the end of this chapter), but what is clear
is that Odin and the warriors who practice his magic — the
berserkir and *úlfhéðnar* as well as sorcerers and heroes like
Sigmund — risk deep dishonor. The distrust of Odinnic
magic and its paradoxical feminization of individuals who
prove their masculinity with violence is only one intellectual
thread in a broader wariness about violence as a means to
an end.

A practical basis for this distrust is evident in the Sagas of
the Icelanders. The mores of independent Iceland deemed
it acceptable in certain circumstances to assert one's will by
force, and while that condition persisted, the last and only
true defense against violence was the threat of violence in
return. The will and the capability to defend oneself became a currency like any other — one coded masculine and

evoked in English with the term "honor." If someone is able to defend himself (or has friends or sons who will defend him), thieves and brigands will respect his honor and leave him alone. However, honor is vulnerable. It is not an innate quality, but something subjective and dynamic, determined fuzzily by collective social judgments. That fragility introduces an intrinsic feedback loop: Honor is the ability to defend against violence; demonstrating an aptitude for violence is the way one accrues honor. Those who are willing to use violence even when doing so damages the social fabric — thus those willing to *over*use violence, even when it is notionally defensive violence — become the richest in the coin of manliness.

Furthermore, because an individual's manliness is a social consensus, it is damaged not only by the failure to defend oneself, but also by insults that suggest that such failure is possible. *Ergi* — with its implication of effeminate incapacity — remains such a potent insult into the Christian period that failure to answer a charge of *ergi* can result in reduced access to legal protections for the victim of the insult. The law codes describe (and proscribe) colorful slanders, such as the accusation that someone "acts as a woman does for a troll every ninth night," but the fear of *ergi* colored any number of everyday social interactions. In one of the starkest cases, *Fóstbrœðrasaga* either depicts or ridicules the resulting worldview by relating that its protagonist Thorgeir "has little to do with women" because he believes that "having sex with them would be an insult to his manhood."

Constant vigilance is necessary against slander, and constant vigilance leads to hypersensitivity. Much saga ink is spilled sussing out insults where they might be hidden because insults, once detected, can rapidly escalate to maiming and death. A harsh word — or the strong suspicion that a word was meant harshly — can and does end friendships in bloodshed. Because kin-groups possess collective honor, the retribution for the original insult must itself be answered with violence, and things can spiral out of control into bloodfeud.

Redressing wounded honor without violence and thus limiting the likelihood that wounded honor will escalate into feud is the core responsibility of the peculiar institution of medieval Icelandic society: its robust, democratic court system. The *Alþingi*, the annual assembly for the recitation of the law and the hearing of suits, was the center of public life, and as such receives extensive treatment in the sagas. *Brennu-Njáls saga* (the jewel of the saga literature) takes a particular interest in legal proceedings and their success and failure in limiting the ability of strong men — of cartoon-Vikings — to get their own way through violence. The saga's tragic power arises from how fleeting the law's successes prove: Despite generational attempts to build a society of laws, the strength of the powerful goes on unchecked, and the feud devours the great families.

The unambiguous heroes of the saga — both killed in their homes in the culminations of separate feuds — are Gunnar of Hlidarend and his friend and counselor Njal Thorgeirsson. The saga does not mumble about why these two are worthy of reverence. After Gunnar wins a lawsuit with Njal's help and spends some time raiding and fighting pirates, the friends reunite to spell out their convictions:

> Njal said . . . "now you have been well tested. . . .
> [T]here are many who will envy you."
> "I want to be on good terms with everyone," said
> Gunnar.

This is a lovely sentiment, but Njal is quick to add that it is out of place in the world of the sagas:

"[Y]ou will often be forced to defend yourself."
"Then it will be important that I should have
justice on my side," said Gunnar.

Gunnar's idealistic sentiment — particularly coming
from such an accomplished warrior — is commendable but
completely misguided. Justice is not definitively on Gunnar's side: In the case they are discussing, Njal's masterful
legal maneuvering only nearly succeeded, and Gunnar
ultimately salvaged the suit by challenging his opponent
to combat. The saga states in so many words that Njal is
Iceland's greatest living lawyer, but even with his help, justice could be obtained only through the martial prowess of
Iceland's greatest living combatant. This is a key critique at
the core of the saga: Iceland's law code relied on violence to
control violence.

In this period, the island was a sparsely settled frontier
beyond the reach of the kings of mainland Europe and their
power to enforce laws. Even if Gunnar had won his legal
case, there were no police or financial authorities to ensure
that he received payment. He, like all plaintiffs, would have
been responsible for collecting damages. Neither did Iceland use prisons to punish what a modern observer would
regard as criminal matters. The complainant was likewise
expected to force the person who harmed him or her to pay
monetary damages. For repeat offenses and truly irreconcil-
able crimes, a perpetrator could be declared an outlaw (one
who could be killed without legal repercussion), but it was
still the responsibility of the plaintiff to kill the outlaw. (If the
claim was pressed on behalf of a woman, it was her responsibility to goad male relatives into the killing; in the sagas, this
is a stock scene, using stock insults invoking, of course, ten-
uously held honor and fragile masculinity.) In short, the law

failed to separate itself from the system of wounded honor and retributive violence that it sought to limit: Without the threat of retribution, damages could go unpaid, the lawful killing of an outlaw could be avenged, and settlements could be refused.

The law offered the *opportunity* to embrace restorative justice over violence, humiliation, and revenge, but only when disputes were pressed by prosocial individuals such as Njal and Gunnar. When parties who preferred violence became involved — as they do in the concluding episodes of *Brennu-Njáls saga* — the law could not stop the feud. In the saga, the troubles begin after Njal's son, Skarp-Hedin, orphans a boy named Hoskuld. Njal does everything in his power to avoid a feud, adopting Hoskuld and raising him to value the law and its promise of social stability. Hoskuld is a perfect student from their first meeting:

> "Do you know what caused your father's death?" asked Njal.
>
> The boy replied, "I know perfectly well that Skarp-Hedin killed him. But there is no need to bring that up again, for it has all been settled with full compensation."

Malefactors try to undermine the peace-settlement, first by telling Hoskuld that his foster brothers (Njal's sons) fear retribution and plot his death. Hoskuld is unshakeable in his trust and in his adherence the spirit of the settlement, and answers that he "would much rather endure death at their hands than do any harm." These same malefactors turn to the Njalssons — aggressive, honor-conscious men who readily believe that Hoskuld intends to betray them. Hoskuld refuses to participate and counts his own life as worth less than forestalling the feud: "I would rather," he says, "that no compensation at all were paid for me than be the cause of suffering to others."

After Njal's biological sons ambush and kill Hoskuld (he prays that God forgive them), Njal laments that he would rather two of them had died than that they broke the settlement with violence against their foster brother. At the *Alþingi*, he clarifies that he would prefer that *all* of his sons had died. Arbitrators design a settlement so expensive that breaking it would be unthinkable, and they call on everyone present to contribute money (a sign of communal support for — and perhaps enforcement of — the settlement). Njal seals the deal with a gift: a fine pair of boots and a cloak.

Enigmatically, the claimant, Flosi, regards the cloak as an insult. Some critics have read it as a unisex garment, implying that accepting a settlement is unmanly (though this interpretation has been called into question). In any case, after Flosi accuses Njal of androgyny (he cannot grow a beard), Skarp-Hedin comes out and mocks Flosi for accepting a settlement in so many words, saying: "We [in contrast to Flosi] have let few [i.e. none] of our kinsmen lie unavenged." The settlement breaks down, and Hoskuld — Njal's great student, who has gone so far as to abnegate his own honor by telling others to forgive his death without settlement — becomes the impetus for the burning-death of peaccable Njal and his extended family. Their own deaths are redressed not with settlement, but with killing in return. It is a compounded tragedy perpetrated by manly, honor-obsessed fighters.

Violence is frightening. It is terrible to behold and worse to endure, but when it becomes a remote or infrequent occurrence — as it has for many of us in the modern, industrialized world — violence can acquire a romance or a mystique. Bringing that sense of romance to these Norse texts is a mistake. In the Viking age proper, violence was tied up with chaos and betrayal, and its most dedicated practitioners — both human and divine — were regarded (sometimes) as antisocial monsters. To the writers of the sagas, violence as a means of proving or defending one's masculine honor was a real and frequent danger, one that threatened to upend the social order through the horror of the feud. When we read Norse literature, we must remember that it does not simplistically valorize indiscriminant violence; it reveals a profound cultural anxiety around damage to fragile masculinity and laments the ultimate failure of cultural projects that attempt to subjugate masculine aggression and violence to the forces that can properly channel them — to foreign kings, to just and wise women and men, and above all to the law.

Further Reading

All quotations from *Njals saga* come from the Penguin edition translated by Magnus Magnusson and Hermann Pálsson. I deeply regret that because of constraints of space, I was unable to treat two sagas that have a great deal to say on issues of masculinity, power, and the law: Hrólfs saga kraka (available in English as Jesse Byock, trans., *The Saga of King Hrolf Kraki* [New York: Penguin, 1999]) and Fóstbrœðrasaga (Lee M. Hollander, trans. and ed., *The Sagas of Kormák and the Sworn Brothers* [Princeton: Princeton University Press 1949]), of which you received a small taste earlier in the essay.

A sweeping synthesis of Norse religion can be found in Neil S. Price, *The Viking Way: Religion and War in Late Iron Age Scandinavia* (Uppsala: Department of Archaeology and Ancient History, Uppsala University, 2002). For gender in the time of the sagas, an important and accessible work is Carol Clover, "Regardless of Sex: Men, Women, and Power in Early Northern Europe," *Speculum* 68, no. 2 (April 1993). A book-length treatment of masculinity and verbal assaults thereupon can be found in Preben Meulengracht Sørensen, *The Unmanly Man: Concepts of Sexual Defamation in Early Northern Society* (Odense: Odense University Press, 1983). For more on bloodfeud and the taunts that get men to continue it, see William Ian Miller, "Choosing the Avenger: Some Aspects of the Bloodfeud in Medieval Iceland and England," *Law and History Review* 1, no. 2 (Autumn, 1983), 159–204. In 2018, The Public Medievalist began an ongoing series, "Gender, Sexism, and the Middle Ages," and Gabrielle Bychowski's essay "Were there Transgender People in the Middle Ages?" (www.publicmedievalist.com /transgender-middle-ages/) goes into greater detail about pre-modern notions of gender fluidity and the social power of clothing in the performance of gender.

#DeusVult

Adam M. Bishop

At the center of much recent discourse of hatred, violence, and intolerance toward Muslims is a two-word Latin phrase: "Deus vult." On social media platforms, #deusvult is associated with far-right politics and particularly anti-Islamic messages. In the United States, mosques in Arkansas were vandalized with the phrase in October 2016, and the words were spray-painted at the University of Southern Maine in November 2016. In Europe, the phrase appeared on a mosque in Scotland in December 2016. The most well-known incident was in August 2017, when some of the white supremacist demonstrators in Charlottesville, Virginia, chanted and carried signs with the phrase. News stories about these incidents correctly report that "Deus vult" is a phrase associated with the crusades. Literally, it means "God wants," "God wishes," or "God wills," but it is usually translated in English as "It is the will of God."

These words come from the very beginning of the crusading movement in 1095. In November of that year, Pope Urban II convened a church council at Clermont in France

(the modern city of Clermont-Ferrand). The council is famous mostly for Urban's closing speech, on November 27,
wherein he called upon the Christians of Western Europe to
send military assistance to the Byzantine Empire in the east,
which was at the time under attack from the Muslim Seljuk
Turks. The resulting military expedition, the First Crusade,
provided some assistance to the Empire but also ended up
marching further south and conquering Jerusalem in 1099.

Several conflicting accounts survive of Urban II's speech
at Clermont, so we don't know exactly what he said. Based
on one or another version, for instance, historians have debated whether the pope originally intended for the expedition to conquer Jerusalem. In one account, that of Robert
the Monk, Jerusalem was the target from the very beginning,
and it is after Urban's speech, with its lurid details about the
supposed cruelties to which Christians had been subjected
by Muslims, that the audience spontaneously exclaims "It is
the will of God!" Whether or not this story about the meeting at Clermont is true, crusaders did use "Deus vult" as a
battle cry during the First Crusade, as well as during other
crusades in the twelfth and thirteenth centuries.

Today, the phrase is probably familiar to anyone with
an interest in the crusades. The story is mentioned in both
popular and academic histories, including, for example, the
very popular and influential history of the crusades written
by the medieval historian Steven Runciman in the 1950s
and more recent histories, for example by Jonathan Riley-
Smith or Thomas Madden. The phrase has made its way
into popular culture, as seen in the 2005 movie *Kingdom of
Heaven* and the massively popular *Crusader Kings* series of
video games.

The phrase has also become popular on the Internet
as a slogan for white nationalists/white supremacists/neo-
Nazis/the "alt-right." These groups have always been very

fond of the Middle Ages in general and the crusades in particular. Over the past few years, medieval historians have started to take notice, and have started speaking out against what they see as misappropriation of crusader and medieval ideas and imagery. Some of the academic backlash has been against the white supremacist idea that medieval Europe was a utopian homeland for white Christians. Historian David Perry has noted that modern white supremacists believe that "once upon a time there was a pure white Europe, building civilization in opposition to the 'other.'"

It is certainly true that medieval Europe was not homogeneously white, and Perry and others, such as the *People of Color in European Art History* tumblr, have been doing admirable work publicizing this information. But there is more to white supremacists' use of "Deus vult" than an imaginary white past. Medieval Europeans may not have had any cohesive sense of whiteness, and hence a clear sense of supremacy based on skin color, but they did make distinctions based on religion. They were very concerned with preserving, restoring, or expanding Christianity throughout Europe, and also, by the time of the crusades, in the Near East and Africa.

There has also been academic backlash against the idea that the crusades were a single monolithic event, that they were always directed against Muslims, or that crusaders all had a single anti-Islamic motivation. It is certainly true that there were other kinds of crusades in Europe against various targets (sometimes even against other Christians), and that the crusaders who fought in the Middle East had many different reasons for joining a crusade.

The crusaders knew that Christianity was once the religion of the entire Roman Empire, in Europe, the Middle East, and Africa. Not long before Urban's speech, the Roman church and the Greek church had been in communion with one another, and the crusaders believed that God wanted them to reunite the two churches, which is what happened (temporarily) in the aftermath of the Fourth Crusade. They remembered that the most important Christian sites in the Holy Land had once been ruled by Christians, even though these sites had been conquered by Muslims in the seventh century, almost 500 years before the crusades. They believed that the holy sites should be returned to Christian rule. And many of the crusaders believed that they had non-Christian enemies in Europe: Jews, whose communities had often existed in Europe long before the arrival of Christianity; Muslims in Spain and parts of Italy; and "pagans" in northern and eastern Europe — these communities were to be expelled, conquered, plundered, and converted.

When Urban II called for the First Crusade, he soon found that he was not the only one who decided what God willed. He envisioned the church leading the wealthy nobility on a relatively well-organized military expedition against the Turks in the Levant, but the First Crusade was preceded by a popular movement in 1096, the "People's Crusade." These crusaders were certain that God wanted them to attack the Jewish communities that they found as they traveled south along the Rhine River. Nearly every crusade thereafter was inevitably accompanied by attacks against the Jews in Europe. The church and secular authorities always tried to protect Jewish communities from crusader attacks, but in the minds of participants in the People's Crusade, Jews were just as much an enemy of Christianity as Muslims.

A nebulous concept such as "what God wants" could easily be appropriated to launch a crusade against almost anyone, far beyond whatever the participants at the Council of Clermont thought it meant. Crusades could also be called against Christians in Western Europe who were considered heretical, as in the church-led Albigensian Crusade against heretics in France in the thirteenth century. Crusaders also believed they could attack fellow Christians in the Byzantine Empire, in military action that was opposed by the church. Every crusade came into conflict with the Byzantines, even the First Crusade, despite its original plan to assist the empire against the Turks. The Fourth Crusade even went so far off course as to conquer the Byzantine capital of Constantinople and to temporarily destroy the empire.

Professional historians have very good reasons to object to the ways that white supremacists have co-opted and abused imagery from the crusades and the Middle Ages. But do white supremacists really misunderstand the crusades? From their own writings and statements, we know that modern white supremacists would like to eradicate Islam from Europe and North America, at the very least, if not from the entire world. We know, because this is what they chanted as they marched through Charlottesville in 2017, that they are afraid of somehow being "replaced" by Jewish people or other people they consider non-white. Like the so-called "Knights Templar International" who are selling homes in the white-only and Christian-only village of Asotthalom in Hungary, white supremacists in general would like to recreate a Christian utopia that they believe must have existed in the past.

In this sense, they are not misusing "Deus vult" at all. Their usage is completely in line with the phrase's original intention. The crusaders really believed that God wanted them to kill Muslims and restore or preserve Christian rule. It is true that demonstrators who chant "Deus vult" have another agenda, white supremacy, that the crusaders would not have recognized. But in their usage and understanding of the slogan "Deus vult," the crusaders would certainly find common ground with modern white supremacists.

Over the past few decades there has been a scholarly debate about why medieval people really went on crusade.

To some extent, at least among professional historians, this debate is a reaction against the arguments of Steven Runciman, who depicted the crusaders as little more than barbarians, intent on destroying the superior civilizations of the Byzantine Empire and the Islamic world. Historians of Runciman's generation often saw the crusaders as violent fanatics, mercenaries who were interested only in personal gain in the wealthier east. This fit in with another popular (and now debunked) theory: that the medieval people who most often went on crusade were the younger sons of European nobility, with no chance to inherit their fathers' properties and with nothing better to do except make war against each other. The church therefore brought them all together and sent them off to conquer the Holy Land.

These scenarios are rather simplistic, and the work done over recent decades to find the true motivations of crusaders has introduced several other interesting possibilities. Modern theories about the motivations of crusaders focus on aspects such as individual piety or family tradition. Crusading, so it is now often argued, was linked to widespread religious attitudes that emphasized concern about the consequences of sin and the need for forgiveness in the eyes of God. It was therefore closely related to other acts of religious devotion such as pilgrimage and making gifts to saints' shrines. If one member of a family went on crusade, then their relatives and descendants were more likely to go on crusade as well. Some went on crusade because they were emotionally distressed over the loss of Jerusalem and the other holy sites in the Near East. Rather than violent fanaticism or a search for material wealth, crusading was an extension of fairly typical medieval Christian beliefs and practices grounded in personal devotion.

When read by non-specialists, this research may seem, in a way, to "rehabilitate" the crusades and individual cru-

saders and, by extension, to open the door for their appropriation by today's white supremacist groups. A bad-faith argument, generated out of the rehabilitation of "Deus vult"
by medieval historians would go something like this: *If the
crusaders were fundamentally pious folks just trying to do
the right thing according to their worldview, then why not
extend the same morally subjective benefit of the doubt to neo-
Nazis?* We are not willing to extend the benefit of the doubt
to Nazis, so why do we extend it to crusaders?

An objection to this argument is that there are many other
aspects of the crusades that can be obscure to non-historians,
aspects that neo-Nazis do not know about, or that they do
not care about or simply do not understand. The crusades
span several centuries and continents, and in a wider historical context, go far beyond a simple war between two religions. One of the more extraordinary outcomes of the First
Crusade was the creation of a European-style kingdom in
the Near East (the so-called "Latin Kingdom of Jerusalem").
The crusaders who stayed in the east, their descendants, and
other Europeans who came to settle there soon learned that
constant warfare and violence were not so useful when trying to establish a functioning society among a much larger
population of Muslims, Jews, and eastern Christians.

The Latin Kingdom of Jerusalem, which lasted for almost
200 years, was a mixture of the various populations that lived
there. This was not a unique situation even in Europe; medieval Spain and Sicily, for example, had similarly diverse
populations. Fulcher of Chartres, one of our sources for the
Council of Clermont, noted that after the First Crusade "we
who were Occidentals have now become Orientals." This
is not to say that the crusader states were a multicultural
utopia by modern standards; Muslims were enslaved and
segregation was the legal norm. It has been argued that in
some ways, the crusades were a very early form of European

colonialism. But the inhabitants of European descent who lived in the crusader states lived, worked, and traded with the native inhabitants of the Near East; they learned new languages and intermarried with eastern Christians, and each side borrowed from each other's cultures. The European settlers developed a different understanding of "Deus vult" than newcomers who arrived on crusade from Europe. Newly arrived crusaders sometimes wanted nothing more than to make war and kill Muslims and could not understand how a mixed society had developed in the Holy Land. Even in the Middle Ages, there was a divide between those who lived in a multicultural society, and new crusaders who wanted to destroy it.

For obvious reasons, these elements of the history of the crusades are not a central aspect of the crusading narrative as it is usually presented and embraced by white supremacists. In fact, in dismissing the important frontier and settlement aspects of crusading, modern hate groups replicate the attitudes of some medieval crusaders, who complained that the settlers in the east had lost their European identity and had become too "eastern," too decadent. And the sense in medieval European Christian accounts that the Latin Kingdom of Jerusalem had lost its western Christian identity is not dissimilar to the claims of white supremacists in America who claim that as a result of immigration and progressive politics, the country has lost its white European and Christian heritage. This may bring a further resonance to their adoption of the crusader "Deus vult" slogan.

The crusades were a complex aspect of medieval history that had wide-ranging effects on three continents over several centuries. Historians rightly argue that they cannot be reduced to one single war waged for one single reason. But the fact that the crusades were complex is not enough to refute appropriation of crusader imagery by white supremacists. Modern supremacists know as well as we do that the crusades were complex. We must not forget that many of the medieval people who actually promoted and fought in the crusades, from popes to aristocratic military commanders to the leaders of popular movements, considered them a clash of incompatible civilizations. White supremacists who chant "Deus vult," dress up as knights, carry crusader flags and banners, and imagine that they are Templars battling against Muslims and protecting the heritage of a white, Christian Europe and North America also believe we are involved in a clash of civilizations. They are not at all misrepresenting the beliefs of medieval crusaders, with whom they would find much common ground.

Further Reading

For more information about various aspects of living in a European crusader society in the Holy Land, see *Tolerance and Intolerance: Social Conflict in the Age of the Crusades*, edited by Michael Gervers and James M. Powell (Syracuse, N.Y.: Syracuse University Press, 2001); Ronnie Ellenblum's *Frankish Rural Settlement in the Latin Kingdom of Jerusalem* (Cambridge: Cambridge University Press, 1998); as well as the Variorum collections of articles by Benjamin Z. Kedar, *Franks, Muslims, and Oriental Christians in the Latin Levant* (Aldershot: Ashgate, 2006), and *The Franks in the Levant, 11th to 14th Centuries* (Aldershot: Ashgate, 1993). A discussion of the motivations of individual crusaders can be found in Jonathan Riley-Smith, "The motives of the earliest crusaders and the settlement of Latin Palestine, 1095–1100," *The English Historical Review* 98 (1983).

Own Your Heresy

J. Patrick Hornbeck II

In October 2015, U.S. Catholic intellectuals were quite literally a-Twitter about an online exchange between Ross Douthat, a self-identified conservative who is a columnist for *The New York Times*, and Massimo Faggioli, a professor of theology then teaching at the University of St. Thomas in Minneapolis. Douthat had written a column entitled "The Plot to Change Catholicism" in which he had charged Pope Francis with scheming to alter what Douthat took to be the Catholic Church's immutable prohibition on the reception of communion by divorced Catholics who subsequently remarried civilly. "Speaking as a Catholic," Douthat wrote, "I expect the plot to ultimately fail; where the pope and the historic faith seem to be in tension, my bet is on the faith." Faggioli responded the day Douthat's column was published. He tweeted that the article "is simply appalling — for his ignorance of basic Catholic theology." Their electronic spat grew heated, until Douthat signed off, telling Faggioli: "Own your heresy."

The outcry from progressive Catholics was swift. Faggioli and a coalition of like-minded theologians complained to the editor of the *Times*, arguing that "accusing other members of the Catholic church of heresy, sometimes subtly, sometimes openly, is serious business that can have serious consequences for those so accused." Jesuit writer James Martin cautioned Douthat: "Please be careful throwing around a word like 'heresy.' That is an extremely serious accusation and in this case unfounded." Indeed, as we will see, in earlier times accusations of heresy entailed the direct threat of execution at the stake. Even in the twentieth and early twenty-first centuries, claims about heresy and dissent have derailed theologians' careers, cost religious men and women their membership in their orders, and generated campaigns of public shaming against supposed religious traitors. Yet despite all this, Douthat was not deterred. In a follow-up column, he charged his progressive opponents with taking the position that "almost anything Catholic can change when the times require it." He doubled down as well on his previous accusation: "I must tell you, openly and not subtly, that this view sounds like heresy by any reasonable definition of the term."

But what, exactly, is heresy? The word comes from the Greek *hairesis*, a noun form of the verb meaning "to personally select or choose." In the first two centuries of Christianity, it evolved from a neutral term, referring to something like a school of thought, into one with strongly negative connotations. By the middle of the second century, *hairesis* had come to mean a very specific kind of choice: a wrong choice, the choice to hold beliefs that diverged from those authorized by church authorities. Those official teachings came to be called "orthodox" (meaning, literally, "right belief"), and church leaders maintained that they had been passed down from Jesus to his first followers and, eventually, to latter-day bishops who considered themselves the successors of the apostles.

Early Christian texts described the conflict between heresy and orthodoxy in stark and sometimes apocalyptic terms. The second-century bishop Irenaeus of Lyons, for instance, laid out in his tome *Against the Heresies* a genealogy of heretical beliefs. Just as orthodox teachings had been handed down from Jesus to the church of his own day, he wrote, so also did heretics stand in a diabolical order of succession, going back to the biblical villain Simon Magus and, beyond him, to the devil. Authors from the relatively obscure Epiphanius of Salamis to the influential Augustine of Hippo assembled catalogues of heresies, identifying and categorizing various species of erroneous belief. And church councils adopted creedal statements that both implicitly and explicitly ruled certain theological views out of bounds. The Council of Nicaea, meeting in 325, adopted a creed that in modified form continues to be used in most Christian churches today. But hardly any contemporary church retains the final sentence of the text that the council approved: "But those who say: 'There was a time when he was not'; and 'He was not before he was made'; and 'He was made out of nothing,' or 'He is of another substance' or 'essence,' or 'The Son of God is created,' or 'changeable,' or 'alterable'—they are condemned by the holy catholic and apostolic Church." Orthodox church leaders associated all these views with the followers of the Egyptian priest Arius, who became, in one scholar's words, the "archetypal" heretic.

Modern theologians have repeatedly reminded us that most doctrinal formulations that came to be labeled heresies started out as competing answers to disputed questions. The condemnation of Arius, for example, emerged from a robust debate among Christian thinkers in the third and early fourth centuries about the relationship between God the Father and Jesus Christ. For many Christians today, it is axiomatic that Christ is equally as divine as the Father: They are "of one substance," as the Nicene Creed proclaims. But prior to (and even after) the Council of Nicaea, early Christians entertained a variety of views about the Father and the Son. Arius may have developed his most controversial idea, namely, that Christ was the first creation of God the Father, out of a desire to ensure that Christians preserved the monotheism that they had inherited from Judaism. Arius was an effective communicator; he attracted many adherents and prompted his opponents to define, and defend, their stance with greater clarity. A combination of theological and political factors, many related to the fourth-century Roman emperor Constantine's desire to ensure uniformity of belief within the Christian faith that he had newly legalized, left Arius on the losing side. Likewise, other Christian thinkers who have gone down in history as heretics constructed alternative theological views that those in power eventually rejected.

By the Middle Ages, discussions about heresy had taken on a distinctively juridical, which is to say legal, character. The category of heresy, while still theological in nature, came in the western church to be defined and policed primarily by the canon lawyers who staffed ecclesiastical courts. One of these, Gratian, included in his twelfth-century compilation, the *Decretum*, a citation from the church father Jerome: "Heresy means 'choice' from the Greek, in other words that choice by which a person chooses that teaching which he thinks to be best." In thirteenth-century England, the theologian and bishop Robert Grosseteste similarly defined heresy as "an opinion chosen by human perception contrary to Holy Scripture, publicly avowed and obstinately defended."

It cannot be overemphasized that, at least from the elev-

enth century through the time of the Protestant Reforma-
tions, heresy was a crime prosecuted in the courts of what
today we would call the Roman Catholic Church. For those
convicted, the charge carried substantial penalties, up to
and including death at the stake. While there are no exact figures, medieval Europe witnessed hundreds (but not,
contrary to the popular imagination, thousands upon thousands) of burnings for heresy.

Ecclesiastical and civil authorities cooperated in the pros-
ecution of heresy. Church courts were able to rely on local
rulers to compel the presence of defendants, who sometimes
were "delated" (referred) to the court by fellow believers and
other times were identified in the course of an investigative
process known as *inquisitio*. When a defendant appeared,
court officials read out a list of specific charges. Perhaps
the defendant had been overheard saying something that
contradicted church teachings; perhaps she or he had been
observed engaging in forbidden practices, such as reading
unauthorized religious literature; perhaps she or he simply
had been noticed in the company of known heretics.

Defendants' options were relatively few in number. If
they had previously been convicted of heresy, they would
immediately be sent to the stake as a "relapsed" heretic. A
first-time defendant could admit that she or he had erred
and ask for forgiveness, could seek to clear her or his name
by calling a specified number of reputable men to speak
on her or his behalf as character witnesses, or could publicly embrace the heterodox beliefs and practices with
which she or he had been charged. In the first instance,
the court usually assigned the defendant one or more forms
of penance, which ranged from public shaming to fines to
restrictions on the defendant's freedom to move about the
land or associate with others. Quite often, courts required
defendants who had confessed ("abjured," in the technical

vocabulary of the day) to wear a badge or be branded on their bodies to indicate that they had committed heresy. Some defendants were able to clear their names through the testimony of others. Relatively few chose open defiance and received the capital sentence that was almost certain to follow. Because the church held that clerics could not shed blood, defendants who were convicted for a second time or were pronounced obstinate were handed over to the civil authorities for the execution of their sentences.

Proceedings against heretics in late medieval England ex-emplified these pan-European dynamics. In the late 1370s, a philosopher and theologian at the University of Oxford, John Wyclif, came to notoriety as the proponent of a number of controversial ideas, including criticisms of the doctrine of transubstantiation, the power of the pope, and the status of religious orders such as the Franciscans and Dominicans. At the same time, Wyclif encouraged (but, contrary to cen-turies of Protestant legend, did not personally undertake) the translation of the Bible into English, and he inspired (but, again, did not to any great extent personally organize) preachers who spread dissenting ideas in communities scat-tered across the English countryside. In comparison to Eu-rope's other kingdoms, England had been relatively free of heresy accusations over the course of the Middle Ages, so in part to preserve their reputation, church authorities re-sponded forcefully to Wyclif and his followers, whom they sometimes dubbed "lollards" (an obscure term of abuse, derived from continental campaigns against heresy, that may originally have meant something close to "loiterers" or "mumblers"). Unauthorized translations of the scriptures and the unauthorized production of religious texts for lay-people were banned. Wyclif and many of his followers were forced from their academic positions or made to recant. Parliament adopted a statute authorizing the death penalty in cases of heresy. And between the last quarter of the four-teenth century and the first quarter of the sixteenth, approx-imately seven hundred trials for heresy took place. Perhaps only one in ten of those charged refused to abjure and were burned; the vast majority of their fellows chose the route of confession and penance, and only a few of them returned to court a second time.

Today, only extreme religious partisans dispute that the death of even one person for her theological convictions is one too many. Yet it is worth pondering why the specter of burning at the stake continues to haunt popular views of the Middle Ages, at least in English-speaking countries, if me-dieval heresy prosecutions were comparatively rare, and death sentences rarer still. To be sure, campaigns against heresy in other parts of Europe were far more violent: The Albigensian Crusade of the early thirteenth century resulted in thousands of deaths, and the Spanish Inquisition of the fifteenth through eighteenth centuries deserves its particu-larly ignominious place in the history of religious brutality. But while not as many heresy defendants suffered in En-gland, their legacy was shaped by the brilliantly effective rhetoric of the first Protestant historians of medieval heresy: men, like John Bale and John Foxe, who sought to identify those who had been persecuted by the Roman church as the forerunners of their own reform movements. Bale famously christened Wyclif the "morning star of the Reformation," and Foxe's *Actes and Monuments* (more commonly known as *Foxe's Book of Martyrs*) depicted medieval churchmen as bloodthirsty, greedy, and diabolical opponents of the gospel. Generations of Protestant worshippers encountered such images of Rome and its prelates in pamphlets, sermons, Sunday school lessons, and history textbooks. (It must be noted, of course, that accusations of and punishments—even capital punishments—for heresy have not been absent

from the histories of Protestant denominations. In this connection, the famous witch trials of the seventeenth-century
American colonial town of Salem, which in medieval terms
would have been trials for sorcery rather than for heresy
proper, are often thought of as belonging to an earlier, and
distinctively benighted, period of history.)

And so, when Ross Douthat chided Massimo Faggioli to
"[o]wn your heresy," he was invoking a concept that has had
life-altering consequences for those accused. Today, heresy
remains a crime in the canon law of the Roman Catholic
Church, where its official definition resembles that of Robert Grosseteste's: "Heresy is the obstinate denial or obstinate
doubt after the reception of baptism of some truth which is
to be believed by divine and Catholic faith."

Thankfully, prosecutions for heresy have been rare in
recent Catholic history, and the Spanish Inquisition ordered
the last execution of a convicted heretic in 1826. But while
the legal device of a heresy trial with its potentially horrific
consequences has fallen into disuse, heresy has retained its
place in churchly rhetoric. A key Vatican office, the Congregation for the Doctrine of the Faith, has taken the place of
what was formerly called the Supreme Sacred Congregation
of the Roman and Universal Inquisition. Particularly under
Popes John Paul II (reigned 1979–2005) and Benedict XVI
(reigned 2005–2013), the Congregation has been active in
defining church teaching and critiquing such Catholic
thinkers as the liberation theologians Leonardo Boff and
Jon Sobrino, the ethicists Charles Curran and Margaret Far-
ley, the theorist of interreligious dialogue Jacques Dupuis,
and the pro-LGBT activists Jeannine Gramick and Robert
Nugent, among many others. One of those the Congregation disciplined, the Australian priest Paul Collins, has gone
so far as to dub it the "modern Inquisition." The penalties
that the Congregation meted out during the previous two

pontificates included the firing of theologians from their professorships, the dismissal of priests and sisters from their orders, and the revocation of individuals' abilities to work in Catholic institutions.

Yet under the current pontificate of Pope Francis, the Congregation for the Doctrine of the Faith has found itself diminished. It now ranks behind several new Vatican offices that Francis has established, it publishes far fewer doctrinal documents, and it has all but ceased publicly to critique individual theologians. In 2017, the pope summarily dismissed its former prefect, the conservative Cardinal Gerhard Müller; as with many of Francis's decisions, both the fact and the circumstances of Müller's departure angered some traditionalist Catholics. In an ironic turn of events, under Francis it has not been the Vatican, but rather those who believe that the pope has gone too far in opening the church to the contemporary world, who have most often employed the rhetoric of heresy. Indeed, in the same year, a group of priests and scholars made public a document they had sent Francis entitled in Latin *Correctio filialis de haeresibus propagatis* ("a respectful correction concerning the propagation of heresies"). They accused him of advancing seven heretical propositions in his 2016 document on marriage and family life, *Amoris laetitia*. While canon lawyers have held for centuries that it is theoretically possible for a pope to commit heresy, public accusations against a sitting pontiff have been exceedingly rare, and the *Correctio filialis* has garnered little support.

As Douthat's critics recognized, to ask an opponent to "own" his heresy is no small matter. For generations of Christians, heresy has been a matter not only of temporal life and death, but also of one's prospects in the afterlife. Church authorities have used heresy charges to discipline both ordinary believers and the intellectual elite, identifying

dissenters not only as theologically incorrect but deserving
of the most stringent punishments. Yet this has not come
without a substantial cost to the institutional church's reputation. It is unclear to what extent the concept, and the rhetoric, of heresy continues to serve the church. But the concept, and the rhetoric, most certainly remain inflammatory.

Further Reading

Malcolm Lambert, *Medieval Heresy* (3rd edition, 2002), remains the classic guide to the many ideas and groups declared heretical from the eleventh through the sixteenth
centuries, though his conclusions are substantially nuanced
by R. I. Moore, *The War on Heresy* (Cambridge: Harvard
University Press, 2012). Rebecca Lyman, "Heresiology: The
Invention of 'Heresy' and 'Schism,'" in *The Cambridge History of Christianity, Volume 2* (Cambridge, UK: Cambridge
University Press, 2007), 296–313, lays out the early Christian background, and Rowan Williams, *Arius: Heresy and
Tradition*, 2nd edition (London: SCM Press, 2001), offers
insights specifically about the Arian controversy. On heresy
in late medieval England, my own *A Companion to Lollardy*
(Leiden: Brill, 2016) attempts to identify key individuals,
contested beliefs, and social contexts.

*I am grateful to the anonymous readers for Fordham Univer-
sity Press for their helpful suggestions on an earlier draft of
this essay.*

Afterword: Medievalists and the Education of Desire

Geraldine Heng

Most of us who are professional euromedievalists[1] today came to the study of the premodern past from defining moments in our own past. A retired Anglo-Saxonist at the University of Texas, Tom Cable, read *La Belle Dame sans Merci*, and, enthralled by the medievalisms of the nineteenth century, decided to investigate their originary cultures. Some, mesmerized by the experience of Latin mass in childhood, may have sought to study a time when Europe was Christendom, rather than Europe. I wanted to know why the King Arthur legend survived 900 years.

For those who study a medieval Mediterranean, or what I've called a Global Middle Ages,[2] an animating moment might have been the lilt of a muezzin's call to prayer, or a glimpse of the samurai history of Japan, or curiosity about Genghis Khan's life in the societies of the Eurasian steppe. Perhaps, reading *Sundiata* for the first time, someone became an Africanist because she was thunderstruck that— hundreds of years before Hollywood needed to fantasize an imaginary Wakanda in Africa—the empires of Mali and Ghana, the kingdom of Zimbabwe, and the Swahili coast had thriving cultures and cities, and dynamic commerce with the world.

Curiosity and desire within our own lives, as professional medievalists—driving forces about which scholars rarely write, schooled as we are by conventions that cordon off *serious* scholarly writing from *confessional* autobiography—thus animate years of study and credentialing, and the careers that have followed. But the fact that a volume like this is needed today—one that asks in its title, *Whose Middle Ages?*—urges that a tipping point has been reached: We've arrived at a moment where we must assess the nature of academic and public desire, and, where necessary, launch a *re-education* of desire.

The essays in this volume are troubled by uses of the past in our present time—instrumental manipulations powered by currents of desire both implicit and explicit in public discourse. Fred Donner counters the paranoid simplifications of Islam in public culture today by meticulously unpacking shari'a law's inherent multiplicities. Helen Young slams popular video games where the freedom to fantasize can celebrate the agency of dragons and magic but does not allow for the existence of non-white peoples in their created worlds. Maggie Williams shows how ignorance and forgetting, yoked to racist intent, deform medieval Celtic symbols to the point where they can be badges to be proudly displayed by neo-fascists.

To racism and Islamophobia, Sandy Bardsley adds the indictment of class: Peasants were 90–95 percent of the medieval population but are conspicuously absent in popular commemorative recovery. To the invisibility of peasants, Katherine Anne Wilson adds the invisibility of craft workers—especially in tapestry production—who resemble the "gig economy" workers and day laborers of today because of the precarity of the piece-work they undertook. Christendom was also nastier than the pious would have it: Monasteries owned half the land and nursed a profitable relationship with the wealthy, Lauren Mancia tartly recalls. Nor does this volume ignore recent pasts: Cord Whitaker movingly remembers how the plantation south was idealized as a medieval pastoral space by defenders of slavery, and William Diebold tackles the Third Reich's manipulation of the medieval German Empire for authority and self-validation.

Some essays unearth neglected native alterities in the Middle Ages, and restore an unruly, multiplicitous archive. David Wacks's restatement of the politics of multicultural, multiracial Iberia contests the whitewashing of medieval Europe's racial history, and refuses any scrubbing of the archive. Ryan Szpiech insists we view Thomas Jefferson's Qur'an within the long history of polemical vilification of Islam's holy book: "Jefferson's Qur'an, expressing both polemical rejection of Islam and also [later] humanist admiration of the civilizations to which it gave rise . . . is . . . a fitting embodiment of the mixed intentions and patent contradictions at the heart of our own modern engagement with the past." And Sarah Guérin points to an irony in today's conservationist politics: The banning of ivory artifacts from public museums will efface the history of Europe's long dependence on medieval Africa's agency in international trade, an agency that is already too often effaced.[3]

The essays in the volume all seek some kind of corrective: to retrograde political movements, the deformation of the past in popular and digital media, and blind spots in our own scholarship—which is to say, they seek to correct how the past is used as a manipulated object. Alarmed about the futures of the past, each essay acknowledges, in individual fashion, that any recovery of a past is colored by where we stand in time and place and affected by the person and community doing the recovering.

Each also assumes, as a fundamental understanding, the intransigence of the past itself—an intransigence that the essays call out for having been insufficiently honored, both in public recoveries for polemical ends and in our own professional neglect of archives that are more unruly and multifarious than we allow. In other words, each essay recognizes in its fashion the *transactional nature* of all present-day encounters with the past, and grasps that an interaction between *it* and *us* is necessarily, continually being revised because of the nature of public and scholarly desire in any given era.

Against the manipulations and appropriations of the past that the essays protest, therefore, what we seek for our own era, if I understand the authors correctly, is a more *ethically responsible*, and *intersubjective* relationship with the past. This is a quest for the kinds of desire, and intersubjective practices, that address the multifariousness of the archive, and do it justice in non-appropriative ways. We wish to forge an *ethical relation* to the past: to weave an interaction that can be responsive to the urgencies of the present (thus acknowledging our situatedness in time and place) while simultaneously *being able to hear* what has not been sufficiently heard in the archives (thus acknowledging that the past, too, has unheard demands).

That search for a responsive, intersubjective relationship to the past that simultaneously honors our responsibilities to the present has driven my own work as well. Troubled by the inadequate tools medievalists had for discussing the treatment of Jews in the European Middle Ages—a racial minority who, in England, were targeted with badges, were herded into towns with a surveillance system for monitoring their livelihoods, were imprisoned en masse for coinage offenses, were forced to endure conversionist propaganda forcibly preached at them, were forbidden social and domestic intimacy with Christians, were legally murdered by the state for trumped-up stories of depravity against Christian children, were taxed to the edge of penury, and then finally were deported as a community when their usefulness was exhausted—I sought a definition of race apposite to premodernity that could bear adequate witness to such atrocities: a definition able to recognize racial treatment and name it for what it was, before a vocabulary of race had coalesced, and that would afford medievalists access to the trenchant resources of modern critical race theory for their analyses.[4]

Modern state racisms, like the edifice of apartheid in South Africa and World War II Japanese American internment camps in the United States, forced a recognition that state apparatuses in medieval England had much in common with modern state apparatuses, and urged an identification of a relationship between the *modern* other, and the *medieval* other, so that the archive of the racial state of medieval England could become visible and name England as the first racial state.[5] The identificatory leap between the modern and the medieval ultimately led to a seven-chapter book, which yielded a diversity of racial archives—on the Romani, the Mongols, Muslims, blackness and Africans, Native Americans, Jews—that needed to be read.

Not surprisingly, the racial urgencies of the present have also moved a number of essays in this volume to engage with medieval race. Pamela Patton attests to how whiteness in the European Middle Ages (and, we might add, today) is signaled not just by skin color but also by clothing, gestures, and bodily proportions—*culture* meets the *biopolitical* in decisions about racial status and belonging, then and now. Race is not confined to the epidermal.

Patrick Hornbeck does not mention race, yet his horror

at the treatment of medieval heretics—who were branded, forced to wear a self-proclaiming badge, put on trial, and executed for their faith—urges that racializing mechanisms can turn on *religion*, the magisterial discourse of the European Middle Ages, just as *science* was the magisterial discourse of the high-modern racial era of the Enlightenment—and even Christians could be racialized. The essays by Donner and Stephennie Mulder, addressing the past, also answer to the exigencies of the present, a time when Muslims—of whatever ethnoracial backgrounds, national origins, or linguistic communities—are being identified as a virtual race at airport security checkpoints, by the media, and in public political discourse.

When they are studied and foregrounded, the archives of race in deep time (the poetic term "deep time" is Wai-Chee Dimock's, adapted from the physical sciences) counter the pernicious nostalgia today for a Europe that might have once been homogenously Caucasian, and for an unproblematized Christianity that was thought to reign supreme in the Middle Ages. This dangerous political fantasy of a pure Caucasian Europe is founded on a willed forgetting, a scrubbing of the past. In fact, medieval archives show us that Jews lived in virtually every country of Europe, intimately ensconced in cities and towns in the heartlands of Christendom. Islamicate settlements in Andalusian Spain and southern Italy and Sicily give the lie to the pretense that Muslims in Europe are a recent phenomenon.

And sub-Saharan Africans, it seems, were everywhere in the European Middle Ages—in Roman Britain, in post-invasion Al-Andalus, in Frederick II's Lucera, even in Guibert de Nogent's twelfth-century France.[6] The diaspora of the Romani ("Gypsies") from India in the eleventh century also saw a dark-skinned race of Asians spread across the face of western Europe and become enslaved in southeastern

Europe, where they labored for monasteries and manorial elites until the nineteenth century

Human trafficking, a flourishing trade at which medieval Italians especially excelled, also ensured the dispersal of Turks, Africans, Arabs, Mongols, Indians, and others as domestic, field, and commercial labor around the Mediterranean. Reading that racial archive, we see that even so-called Caucasians in the medieval West fail to be really "white": Higher prices paid for young female slaves of reproductive age, and their disproportionate representation in the slave markets and records of sale over male slaves, means that an unfathomable number of today's "white" Europeans (including nativists themselves) have descended from intermixed human DNA. Young female slaves, deployed predominantly as domestic labor and intruded into households—as historians have repeatedly demonstrated—furnished sexual recreation for their masters and bred new, mixed races.[7]

Remarkably, scientists have even discovered shared DNA between Native Americans and Icelanders: Among all the races of the world, the C1e gene element is shared *only* by Icelanders and Native Americans—a discovery that will perhaps not surprise those of us who study the Vinland sagas, which register the kidnap and abduction of two Native boys from the North American continent, who are forcibly transferred back to Europe, taught Norse, and Christianized.[8]

Sifting through the medieval archives of race delivers a multiracial, multireligious ethnoscape that undercuts the fantasy that an earlier Europe was the opposite of Europe today, a continent containing global populations from everywhere and a diversity of faiths. Medieval Europe *already* contained people from everywhere and a diversity of faiths—Jews, Arabs, Turks, Africans, Mongols, "Gypsies," steppe peoples, and others—and its unruly archives refuse the fiction that a singular, homogenous, communally unified Caucasian race solely inhabited the continent. White Europeans weren't even solely white. The nostalgia for a white Europe that existed as a historical inheritance—and not as an idea manufactured by centuries of assiduous identity-construction—is thus exposed as the spurious fantasy of contemporary European politics and political factions. The archives of race in deep time productively answer to the racial politics of the contemporary European now.

If attention to domestic alterities within medieval Europe is essential to our understanding of the present, beyond the horizon of the euromedieval remains exigent work to be accomplished in early global studies. After all, globalization is the one inescapable condition of our world today—a twenty-first-century world where new technologies, new modes of transnational labor and post-Fordist industrialization, and political and economic interdependencies have transformed the character of international politics. Yet globalism itself is a centuries-old phenomenon, and the nascent field of early global studies asks to be expanded, deepened, and complexified, if we are to better understand the world and its sociocultural and historical relations.

World-systems theorists, of course, have charted an economically interlinked world in the *modern* era, and Janet Abu Lughod has valuably applied their economic models to the thirteenth-century world. But world-systems theories primarily present *economic* models, neglecting to thicken our grasp of culture, society, religion, climate, animals, plants, bacteria, ecoscapes, architecture, art, music, class, gender, sexuality, race, cities, stories—that whole human-life cycle and environmental habitus that medievalists of many disciplines so ably study. Scholars positioned in the global south have also taken exception to how the economic models of world-systems turn on the postulation of economic *centers* and *peripheries*, relegating their locales in the world to permanently subordinate status on the fringes of civilizations elsewhere that are privileged with important, central status.

In calling for a widening of our attention to a global past beyond the boundaries of Europe and the Mediterranean, I should add that the gains to be had are not minor. For instance: Viewing Spain's persecution and expulsion of Jews and Moriscos—a moment of defining what it means to be Spanish that is constitutive of the early Spanish nation—within the global context of Spain's colonization of the so-called New World and Philippines, opens a window into how nationalism and colonialism work as twinned, colluding forces in communal identity-formation.

Just as it forcibly emptied itself of people it saw as belonging elsewhere in the world, and not in Spain, Spain under the Catholic monarchs also made its governance bloom elsewhere in the world. This *contraction* of the nation, as it evacuated undesirables who were being named as aliens through expulsion, exists in ironic tandem with the concomitant *expansion* of the nation's borders around the world, as Spain's global-colonial ambitions incorporated peoples far more alien than Jews and Muslims under the Spanish umbra. The spread of Spanish national boundaries outward, through the incorporation of Hispanized colonies around the globe, affirms Spanish national and global identity as mutually interlocking and co-constitutive. The complicity of the forces of nationalism and colonialism-globalism that creates Spain's identity is, of course, visited upon bodies that are selectively deemed alien/unassimilable, and alien/assimilable, depending on the political priorities of the mechanism of racial sorting that powers the nationalist-colonialist project.

Looking past Spain, and well into the modern era, we see similar dynamics of complicity between nationalist and colonialist forces working in tandem in the era of Europe's maritime empire-formation around the world, as European nations colonized India, Africa, Indonesia, the Malay archipelago, Burma, Vietnam, the Caribbean, Egypt, Algeria, and so on, while consolidating what it meant to be English, French, Dutch, Portuguese, Spanish. I've argued that the disciplinary field known as postcolonial studies would be significantly enriched by a sophisticated knowledge of the medieval past, rather than dismissively assuming the deep past was a pre-political era with no bearing on the modern, and thus of little interest to scholars unmoved by antiquarianism ("Reinventing").

I've also argued that a global perspective in deep time transforms our understanding of time itself, as well as our understanding of modernity ("Early Globalities"). For instance: Many markers of modernity already appear in what we think of as premodern time, so much so that, looking globally, we see modernity itself to be a repeating, transhistorical phenomenon, with a footprint in different vectors of the world moving at varied rates of speed. Key examples are the iron and steel industries of China: The Sinologist Robert Hartwell's data tell us that seven hundred years before Western Europe's "Industrial Revolution," the tonnage of coal burned annually in eleventh-century Song China's iron and steel industries was already "roughly equivalent to 70% of the total amount of coal used by all metal workers in Great Britain at the beginning of the 18th century" (Hartwell 1967, 122; also 1962).

Mass-market industrial production of ceramics, as early as the Tang era (fl. 618 to 907 CE) also suggests that a millennium before similar commercial production in the West, mass-produced Chinese ceramics were already the rage in the international export market.[9] We've long been aware of the circulation of paper money, movable type, printing, and gunpowder in China's long eras of premodernity. What does it mean, therefore, to insist that the Scientific and Industrial Revolutions *only* began in the West, or to insist that there was *only one single* industrial or scientific revolution? Shouldn't we be speaking of *revolutions*, that occurred, and recurred, around the world across macrohistorical time?

A perspective like this, of what since 2004 I've been calling a *Global Middle Ages*, offers us a view of history not as simple and linear, but as oscillating between inscriptions, ruptures, and re-inscriptions, as phenomena that are tagged "modern" or "premodern" recur over *la longue durée* — each time with difference, each time not identically as before — around the world. Study of the global past in deep time can position critical responses to the tired old foundational narratives of the present, which are endlessly repeated, in the academy and in public life, and can decenter the tenacious claim of a unique European genius, essence, climate, mathematical aptitude, scientific bent, or other environmental, societal, or cognitive matrix guiding destiny in the so-called "rise of the West," a claim that has long positioned the rest of the world as always catching up.

Instead, premodern China's history attests to the difficulty of building continuously on technological and scientific innovations in the context of repeated territorial invasion and political and social disruption. China's example restores an acknowledgment of the role of *historical contingency* — of *randomness and chance* — as operative forces in the shaping of civilizational history. Rather than ascribe a unique genius to the West, restoring contingency to centrality as an operative force in the making of civilizational history perhaps better honors the scholarly imperative of an ethical and non-appropriative relation to the past. Moreover, China's modernities-*within*-premodernity also usefully guide us to an understanding of the *plural nature* of time — to see that different, even colliding, temporalities can be enfolded and co-exist within a single historical moment, which would help us to make sense of not only premodern worlds, but also of societies *today* around the globe, which can seem modern, postmodern, and premodern all at once.

It must be said that the kind of global work for which I am calling requires more than mere descriptions of an interconnected past across the planet and its regions. The essays in this volume make plain that scholarly retrievals of the past are always freighted: Decisions are made on where to afford attention and what to ignore; data are sifted and evaluated for what particular significance should be highlighted; and conclusions are drawn to deliver the widest, or the narrowest, implications of the scholarship to the academic community.

The essayists in this volume attest well their conscious understanding of what kinds of scholarship would support a responsive, ethical relationship to a multifarious past and that would correlatively also be responsible to the urgent demands of the present. An articulated consciousness of this kind—of one's situatedness and one's responsibilities—is imperative for the re-education of scholarly desire, whether we are continuing our current projects or developing larger, global projects.

For a coda, I should confess that in addition to the effort of renewing an ethical relationality to the past, those of us willing to undertake transnational-globalist work will also require the courage of renewing autodidacticism and collaboration. After long processes of credentialing, few euromedievalists (and the large majority of contributors to this volume are euromedievalists) have the luxury of appending years in which to learn, say, Uighur-Mongolian or Pali, to the scholarly resources they might need for larger projects. Collaboration with premodernists who are not our usual interlocutors will be legion, and new collaborative models will need to be sought and found to lead academic scholarship into a wide-ranging transhumanist future. In this, as in our current efforts to correct the misappropriations of the past we find today, the re-education of our desire is imminent.

Notes

1. When scholars refer to "the Middle Ages," they usually mean the *European* Middle Ages, though in recent years a broadening understanding of Europe's debt to Jewish and Islamic intellectual, social, and commercial cultures, and Europe's intertwined relations with the Islamic and Jewish worlds has emerged—often acknowledged through the resuscitation of Fernand Braudel's concept of a "medieval Mediterranean." I use the term "euromedievalist" to distinguish scholars of the European Middle Ages from Indologists, Sinologists, Africanists, Eurasianists, and so on, who work in premodern periods that they sometimes also identify as medieval.

2. This imperfect term, the "Global Middle Ages," registers the politically and epistemologically freighted nature of the vocabulary we must use in order to communicate intelligibly with our fellow scholars. Autocritique of the term, in a founding work-shop at the University of Minnesota in 2007 and later in print, registers the problematic nature of applying the idea of European time, and its "Middle Ages" (another problematic term devised by Renaissance historiography to name an interval between two ages of authenticity and authority, Greco-Roman antiquity and its renascence) to the rest of the globe, where asynchronous tempo-ralities exist. However, autocritique has yet to deliver a universally accepted alternative naming. The codirectors of the Global Middle Ages Project (G-MAP), a consortium I founded and lead, are thus resigned to the use of the term until such time as better alternate naming becomes feasible. We also repeatedly remind that asynchronous eras are studied by premodernists around the world.

Correlatively, while we ourselves do not preemptively apply the term "medieval" or "Middle Ages" to other zones around the world, with their varied and different temporalities, societies, and cultures, scholars of other zones have sometimes *themselves* used the term "medieval" or "Middle Ages" to describe their own historiography—say, by referring to "medieval India," or "medieval Japan," or to an "Islamic Middle Ages" or a "North American Middle Ages." Such applications, by scholars of non-European studies themselves to their own geo-cultural zones and temporalities, thus have a different valence from occasions when euro-medievalists willy-nilly describe the rest of the world by exporting vocabulary typical of the European Middle Ages, and avoids the risk of an inadvertent intellectual colonization through language.

3. I apologize for not being able to cite every contribution to this volume in my short essay, and I did not have access to the full manuscript at the time of writing what has become the volume's Afterword.

4. My working definition is that "race" is one of the primary names we have—a name we retain for the commitments it recognizes—for a repeating tendency, of the gravest import, to demarcate human beings through differences among humans that are selectively identified as absolute and fundamental, so as to distribute powers and positions differentially to human groups. In race-making, strategic essentialisms are posited and assigned through a variety of practices: This suggests that race is a structural relationship for the management of human differences, rather than a substantive content.

It is important to note that *religion*—the paramount source of authority in the European Middle Ages—can function both socio-culturally *and* biopolitically in the medieval period: subjecting peoples of a detested faith, for instance, to a political theology that biologizes, defines, and essentializes an entire community as absolutely and fundamentally different in an inter-knotted cluster of ways, so much so that *nature* and *culture* are not bifurcated spheres in medieval race-making.

5. Work of this kind is made possible by, and stands on the shoulders of, generations of accumulated scholarship on Jews in medieval England, whether or not that accumulated scholarship

has named the treatment of medieval Jews as *racial* per se. See Chapter 2 of my *The Invention of Race in the European Middle Ages* for a bibliography. While the archive of medieval English and European Jews has received increasing attention, other racial archives—like that of the Romani, or the Cagots, or even the Mongols—remain underexposed and invite attention.

6. See Chapter 4 of my *Invention of Race*. The essay on immigration, by Mark Ormrod, has also found a "'James Black of Inde,' who lived in Dartmouth in Devon in 1434" in the records of late-medieval England (see also Ormrod's essay in this volume).

7. See Chapter 3 of *Invention of Race* for a bibliography on the medieval slave trade, and Chapter 7 on the Romani.

8. See Ebenesersdóttir et al., and Chapter 5 of *Invention of Race*.

9. See Heng, "An Ordinary Ship," which discusses the industrial mass production of export ceramics in Tang China, as part of a new book project, *Early Globalities: The Interconnected World, 500–1500 CE*. For mass production of ceramics in China slightly later, from the tenth through fourteenth centuries, see Billy So.

Works Cited

Dimock, Wai-Chee. *Through Other Continents: American Literature Across Deep Time*. Princeton: Princeton University Press, 2006.

Ebenesersdóttir, Sigríður Sunna, Ásgeir Sigurðsson, Frederico Sánchez-Quinto, Carles Lalueza-Fox, Kári Stefánsson, and Agnar Helgason. "A New Subclade of mtDNA Haplogroup C1 Found in Icelanders: Evidence of Pre-Columbian Contact?" *American Journal of Physical Anthropology* 144 (2011): 92–99.

Hartwell, Robert. "A Cycle of Economic Change in Imperial China: Coal and Iron in Northeast China, 750–1350." *Journal of the Social and Economic History of the Orient* 10 (1967): 102–59.

———. "A Revolution in the Chinese Iron and Coal Industries During the Northern Sung, 960–1126 A.D." *Journal of Asian Studies* 21, no. 2 (1962): 153–62.

Heng, Geraldine. "Early Globalities and Its Questions, Objectives, and Methods: An Inquiry into the State of Theory and Critique." *Exemplaria* 26, nos. 2–3 (2014): 234–53.

———. *The Invention of Race in the European Middle Ages.* New York: Cambridge University Press, 2018.

———. "An Ordinary Ship and Its Stories of Early Globalism: Modernity, Mass Production, and Art in the Global Middle Ages." *The Journal of Medieval Worlds* 1, no. 1 (2019): 11–54.

———. "Reinventing Race, Colonization, and Globalisms Across Deep Time: Lessons from the *Longue Durée*." *PMLA* 130, no. 2 (2015): 358–66.

So, Billy K. L. *Prosperity, Regions, and Institutions in Maritime China: The South Fukien Pattern, 947–1368.* Cambridge: Harvard University Press, 2000.

Appendixes

Appendix I: Possibilities for Teaching—By Genre

Whose Middle Ages? can be taught in its entirety according to the order and themes provided in the Table of Contents and Part introductions. However, many other disciplinary and thematic paths through the book can be charted, each with its own appeal to a different readership, teaching style, or course. In the text that follows, we have suggested some of these alternative arrangements, first dividing the essays roughly by discipline, then highlighting thematic clusters of essays that may be of use in particular courses.

Art History

Bleeke, "Modern Knights, Medieval Snails, and Naughty Nuns"

Guérin, "Ivory and the Ties That Bind"

Patton, "Blackness, Whiteness, and the Idea of Race in Medieval European Art"

Williams, "'Celtic' Crosses and the Myth of Whiteness"

Wilson, "The Hidden Narratives of Medieval Art"

History

Bardsley, "The Invisible Peasantry"
Bishop, "#DeusVult"
Cerbone, "Real Men of the Viking Age"
Diebold, "The Nazi Middle Ages"
Mulder, "No, People in the Middle East Haven't
  Been Fighting Since the Beginning of Time"
Ormrod, "How Do We Find Out About Immigrants
  in Later Medieval England?"
Paul, "Modern Intolerance and the Medieval Cru-
  sades"
Teter, "Blood Libel, a Lie and Its Legacy"
Wacks, "Whose Spain Is It Anyway?"

Law

Donner, "Who's Afraid of Shariʻa Law?"

Literature

Tyler, "England Between Empire and Nation in
  'The Battle of Brunanburh'"
Whitaker, "The Middle Ages in the Harlem Renais-
  sance"

Popular Culture

Young, "Whitewashing the 'Real' Middle Ages in
  Popular Media"

Theology

Hornbeck, "Own Your Heresy"
Mancia, "What Would Benedict Do?"
Reeves, "Charting Sexuality and Stopping Sin"
Szpiech, "Three Ways of Misreading Thomas Jeffer-
son's Qur'an"

Appendix II: Possibilities for Teaching — By Course Theme

American Studies

Mancia, "What Would Benedict Do?"

Szpiech, "Three Ways of Misreading Thomas Jefferson's Qur'an"

Whitaker, "The Middle Ages in the Harlem Renaissance"

Williams, "'Celtic' Crosses and the Myth of Whiteness"

Area Studies (Outside the United States)

Germany

Diebold, "The Nazi Middle Ages"

Teter, "Blood Libel, a Lie and Its Legacy"

Middle East

Donner, "Who's Afraid of Shari'a Law?"
Mulder, "No, People in the Middle East Haven't Been Fighting Since the Beginning of Time"

Ireland

Williams, "'Celtic' Crosses and the Myth of Whiteness"

Spain

Wacks, "Whose Spain Is It Anyway?"

UK

Ormrod, "How Do We Find Out About Immigrants in Later Medieval England?"
Tyler, "England Between Empire and Nation in 'The Battle of Brunanburh'"

Communications Theory

Teter, "Blood Libel, a Lie and Its Legacy"
Whitaker, "The Middle Ages in the Harlem Renaissance"
Young, "Whitewashing the 'Real' Middle Ages in Popular Media"

Current Affairs

Bishop, "#DeusVult"
Diebold, "The Nazi Middle Ages"

Donner, "Who's Afraid of Shari'a Law?"
Mancia, "What Would Benedict Do?"
Ormrod, "How Do We Find Out About Immigrants in Later Medieval England?"
Paul, "Modern Intolerance and the Medieval Crusades"
Tyler, "England Between Empire and Nation in 'The Battle of Brunanburh'"

Gender

Bleeke, "Modern Knights, Medieval Snails, and Naughty Nuns"
Cerbone, "Real Men of the Viking Age"

Global History

Donner, "Who's Afraid of Shari'a Law?"
Guérin, "Ivory and the Ties That Bind"
Mulder, "No, People in the Middle East Haven't Been Fighting Since the Beginning of Time"
Ormrod, "How Do We Find Out About Immigrants in Later Medieval England?"
Paul, "Modern Intolerance and the Medieval Crusades"
Wacks, "Whose Spain Is It Anyway?"

History and Theory of Race

Patton, "Blackness, Whiteness, and the Idea of Race in Medieval European Art"
Whitaker, "The Middle Ages in the Harlem Renaissance"

Williams, "'Celtic' Crosses and the Myth of Whiteness"

Young, "Whitewashing the 'Real' Middle Ages in Popular Media"

Jewish Studies

Teter, "Blood Libel, a Lie and Its Legacies"

Wacks, "Whose Spain Is It, Anyway?"

Medieval Life

Bardsley, "The Invisible Peasantry"

Cerbone, "Real Men of the Viking Age"

Hornbeck, "Own Your Heresy"

Ormrod, "How Do We Find Out About Immigrants in Later Medieval England?"

Social Class

Bardsley, "The Invisible Peasantry"

Bleeke, "Modern Knights, Medieval Snails, and Naughty Nuns"

Wilson, "The Hidden Narratives of Medieval Art"

Warfare

Bishop, "#DeusVult"

Cerbone, "Real Men of the Viking Age"

Mancia, "What Would Benedict Do?"

Paul, "Modern Intolerance and the Medieval Crusades"

Tyler, "England Between Empire and Nation in
  'The Battle of Brunanburh'"

Western Civilization

This volume is intended to complicate popular understandings of the place of the Middle Ages in history, particularly
as the medieval period is sometimes presented in "Western
Civilization" courses. The book as a whole and each of the
individual essays addresses critical questions around how
we use the medieval past to construct and think about "the
West."

You can also refer to the "History" section in Appendix I.

Contributors

Sandy Bardsley is Professor of Medieval History at Moravian College in Bethlehem, Pennsylvania. Her work focuses on women and gender in late medieval England.

Adam M. Bishop obtained his PhD in medieval studies from the University of Toronto in 2011. He is currently an independent scholar researching the legal system of the crusader Kingdom of Jerusalem.

Marian Bleeke received her PhD in art history from the University of Chicago. She has taught at Beloit College, Southern Illinois University at Carbondale, and the State University of New York at Fredonia, and is currently Associate Professor of Art History and Director of General Education at Cleveland State University. Her first book, *Motherhood and Meaning in Medieval Sculpture: Representations from France, c. 1100–1500*, was published by Boydell and Brewer in 2017.

Will Cerbone holds an MA from the University of Toronto's Centre for Medieval Studies. He is a writer and an editor of scholarly books in New York.

William J. Diebold is the Jane Neuberger Goodsell Professor of Art History and Humanities at Reed College. He has published extensively on early medieval topics, including his book *Word and Image:*

An Introduction to Early Medieval Art (Routledge, 2001). He has taught these areas at Reed since 1987, and participates in the College's humanities program, teaching both ancient Mediterranean and modern European courses.

Fred M. Donner is the Peter B. Ritzma Professor of Near Eastern History at the University of Chicago, where he has taught since 1982. He received his PhD from Princeton University in 1975 and has researched and written mainly on early Islamic history, Islamic historiography, and the Qur'an.

Sarah M. Guérin is Assistant Professor of Medieval Art at the University of Pennsylvania. Her research examines medieval ivory carving and has focused on the inter-regional trade networks that enabled exchange, work that has appeared in such journals as the *Journal of Medieval History*, *al-Masaq*, and *The Medieval Globe*. She is presently working on a monograph treating the first century of Gothic ivory carving called *Ivory Palaces: Material, Belief, and Desire in Gothic Sculpture*.

Geraldine Heng is Perceval Professor in English and Comparative Literature, Middle Eastern Studies and Women's Studies, at the University of Texas in Austin. The author of *Empire of Magic: Medieval Romance and the Politics of Cultural Fantasy* (Columbia, 2003, 2004, 2012), *The Invention of Race in the European Middle Ages* (Cambridge, 2018), and *England and the Jews: How Religion and Violence Created the First Racial State in the West* (Cambridge, 2018). She is also the founder and director of the Global Middle Ages Project (www.globalmiddleages.org). She is currently researching and writing *Early Globalisms: The Interconnected World, 500–1500 CE*.

J. Patrick Hornbeck II is Chair and Professor of Theology at Fordham University. He is author of *What Is a Lollard?* (Oxford University Press, 2010), *A Companion to Lollardy* (Brill, 2016), and *Remembering Wolsey* (Fordham, 2019), as well as coeditor of *More Than a Monologue: Sexual Diversity and the Catholic Church* (Fordham, 2014) and *Europe After Wyclif* (Fordham, 2016).

Lauren Mancia is Assistant Professor of History at Brooklyn College. She is a scholar of the Western European Middle Ages, with specialties in medieval Christianity, the history of emotions, and medieval monasticism. She has published on her scholarly interests both in peer-reviewed academic journals and in publications for wider, more general audiences.

Stephennie Mulder is Associate Professor of Islamic Art and Architecture at the University of Texas at Austin. She is a specialist in Islamic art, architectural history, and archaeology. Her research interests include the art and architecture of Shi'ism; the intersections between art, spatiality, and sectarian relationships in Islam; anthropological theories of art; material culture studies; theories of ornament and mimesis; and place and landscape studies. Mulder works on the conservation of antiquities and cultural heritage sites endangered by war and illegal trafficking.

W. Mark Ormrod, Emeritus Professor of History at the University of York, is the author of many books and articles on the politics and political culture of later medieval England, including *Political Life in Medieval England, 1300–1450* (Macmillan, 1995) and *Edward III* (Yale, 2011). He has collaborated extensively with the National Archives of the United Kingdom on the cataloguing and editing of medieval document collections. He was Principal Investigator of the major project "England's Immigrants, 1330–1550," funded by the Arts and Humanities Research Council of the United Kingdom (2012–15), and (with Bart Lambert and Jonathan Mackman) has coauthored *Immigrant England, 1300–1550* (Manchester University Press, 2019).

Pamela A. Patton is Director of the Index of Medieval Art at Princeton University. Her publications include two monographs, *Pictorial Narrative in the Romanesque Cloister* (Peter Lang, 2004) and *Art of Estrangement: Redefining Jews in Reconquest Spain* (Penn State, 2012), and the edited volume *Envisioning Others: Race, Color, and the Visual in Iberia and Latin America* (Brill, 2016). She serves as coeditor of the journal *Studies in Iconography* and as an area editor for the *Oxford Bibliographies in Art History*. Her current research and forthcoming publications concern the depiction and meanings of skin color in medieval Iberia against the backdrop of a multiethnic, multicultural Mediterranean. Before joining the Index in 2015, she was Professor of Art History at Southern Methodist University.

Nicholas L. Paul is Associate Professor of History at Fordham University. He received his MPhil in Medieval History and PhD in History from Cambridge University. His previous publications include *To Follow in Their Footsteps: The Crusades and Family Memory in the High Middle Ages* (Cornell, 2017) and the coedited collections *Remembering the Crusades: Myth, Image, and Identity* (Johns Hopkins, 2012), and, with Laura K. Morreale, *The French of Outremer: Communities and Communications in the Crusading Mediterranean* (Fordham, 2018).

David Perry — Professor of Medieval History at Dominican University from 2006 to 2017 — is a columnist for *Pacific Standard Magazine* and a freelance journalist covering politics, history, education, and disability rights. His scholarly work focuses on Venice, the Crusades, and the Mediterranean world. He is the author of *Sacred Plunder: Venice and the Aftermath of the Fourth Crusade* (Penn State, 2015).

Andrew Reeves earned his PhD from the University of Toronto's Centre for Medieval Studies in 2009 and is an Associate Professor in the Department of History and Political Science at Middle Georgia State University. His research covers how laypeople and lower-ranked clergy interacted in the later Middle Ages. His 2015 book, *Religious Education in Thirteenth-Century England: The Creed and Articles of Faith* (Brill, 2015), shows how clergy taught the basics of Christian doctrine to laypeople.

Ryan Szpiech is Associate Professor at the University of Michigan, Ann Arbor. His most recent book is *Conversion and Narrative: Reading and Religious Authority in Medieval Polemic* (University of Pennsylvania, 2012), and he is also currently editor-in-chief of the journal *Medieval Encounters*.

Magda Teter is the Shvidler Chair in Judaic Studies and Professor of History at Fordham University. She received her PhD in History from Columbia University in 2000. She specializes in early modern religious and cultural history, with emphasis on Jewish–Christian relations, the politics of religion, and transmission of culture among Jews and Christians across Europe in the early modern period. She is the author of *Jews and Heretics in Catholic Poland* (Cambridge University Press, 2005) and *Sinners on Trial* (Harvard, 2011).

Elizabeth M. Tyler is Professor of Medieval Literature. Her research and teaching focuses on the literary culture of England from the ninth to the twelfth century, that is from the time of Alfred the Great to the time of William of Malmesbury and Geoffrey of Monmouth. Situated at the intersection of literary study with intellectual, social, and political history, her work stresses the international nature of English literature and draws attention to the key role England plays in the flourishing of European literary culture across the early and high Middle Ages.

David A. Wacks is Professor of Spanish at the University of Oregon. He is author of *Framing Iberia: Frametales and Maqamat in Medieval Spain* (Brill, 2007), winner of the 2009 La corónica award; and *Double Diaspora in Sephardic Literature: Jewish Cultural Production before and after 1492* (Indiana, 2015), winner of the 2015 National Jewish Book Award in the category of Sephardic Culture. He is coeditor, with Michelle Hamilton, of *The Study of al-Andalus: The Scholarship and Legacy of James T. Monroe* (ILEX Foundation, 2018). His most recent monograph, *Medieval Iberian Crusade Fiction and the Mediterranean World*, is forthcoming in 2019 from University of Toronto Press. He blogs on his current research at http://davidwacks.uoregon.edu.

Cord J. Whitaker is Assistant Professor of English at Wellesley College where he researches and teaches late medieval English literature, especially Chaucer and romance. His research also focuses on medieval religious conflict and the history of race. He received his MA and PhD from Duke University.

Maggie M. Williams teaches at William Paterson University in New Jersey. She is a co-founder and Core Committee member of the Material Collective, and Series Editor of the Collective's imprint from punctum books, Tiny Collections. In the past, she has worked on medieval stone crosses in Ireland, and her 2012 book *Icons of Irishness from the Middle Ages to the Modern World* (Palgrave Macmillan, 2012) deals with the use of such imagery in the nineteenth and twentieth centuries. More recently, she has been researching the white supremacist uses of the so-called "Celtic" cross.

Katherine Anne Wilson is Senior Lecturer in Medieval History at the University of Chester. Her research interests lie in understanding the relationship between social and cultural change, and shifting patterns in the use of material culture in the later Middle Ages. She works and publishes on the biographies of producers and consumers of objects in medieval courts and urban centers as well as on the circulation of objects across medieval Europe.

Helen Young is a Lecturer in Literary Studies at Deakin University, Australia. Her current research interests are in medievalism and critical whiteness studies. She is most recently the author of *Race and Popular Fantasy Literature: Habits of Whiteness* (Routledge, 2016).

About the Editors

Andrew Albin is Assistant Professor of English and Medieval Studies at Fordham University and a member of the faculty of Fordham University's Center for Medieval Studies.

Mary C. Erler is Distinguished Professor of English at Fordham University and a member of the faculty of Fordham University's Center for Medieval Studies.

Thomas O'Donnell is Co-Chair, Comparative Literature, Associate Professor of English and Medieval Studies, and a member of the faculty of Fordham University's Center for Medieval Studies.

Nicholas L. Paul is Associate Professor of History at Fordham University. He received his MPhil in Medieval History and his PhD in History from Cambridge University. His previous publications include *To Follow in Their Footsteps: The Crusades and Family Memory in the High Middle Ages* and the co-edited collection *Remembering the Crusades: Myth, Image, and Identity*.

Nina Rowe is Associate Professor of Art History and a member of the faculty of Fordham University's Center for Medieval Studies.

David Perry — Professor of Medieval History at Dominican University from 2006 to 2017 — is a columnist for *Pacific Standard* magazine and a freelance journalist covering politics, history, education, and disability rights. His scholarly work focuses on Venice, the Crusades, and the Mediterranean world. He is the author of *Sacred Plunder: Venice and the Aftermath of the Fourth Crusade*.

Geraldine Heng is Perceval Professor in English and Comparative Literature, Middle Eastern Studies, and Women's Studies at the University of Texas in Austin. She is the author of *The Invention of Race in the European Middle Ages*.